# Student Teaching and Field Experiences Handbook

**Betty D. Roe**
*Tennessee Technological University*

**Elinor P. Ross**
*Tennessee Technological University*

**Paul C. Burns**
*University of Tennessee*

*105101*

Charles E. Merrill Publishing Company
*A Bell & Howell Company*
Columbus  Toronto  London  Sydney

Published by
Charles E. Merrill Publishing Co.
*A Bell & Howell Company*
Columbus, Ohio 43216

Typeface: Benguiat
Production Editor: Molly Kyle
Cover Design: Tony Faiola

Photo credits: pp. 9, 182—Ben Chandler; pp. 82, 95, 107, 137, 148—Paul Conklin; pp. 1, 75—Vivienne della Grotta; p. 19—Eastman Kodak Company; pp. 51, 68—Larry Hamill; p. 221— Harvey R. Phillips/Phillips Photo Illustrations; pp. 39, 57, 63, 152, 170, 201— C. Quinlan; p. 112— *Resource Teaching*, Charles E. Merrill, 1978; pp. 8, 115, 165, 179, 206, 233—Strix Pix.

Library of Congress Catalog Card Number: 83-62905

International Standard Book Number: 0–675–20169-1

Printed in the United States of America

3  4  5  6  7  8  9  10—88  87  86  85

*Because of his untimely death during the last stages of preparation of this book, we would like to dedicate this book to the memory of Paul C. Burns, a prolific writer, an outstanding educator, and a good friend.*

# Preface

This *Student Teaching and Field Experiences Handbook* is designed for students who are teaching in schools during their teacher-preparation programs, either in pre-student teaching practicum courses or as actual student teachers. The text is a practical guide for college students who are directly involved with elementary and secondary students.

Each chapter opens with an introductory vignette to initiate discussion of the material in the chapter. Questions following each vignette encourage reflection, and discussion questions at the end of the chapters encourage reflection over all the material in the chapter and ways to apply the information. Selected references guide students to additional reading.

The first three chapters help the student get ready to teach. The first chapter addresses professional ethics and legal status, stress, and instructional resources, all of which students need to know as background for engaging in teaching activities. Chapter 2 focuses on the relationships a student teacher or practicum student will have with other people in the school. Chapter 3 gives practical suggestions about observation and planning.

The next six chapters address specific teaching problems. Chapter 4 offers practical suggestions about discipline—many student-teachers' number one worry. Chapter 5 provides information on several important aspects of classroom management: grouping, scheduling, record keeping, and classroom environment. Chapters 6 and 7 cover teaching strategies and other school activities—motivation, teaching techniques, creative activities, study skills, functional learning activities, extracurricular activities, and student supervision. The exceptional student receives attention in chapter 8. Because of mainstreaming, all student teachers need information on this topic. Chapter 9 deals with methods of evaluation, and student teachers are asked to evaluate both their students and themselves.

The final chapter provides information about entering the teaching profession, with suggestions for locating and applying for positions and information about continuing one's professional growth after obtaining a position.

Six appendixes offer additional helpful information in the form of sample lesson and unit plans and a handwriting refresher.

Throughout the text, case studies focus on situations student teachers may encounter. Analyzing these case studies and considering the other discussion questions in the chapter are good seminar activities for student teachers and practicum students.

This book is not meant to supply all the information students generally require in their methods courses. Rather, it will remind them of what they already know, fill in some gaps that are often not covered by methods courses, offer practical suggestions, and provide a setting for critical analysis of teaching activities. The orientation is toward practical suggestions rather than theory.

We hope this handbook will give prospective teachers greater confidence as they prepare for their profession, and that it will make the preparation more enjoyable.

# Contents

# 1
## General Background

Miss Smilansky, the student teacher, notices that Debbie is dull and listless in class and sometimes has bruises on her body. Miss Smilansky is concerned about Debbie and wants to help. Mr. Huang is the cooperating teacher.

Miss Smilansky (trying to gain Debbie's confidence): Debbie, tell me what you like to do when school is out.

Debbie: Nothing.

Miss Smilansky: Where do you live?

Debbie: Over by the cannery.

Miss Smilansky: You must do some things for fun.

Debbie: Nope.

Miss Smilansky (two weeks later, still patiently trying to bring Debbie out of her shell): Debbie, you really look nice today.

Debbie: Yeah. My cousin gave me this new shirt.

Miss Smilansky: I think you could be a really good student in class, but sometimes you look so sleepy. What time do you go to bed?

Debbie: About midnight, sometimes later.

Miss Smilansky: Couldn't you try to get to bed earlier than that? I'll bet you could really do well if you got enough sleep.

Debbie: I can't never get to sleep before then.

Miss Smilansky: Why? Surely you can go to bed earlier than that?

Debbie: I don't want to talk about it.

Miss Smilansky (after another two weeks): Debbie, have you tried to get to bed any earlier? You know, it would really help you. You fell asleep during English today.

Debbie: I know. I really want to, but I just can't.

Miss Smilansky: Why don't you tell me about it?

Debbie (sighing and looking doubtful): Would you promise you wouldn't tell nobody? Nobody at all?

Miss Smilansky: I promise. I won't ever tell anybody.

Debbie: Well, see, it's like this. My dad comes home, then he starts drinking. He's O.K. at first, but then he starts getting real loud and mean. Then he starts beating on me and my mom. We try to get away from him, but he's too strong. There ain't nothing we can do about it. Now don't tell nobody or that'll only make it worse.

Miss Smilansky (very concerned after this disclosure): Mr. Huang, do you know anything about Debbie and her family?

Mr. Huang: I know something about them. That's a mean bunch. You'd better not mess with them. Stay out of it.

Miss Smilansky decides to talk to her university supervisor about the situation. He shares her concern and realizes that this is probably a case of wife and child abuse. He advises Miss Smilansky to notify the Department of Human Services. Miss Smilansky does so, and they agree to investigate the matter. Miss Smilansky is now worried that Debbie will find out she told them and asks them to be discreet.

Debbie (one week later with dark bruises on her arms and a bruise under her left eye): I thought I could trust you not to tell. I should've knowed better. All you teachers are just alike. You sent the welfare person out and she asked my dad a bunch of questions. He figured I'd been blabbing so he really laid into me and my mom last night. Now it's worse than ever. I wish I'd never told you!

1   Do you think Miss Smilansky did the right thing in involving the Department of Human Services? Are there laws about reporting suspected child abuse? Check with your local agency and find out how this situation should be handled.
2   Is there anything Miss Smilansky can do to restore Debbie's trust? How might she try to do this?
3   Do you believe it is ever right to share a student's confidences with someone else after you promise not to tell? If so, under what circumstances?
4   It appears that things are indeed worse after Miss Smilansky became involved. Should Miss Smilansky have taken Mr. Huang's advice?
5   What would you have done in a similar situation?

## Getting Ready

You are about to enter the teaching profession. Before you become a fully qualified teacher, you will have many experiences working with students under the guidance of a cooperating teacher and a university supervisor. With their suggestions and your knowledge, you will discover many techniques for helping students learn. Your introduction to teaching will be gradual, so you will be prepared to assume additional responsibilities as you encounter them.

When you begin teaching, your point of view will change. As a student, you have worried about paying attention to dull teachers, spending long hours doing homework, and taking tests. As a teacher, you will have different concerns. How do you prepare informative lessons that will keep each student interested? How do you find the time to plan tomorrow's lessons after teaching all day? How do you make up tests that will truly evaluate what each student has learned?

Teaching is both a wonderful opportunity and a serious responsibility. Teachers never really know the extent of their influence. What you teach may affect students in such a way that they will in turn influence others. As you teach, be sensitive to the needs and feelings of your students and let them know that you believe in their ability to succeed.

# Professional Ethics and Legal Status

Am I allowed to express my own political opinions when I teach? Can I do anything I want to do in my free time? Should I talk about my students with other teachers? What should I do if I suspect a student in my class is using drugs? You may be wondering about the answers to questions such as these. A professional code of ethics (see Appendix B) and school law should serve as guides for your behavior.

## Ethical Responsibilities to Students

Your primary concern as a student teacher should be for the students you teach. A good student teacher can enrich the students' education; a poor student teacher merely wastes valuable learning time. As a guest of the school, you owe the students your very best efforts in providing worthwhile learning experiences.

Each student is entitled to your courtesy and consideration, regardless of her or his physical appearance, socioeconomic status, race, creed, or ethnic origin. You will find that it is much easier to get along with some students than with others, and you will be tempted to have "teacher's pets." Students may compete for your attention with notes and little gifts, but you should be impartial in the way you treat them. Never embarrass or humiliate students who do not measure up to your expectations.

Your classroom should have a democratic atmosphere. Students should be allowed to express their opinions and different points of view. Don't impose your own religious or political views on them, and be careful to present both sides of controversial issues.

Students who confide in you expect you to keep their secrets. It would be unethical to take advantage of the information they share with you, or to embarrass them by revealing their information to other people. There may be times, however, when you feel the information they confide in you may bring harm to them or to others. They may be concealing information sought by the police or may need psychological help you cannot provide. In these cases, and in the case of Debbie and Miss Smilansky, it is usually a good idea to discuss the information with someone in authority who will respect the student's confidence and know what to do.

You may overhear teachers talking, particularly in the faculty lounge, about some of the students. It is unethical for you to openly and informally discuss a student's character, personality, appearance, or behavior in a disparaging way. Such conversations violate students' rights to privacy, and you should avoid them.

Students also have the right to confidentiality in the grades they receive. You shouldn't post grades or read them aloud unless you use some identification other than the student's name. When you return papers, make sure that only the student receiving the paper can see the grade.

## Ethical Responsibilities to the Profession

You should be proud to be entering the teaching profession, and you will want to act appropriately. Dress and behave in such a way that your students and colleagues will respect you. Try to get along with your co-workers. Show respect for people in authority, even if you don't always agree with them. Be sure to express appreciation to the school in which you do your student teaching for assisting you in your education. Remember also that you are a representative of your college or university, and your behavior is a reflection on that institution.

You should also observe certain ethical standards regarding tutoring. Don't tutor students assigned to your classes for pay unless no other qualified person is available.

When you look for a teaching job, be completely honest with school district personnel about your qualifications and professional preparation. Don't apply for any position already held by a qualified teacher.

You have a responsibility to support your profession and to stay up-to-date. One way to become profesionally active is to join a professional organization. Many professional organizations offer student memberships at reduced rates. Your university supervisor can probably suggest one or two appropriate organizations for you to join and help you find information about them.

## The Law and Student Teaching

You will need to know your legal rights, responsibilities, and liabilities as a student teacher. Since local and state laws differ and change frequently, be sure to find out what your legal status is in the school system where you are teaching.

**Child abuse** Laws in all 50 states require you to report cases of suspected child abuse, and laws in 42 states specifically direct school personnel to report suspected child abuse. Since at least 50 percent of child abuse cases involve school-aged children, educators can play a key role in identifying and reporting individuals who have been abused. If school personnel neglect this responsibility, they may endanger a child's well-being and contribute to the recurrence of abuse.[1]

[1]Samuel B. London and Stephen W. Stile, *The School's Role in the Prevention of Child Abuse* (Bloomington, Ind.: Phi Delta Kappa Educational Foundation, 1982).

Learn to recognize these signs of possible child abuse:

1 Physical abuse—lacerations, missing teeth, fractures, rope burns, cigarette burns, bruises
2 Neglect—constant fatigue, excessive hunger, lack of cleanliness, body odor
3 Sexual abuse—difficulty in walking or sitting, torn or stained underclothes
4 Emotional maltreatment—low self-concept, behavioral extremes, frequent temper tantrums, demand for affection

Not every child who exhibits one of these characteristics has been abused, but a combination of these factors, frequent recurrence of injuries, or excessive behavioral maladjustment may justify your suspicion. If you have reason to suspect a student is being abused, first talk it over with your cooperating teacher. Perhaps he or she is already aware of the problem or has noticed the same symptoms. Then a school employee—perhaps a teacher, school nurse, or principal— should interview the student in a relaxed, nonthreatening manner. The interview should be conducted privately, and the school authority should assure the child that the conversation will be confidential unless it becomes necessary to contact an agency for help. If further action is necessary, school authorities will then follow appropriate procedures for reporting the situation.

If there are abused children in your classroom, you can offer support in a number of ways. Be understanding and patient with them. Be a model of behavior for them to follow so they realize there are better ways to deal with frustrations and disappointments than with physical violence. Focus on their strengths and find ways for them to experience success. Praise them whenever there is cause. Be sensitive to their problems and willing to listen if they need to talk about their feelings.

**Negligence** School personnel are responsible for the protection of students while they are in school. When an accident or injury occurs to a student, you may be held liable if you are in charge and negligence, or extreme carelessness, can be proved. In determining negligence, a court of law considers whether or not the person in charge exercised reasonable care and acted sensibly. If, for example, on a day when you are responsible for the class, an accident occurs while you are out of the classroom, you could be found negligent if your presence most likely would have prevented the accident from happening.

Accidents are apt to occur when unusual events are taking place. Each student who goes on a field trip should bring a parental permission note, but even so, you can be held liable if you are negligent. When animals are brought to school, you are responsible for seeing that they are kept under control so that no students are injured.

You can purchase liability insurance to protect yourself from lawsuits. Liability insurance is available through professional societies at greatly reduced student rates, or you may include it as part of your home-owner's general policy.

**Discipline** Recent U. S. Supreme Court decisions held that corporal punishment does not violate the Eighth Amendment barring cruel and unusual punishment. The Court supported your right as a teacher to use corporal punishment even over parental objections. Although corporal punishment has been banned by some states and in some local districts, other school systems permit corporal punishment as a way of controlling student behavior.

Certain due process procedures have been established for administering corporal punishment.

1 Corporal punishment should rarely be used in a first-offense situation.
2 Students should know what types of misconduct could lead to corporal punishment.
3 An adult witness should be present when someone administers corporal punishment.
4 The student should be informed in front of the adult witness of the reasons for the punishment.
5 The disciplinarian should inform the student's parents of the reason for administering corporal punishment, if requested to do so.

As a student teacher, you should avoid using corporal punishment. If a student doesn't seem to respond to any other form of discipline, you might consult with your cooperating teacher about how to handle the problem.

**Public Law 94–142** You will probably find more students with physical, mental, or emotional handicaps in regular classes than there were when you were attending school. Enactment of Public Law 94–142—the Education for All Handicapped Children Act of 1975—has resulted in a number of changes regarding placement and treatment of handicapped children in the schools. Instead of being placed in special classes, many handicapped children are now "mainstreamed" into regular classrooms. The rationale for this policy is that both handicapped and "normal" children benefit from the increased academic and social interaction.

You will have an opportunity to observe and work with these students on a daily basis. Because the law requires each handicapped student to have an Individual Educational Plan (IEP), you

*Because of P.L. 94–142, there are probably more handicapped students in regular classrooms than there were when you attended school.*

may participate in developing and implementing such a plan. (See chapter 8 for a sample IEP.)

**Search and seizure**   Courts have generally ruled in favor of allowing school officials to conduct searches and seizures. Searches consist of looking for illegal goods; seizures involve confiscating illegal goods. Some of the items usually prohibited in schools are drugs and drug paraphernalia, weapons such as knives and guns, and obscene materials.

The Fourth Amendment to the Constitution gives individuals freedom from unreasonable searches and seizures. Weighing this freedom against a safe and drug-free school environment, however, the courts usually rule in favor of the schools. Searches and seizures are increasing as drug use and violence in schools become greater problems.

If you suspect a student possesses something illegal, discuss the matter with your cooperating teacher. If evidence warrants an investigation, a school official can be asked to search the student's locker. Do not conduct the search yourself, and do not search a student's body or clothing for suspected harmful items.

**Copyright laws**   The U. S. Copyright Act contains certain provisions for photocopying material. You need to know what you can copy and how many copies you can make without violating the copyright law. Some magazines and journals state their photocopying policies on the title page of each issue. When reproduction of

*Copyright law does not permit duplication of consumable materials (worksheets, standardized tests, ditto sheets) without permission from the publisher.*

certain material is clearly prohibited, you may still write to the publisher for permission to use the material.

There are several guidelines for determining whether material can be photocopied under the "fair use" policy. Generally, "fair use" is observed when photocopying material has no effect on its demand. For instance, you can make a copy of an article or selection, but you can make multiple copies of only a very small portion of a work. You are not permitted to copy consumable materials, such as workbook pages, standardized tests, and ditto sheets, unless permission is granted by the publishers. You cannot reproduce substantial parts of materials for public performances, including sheet music and plays. If a work is out of print or unavailable, however, the policy of "fair use" generally allows you to photocopy it.

**Private lives of teachers**    Teachers have advanced considerably since the days when they were forbidden to drink or smoke, and married women were not permitted to teach. Today, teachers are granted a great many privileges, but their behavior is still sometimes challenged and brought before the courts.

Some general guidelines for behavior have been established as a result of case law. As you begin your student teaching, you should find out if there are any published or generally accepted rules regarding these matters. Dress, grooming, and sexual behavior usually come under the teacher's right to privacy, unless it can be proved that the teacher's appearance or lifestyle affects his or her teaching. Teachers, as well as students, have the right to refuse to participate in patriotic ceremonies. They are also free to oppose school policies by speaking out against them or by writing letters that appear in local newspapers. As a student teacher, however, you would be wise to act with discretion and avoid antagonizing people.

### Academic freedom

Congress shall make no law respecting an establishment of religion, or prohibiting the free exercise thereof; or abridging the freedom of speech, or of the press; or the right of the people peaceably to assemble, and to petition the government for a redress of grievances.
—First Amendment, United States Constitution

A great deal of controversy has arisen over recent interpretations of the First Amendment. There have been many court cases dealing with censorship of materials and subjects for instruction, as well as with school prayer and Bible reading. The issues of morality, politics, racism, and religion form the basis of most attacks by censors.

Teachers sometimes face the dilemma of using uncontroversial and generally acceptable materials, or materials relevant to living in contemporary society that may offend some citizens of the community. When you deal with controversial issues, you risk confrontations with parents and public criticism. Teachers who use books or teach subjects that have been specifically forbidden by the board of education may be dismissed. These are some points to consider in determining whether or not to use controversial materials in your classroom:

1  Is the material you plan to use appropriate for the maturity and age level of the students?
2  Is there a valid educational reason for using the material?
3  Is there any policy established by the board of education to prohibit use of the material?

In *Abington Township School District* v. *Schempp,* 1963, the U. S. Supreme Court ruled that school prayer and Bible reading violated the constitutional provision for separation of church and state. Because of different interpretations of the law, however, schools in some states permit silent periods of meditation or voluntary school prayer.

## Stress

As a student teacher, you face many pressures: teaching lessons for the first time, preparing to enter the job market, and handling social, family, and monetary demands. These pressures can cause stress, and stress can affect your teaching performance. It can also affect your physical and emotional well-being. How you deal with stress will determine to a great extent how successful you will be in teaching.

## Understanding Stress

Stress is an intense degree of nervous tension which results from anxiety. It occurs when people are unable to cope with the demands of a situation. The most stressful situations are those that people are least able to control. An increase in teacher stress and subsequent "burnout" has become a major concern in the teaching profession. In a survey of 9,000 teachers, 75 percent indicated that their absences from school were often related to stress and tension.[2]

This high rate of stress is caused by many factors, including lack of respect from students, potential student violence, run-down school buildings, and unreasonable expectations from the public. Teachers are held accountable for helping students attain certain levels of achievement, yet they find they must also act as counselors and stand-in parents. They are pressured to individualize, evaluate, motivate, and maintain discipline. Good teachers combine all their knowledge, skill, and training in their daily encounters with students.

Although too much stress can cause physical and emotional problems, a certain amount of stress is desirable. Stress can give you a burst of energy and get your adrenalin flowing. In the right amount, it will enable you to "rise to the occasion" and put forth the extra energy to get the job done. People react differently to potentially stressful situations. You may consider these situations challenging and stimulating, or you may become anxious and tense. How would you react if your cooperating teacher asked you to take over the class unexpectedly when a parent came for an unscheduled conference?

## Sources of Stress

Any situation involving worry or tension may cause stress. You may encounter some of these sources of stress:

1   Choice of career—You may be wondering if you should be in the field of education after all. Perhaps you are finding it more difficult to work with students and to help them learn than you expected.
2   Expectations of others—Your parents, your former teachers, or family friends may have always expected you to grow up and be a teacher. You may be worried now that you are not able to live up to their expectations.
3   Effectiveness of teaching—The range of interests and

[2]William C. Miller, *Dealing with Stress: A Challenge for Educators* (Bloomington, Ind.: Phi Delta Kappa Educational Foundation, 1979), p. 7.

abilities within any classroom is so wide that it is nearly impossible to fully meet the needs of every student. You may become frustrated because you cannot reach each student, regardless of how hard you try.

4   Evaluation by supervisors—Being evaluated is probably a stressful time for you. You worry about how your supervisors regard your efforts, especially if they observe one of your less successful lessons.

5   Appreciation for your efforts—Teaching requires a great deal of outside preparation: writing daily lesson plans, grading papers, making up tests and worksheets, setting up audiovisual equipment, developing materials, and planning units. It may seem that your efforts go unnoticed and unappreciated.

6   Job market—The job market may be tight when you graduate and seek employment. You may worry about how you will support yourself if you can't get a teaching job.

Some sources of stress originate in situations outside yourself. Clouds gather and thunder booms. Jackhammers reverberate as construction begins on the new addition. Tony interrupts to tell you he's going to be sick. The first snowflake drifts down lazily. A parent enters with the cupcakes for this afternoon's Halloween party. The principal makes an announcement over the intercom. Any of these events can turn a well-ordered classroom into chaos, and chaos is a cause of stress.

Other external sources of stress generally center around circumstances such as these:

1   Too much work for the time available—You find you are staying up late at night and working weekends to get everything done. You have practically no free time and not enough social life. The day moves too quickly, and extra responsibilities—working on the school newspaper, bus duty, playground supervision—further intrude on your time.

2   Unpleasant working environment—Not everyone faces this problem, but those who do are disturbed by overcrowded classrooms; poorly maintained buildings; and/or old, drab schools with poor lighting in potentially dangerous inner-city neighborhoods.

3   Lack of resources—Some schools have old audiovisual equipment in need of repair. Books and materials you would like to use with your unit may be unavailable or outdated. Films may need to be ordered so far ahead of time that they cannot reach you in time to be used.

4   Poor relationships with co-workers—You may not get along with your cooperating teacher or other personnel. You

may feel they are not interested in helping you, expect too much from you, do not give you enough freedom, or are too critical.

## Negative Consequences of Stress

If you allow stress to affect you negatively, you may develop physical and emotional reactions. Some of these are probably already famil- iar to you—sweaty palms, rapid breathing and heartbeat, tense muscles, and queasy stomach. This kind of stress is normal and temporary. When stress is intense and prolonged, however, you may develop headaches, high blood pressure, or insomnia. You may also become depressed and undergo a change in personality.

Not only will continued stress affect you physically and emotionally, it will also have a detrimental effect on your teaching. You will tend to be irritable, grouchy, and cranky. You will become impatient and short-tempered with your students. You may be sar- castic and find fault easily.

When you are under stress in the classroom, it is common to hurry. You talk fast and don't allow enough time for students to answer your questions. Instead of probing more deeply into a discussion, you rush on to the next topic. You try to cram too much into a lesson, and try to do too many things at once. You may grab a sandwich, grade papers, and supervise your class during lunch pe- riod instead of using this time to relax.

## Positive Responses to Stress

There is no doubt that teachers encounter stressful situations in their profession. What makes the difference between job satisfaction and teacher burnout is the way teachers cope with these situations. Many teachers are able to maintain their commitment to students and their dedication to teaching. They keep their sense of humor, take a sincere interest in their students' needs, and teach lessons skillfully. They think of teaching as a challenge and an opportunity instead of just another exhausting day filled with discipline problems and papers to grade. These teachers enjoy their work because they know how to manage stress.

Figure 1-1 describes several stressful situations, reactions to them, stress ratings, and avoidance/management strategies. The ratings rank from 1 (lowest stress) to 10 (highest stress). Make a similar chart for one day of your student teaching, including your own ideas for avoidance/management strategies. If four or more stressful situations are rated 8 or above, you will need to give serious attention to reducing the stress in your life.

**Attitudes**   Your attitude toward yourself is important in how you handle stress. Recognize and accept your strengths and weak- nesses. Instead of envying another student teacher's artistic talent, make the most of your own special skills. For instance, if you can play a guitar, find a way to include a guitar selection in your lesson. If you can do some magic tricks, use magic to get the students' attention when you introduce a lesson. Know your limitations as well, and don't try to do something that probably won't succeed.

Be well prepared for each lesson. Thorough knowledge of content and methods will help you feel confident and self-assured as you teach. Then, even if things don't go exactly as you expect them to, you can complete the lesson so the students get the message.

Think positively! Don't say to yourself, "I'll never get all this work finished" or "these students are impossible." Instead, tell yourself, "I really got that point across" or "I think I'm finally making some headway."

Avoid worrying. Many things you worry about never happen. Other things work themselves out without the serious consequences you feared. Worrying doesn't solve problems; it only makes you less effective as a teacher. Don't worry about things you can't change. Do something about things you *can* change. Feeling guilty or worrying about something you did earlier doesn't change what happened. Remembering unpleasant scenes only makes you uncomfortable. Things won't always go well, but it's important to keep the day's events in perspective. Perhaps only three things went wrong, but as many as twenty went well. Focus on the good things that happened.

**Relationships**   Find time to be with friends during student teaching. Some friends should be outside the field of education so you can get your mind off school. You need to forget your students and teaching obligations for awhile and laugh and talk about other

**Figure 1-1   A Typical Day of Student Teaching**

| Time | Stressful Situation | Reactions | Rating | Avoidance/ Management Strategies |
|---|---|---|---|---|
| 6:30a.m. | Can't decide what to wear. Out of cereal for breakfast. Can't find car keys. | Felt rushed, tense, annoyed at self, hungry. | 4 | Decide what to wear the night before; check food supplies and keep adequate stock; always put car keys in same place. Set alarm clock 15 minutes earlier to allow for unexpected problems. |
| 7:20a.m. | Have to wait 10 minutes for car pool passenger. | Hated to waste time, especially after rushing around to get ready. | 5 | Use waiting time productively. Check over lesson plans, think about what to do about the problems Manuel is having. |

| | | | |
|---|---|---|---|
| 7:45 a.m. | Ditto machine is out of fluid. Will have to write lesson on board instead of passing out worksheets. | Wasted more time, fell behind schedule. | 5 | Keep a day or two ahead with worksheets. Have other activities in reserve for unforeseen emergencies. |
| 9:15 a.m. | Fire drill while introducing lesson. Students are excited and won't settle down again. | Felt angry with school for ruining my lesson. Why can't they have fire drills when nothing is going on? | 8 | Can't avoid fire drills. Need to stay more relaxed, give students more time to get back to the lesson. Don't push them—or myself—so much. |
| 11:30 a.m. | Juan pulled a knife on José. Kids gathered around. Looked like a mean fight was coming. | Panic! Didn't know how to handle this one. Stood there like an idiot. Principal stopped it. | 8 | Must check with teacher about what to do. Need to be prepared to deal with this next time. |
| 1:45 p.m. | Spied the university supervisor out of the corner of my eye as he entered to observe my lesson. | Couldn't remember what I was supposed to say next. Worried about the students' restlessness. | 9 | Be well prepared and know exactly what to do. Don't let the students get out of control. Do the best job I can and forget about Mr. Henry's being there. |
| 3:00 p.m. | Cliff's mother accused me of being unfair to him. She claimed Cliff says I am "picking on him." | Felt unjustly accused, completely bewildered by her unfair statement. Wanted to shout, "It's not true!" | 9 | There has been a misunderstanding. Discuss the matter calmly. Find out why Cliff feels this way. Possibly include him in our conversation. Don't get angry! |
| 7:30 p.m. | Left my teacher's manual at school. Will have to wait till morning to plan my lessons. Probably won't do well. | Felt disgusted with myself for forgetting it, worried about not being prepared for tomorrow's lesson. | 5 | Can I find an extra copy of the manual in the store room to keep at home? Need to put everything to take home in a special place so I won't forget. Get some any-occasion ideas to fill in. |
| 10:00 p.m. | Just realized I have to put up a bulletin board tomorrow! I'll have to make it tonight. | Felt overwhelmed with so much to do and not enough time, angry at supervising teacher for making so many assignments. | 8 | Keep a calendar of due dates. Try to keep ahead on assignments. Must get my sleep or I'll be a nervous wreck the next day. |

things. You will also want some friends in whom you can confide about problems with your student teaching. By sharing your difficulties with each other, you may see things from a different point of view and be willing to try a new approach.

Your working relationships with supervisory personnel and other student teachers are also important. If you have a conflict with someone, it is usually best to discuss the problem with that person instead of worrying about it. Perhaps it is based on a misunderstanding and can be readily resolved. If there is simply a personality conflict or a basic difference in point of view, accept the situation and get along the best you can. The relationship is only temporary.

Don't forget that your students may also be under stress. They don't know exactly what to expect from you. Let them know what your standards of behavior are and what will happen if they violate them. Give warnings only when you are prepared to carry them out. Give assignments clearly so students will know what they are to do. Show them that you care and are willing to help. Be fair and consistent. If you can relieve your students' stress, they will perform better for you.

**Dealing with stress**   One of the first steps in dealing with a problem that produces stress is to decide whether the problem is really *yours*. If it isn't, turn it over to the person responsible for it. If it is your problem, brainstorm ways to solve it. If you don't know how to solve it, get help. Then proceed to solve the problem the best way you can.

When you feel stress because you have so many things to do, make a list of what must be done, in order of importance. Consider what must be done right away, so it will be completed when it is needed, such as starting a science experiment that takes two weeks to reach fruition. Set deadlines for getting these things done and stick to your schedule. As you finish each task, check it off. This way you are aware of your accomplishments and aren't as likely to fall behind.

Don't worry about assignments because they seem too big. Break them into manageable chunks and work on them a piece at a time. Do the hardest parts first and save the most interesting tasks until the end. Each time you successfully complete one portion of the assignment, you will be motivated to try another until you are finished.

Keep your sense of humor. Be able to laugh with the children at your own mistakes. It is better to laugh with them when something goes wrong than to get angry. Even though it may not seem funny when it happens, you may see the humor later. Besides, laughter reduces stress, while anger increases it.

Feel free to say "no" to people when you feel you can't handle another responsibility. Do what is required of you and a little more, but don't accept unreasonable demands on your time. Someone may be taking advantage of your good nature. If you take on more responsibilities than you can manage, you will not do well in anything.

**Taking action** Some activities will keep stress from getting the better of you. Exercise—jogging, walking briskly, playing tennis or racquet ball, working out in the gym—is good for you as a change

**Figure 1-2  Analyzing Stress**

1.  Identify a recent stressful situation. _____

   _____

2.  Why did this particular situation cause you to feel stress? _____

   _____

3.  How did you react? _____

4.  Could the situation have been avoided? If so, how? What else could you have done? _____

   _____

5.  Should you have reacted differently? What else could you have done?

   _____

   _____

   _____

6.  What was most effective in helping you overcome your feelings of stress?

   _____

   _____

   _____

7.  Could you have used this situation in a positive way? How? _____

   _____

   _____

8.  How could you have reduced the intensity of the stress? _____

   _____

   _____

9.  If the same thing happens again, how can you manage the stress better?

   _____

   _____

of pace. Even though these forms of exercise can be physically tiring, they leave you with a pleasant, relaxed tiredness, rather than the tense exhaustion you may feel at the end of a school day. Be careful to avoid highly competitive games, though, or you may defeat your purpose of reducing stress.

Getting enough sleep is important in staying fit for the classroom and avoiding nervous tension. For some people, a nap after school relieves that drained-out feeling. When you go to bed, try not to go over what happened in school or what you plan to do tomorrow. You need to relax before you can sleep, so try reading a magazine or watching an entertaining television show. Exercising before going to bed may make you physically tired enough to go right to sleep.

You can't do schoolwork all the time, so turn to hobbies or relaxing mental activities for those free times when you are alone. Read a novel or solve a crossword puzzle. Do something easy that keeps your mind involved in a different sort of mental activity. You can't worry about school when you are thinking about something else.

You may want to fill out the questionnaire in Figure 1-2 to analyze how you manage stress. Most reactions to stress fall into one of four categories: freeze, flee, fight, or compromise. Think about your reaction and choose the appropriate category. If you use the questionnaire for more than one stressful situation, you may discover a pattern of reactions to stress and ways of overcoming stress. Learn your most effective ways of dealing with stress and use these techniques to relieve future stressful situations.

## Instructional Resources

People learn best what they experience. Much learning takes place through listening and reading, but learning is likely to be more meaningful and lasting if it is supplemented with experiences. Sometimes these experiences can be direct, as in field trips and experiments; other times, indirect, as in films and visits from resource people.

You can find instructional resources nearly everywhere. You can obtain audiovisual materials through the school, public library, college resource center, and local and state agencies. You can make games and activities for teaching specific skills. The community is rich in resources. Many home decorating and supply stores give away scraps of materials that can be used for various purposes in the classroom. Industries, farms, and parks provide opportunities for field trips. People in various occupations can serve as resource persons. If you use your imagination, you will find ways to take advantage of the resources that abound in your school and community.

## Audiovisual Media

A wide variety of audiovisual media is used in many ways in schools today. You should plan to use them as alternatives to, or along with, traditional teaching approaches. To do so, you need to know *where* to get these materials, *when* to make use of them, *how* to use them, *why* they will enhance your lesson, and *which type* is most appropriate for your purpose.

**Selecting audiovisual media**   When you meet with your co-operating teacher, discuss what units, skills, and activities you will be expected to teach. Decide what materials you might want to use in connection with these teaching areas, then check to see what materials are available. Some materials may have to be reserved or ordered well in advance of the time you actually plan to use them.

One of the first things you should do is to become acquainted with the school librarian or media specialist. Find out what resources are available in your school. Most school media centers have supplementary reading materials, newspapers and periodicals, reference books, maps and globes, files of photographs and slides, filmstrips, art prints, audiotapes, transparencies, charts and posters, models and exhibits, and a limited supply of films.

*Be sure to familiarize yourself with audiovisual equipment before you use it in class.*

After assessing the holdings of the school media center, you may wish to explore other possibilities. One place to look for additional materials is the school system's central office, which may have a systemwide file of resource materials. Another source is the public or regional library. You may be able to order films from the state Department of Education or check out resource materials from your university.

Materials are also available from other places. The Public Documents Distribution Center (Pueblo, Colorado 81009), various state departments and agencies, and business and industries will send you free and inexpensive materials. Locally, you can get maps and other printed materials from the Chamber of Commerce, banks, local industries, and the Department of Health.

If you still can't find what you need, you may want to make simple materials yourself, such as transparencies, slides, mounted pictures, or teaching games. Some of these materials should be protected by laminating them or covering them with clear contact paper. A good way to begin a collection of teacher-made games and activities is to make some on the insides of file folders. Write the directions on the outside of each folder. You can then label and organize these activities according to skills. (See Figure 1-3 for an example of a teacher-made language arts game.)

There are a number of factors to consider in selecting audiovisual materials to use with a particular lesson. Be sure you do not decide to use them simply to impress your cooperating teacher, fill up instructional time, or entertain the students. Consider these criteria in choosing materials:

1  Relevance to lesson—Make sure the audiovisual material actually helps to carry out the objectives of the lesson you are teaching. Does it get the points across in the best way possible? Is this medium the most appropriate for your purpose? Will it stimulate discussion and lead to further study?

2  Appeal to students—Be sure the material is suitable for the students' age level and that it will hold their attention. Students should have sufficient background information to appreciate the presentation.

3  Quality of materials—Check your materials to make sure they are well designed and of high technical quality. The material should be accurate, current, and in good taste.

4  Objectivity—Examine your material for bias, propaganda, and controversy. If there is bias, help your students to see the other point of view. Point out misconceptions that arise as a result of propaganda techniques. If the material is controversial, be sure that each side receives equal emphasis. Free materials are often available to class-

**Figure 1-3  Teacher-made Language Arts Game**

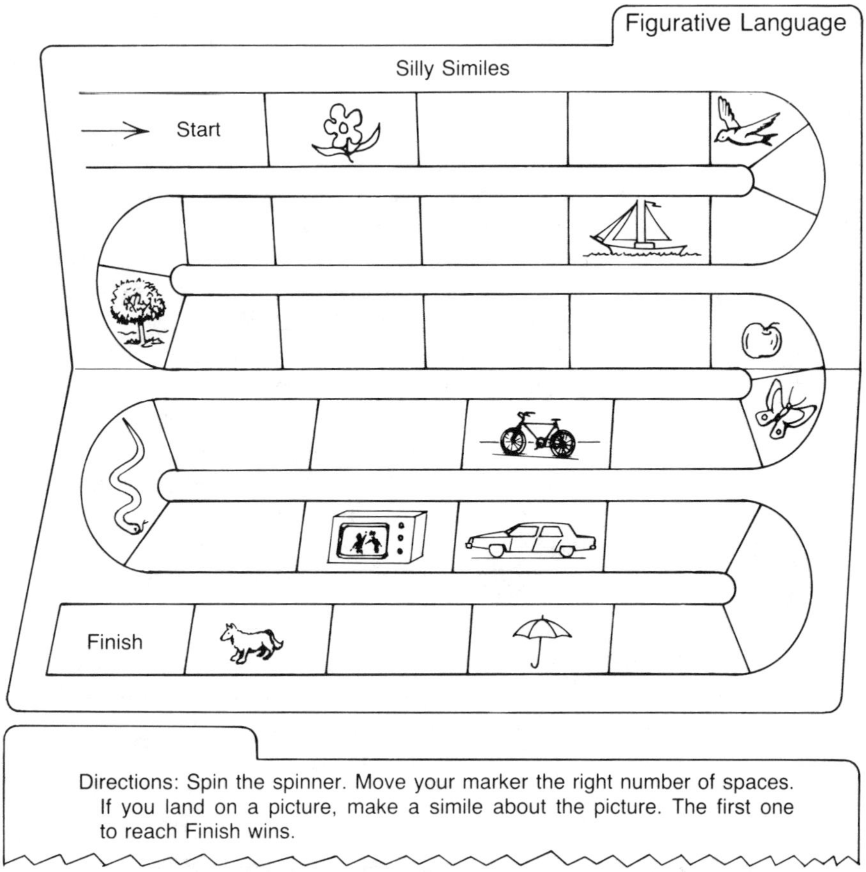

Figurative Language

Silly Similes

Start

Finish

Directions: Spin the spinner. Move your marker the right number of spaces. If you land on a picture, make a simile about the picture. The first one to reach Finish wins.

room teachers for the purpose of advertising a product or advancing a particular point of view. Be cautious about using these materials.

5  Practical considerations—Be sure you know how to operate the equipment you need for presenting your material. Check in advance to see that both material and equipment will be available when you need them. Allow enough time to introduce the lesson, present the audiovisual material, and follow it up. Allow extra time in case something goes wrong. Prepare a suitable place for your presentation. The checklist in Figure 1–4 will help you use audiovisual materials efficiently.

**Effective use of audiovisual media**  Audiovisual media can be used for many purposes: introduction and orientation to a new area of study, representation of events and processes, and individualized learning experiences. They arouse students' interest and curiosity as you introduce a new topic. A display of brightly colored photographs of wild animals, a recording of medieval madrigal music, or a film of a slowly opening flower are stimuli for learning. Since students have become accustomed to acquiring ideas and information through television, an audiovisual presentation is more likely to catch their attention than a textbook.

You can use certain types of audiovisual media to individualize instruction according to the learner's style or special needs. If the same information is available in the classroom in different forms, learners can choose the form that best suits their way of learning. For instance, a student who has great difficulty with reading can listen to a tape about the African jungle. Another student who has trouble visualizing what is read might operate a filmstrip projector and watch pictures of the jungle. A third student who is an excellent reader might prefer to read about the jungles of Africa from several reference books. Visually handicapped students may need to use recordings or large-print materials.

When you use audiovisuals, prepare carefully for your lesson by previewing the material and reading the accompanying study guide or lesson plan. Create a feeling of readiness and anticipation among the students by raising questions and telling them what they

**Figure 1-4   Checklist for using audiovisual equipment**

Preparation:
_____ Reserve or check out necessary materials and equipment.
_____ Preview material to make sure it is appropriate and in good condition.
_____ Prepare related materials for introduction or follow-up activities.
_____ If each student is to receive a copy of related materials, count the copies to make sure you have enough. Plan for efficient distribution.
_____ Arrange audience seats so everyone can see.
_____ Consider the location of handicapped students by placing those with visual or auditory difficulties near the front and providing places for students in wheelchairs.
_____ Check the room's temperature, ventilation, and lighting.
_____ Eliminate distractions as much as possible.

Equipment:
_____ Practice operating it until you feel sure of yourself.
_____ Set it up in advance so that it is ready to use (check focus, position on screen, size of image, etc.).
_____ Have an extra bulb on hand, and know how to replace the old one.
_____ Get an extension cord or an adapter if you need one.
_____ Avoid having cords where the students will trip over them.
_____ Check the cleanliness of the lens and other vital parts of the equipment.

can expect to learn. Relate the audiovisual material to what they are studying; make it a part of your overall instructional plan. Explain any unfamiliar terms or concepts that will be used.

During the presentation, observe the students' reactions. There may be some points they do not seem to understand or some parts that do not hold their interest. You may be able to interrupt the presentation, but more likely you will need to bring these matters up during your follow-up discussion. You should take notes of your observations so you can recall anything that needs to be mentioned later.

The follow up is based on the audiovisual presentation but is not limited to it. In fact, the presentation may serve primarily as a taking-off point. Follow-up activities may consist of a lively discussion, the application of concepts to real situations, or experiments, projects, and reports. Students may be divided into groups to pursue special interests, and the projects may continue over an extended period of time. Pupil participation in follow-up activities is essential for learning to take place.

## Case Study: Breakdown of a Lesson

Mr. Kuo, the student teacher, is introducing a unit on Scandinavia in social studies by showing his students a film about the region. He has reserved the film and equipment, set it up, and is ready to begin. Mrs. Colby is the cooperating teacher.

Mr. Kuo: Everybody sit down and be quiet. We're going to see a film.

Students (shuffling to their seats and mumbling): Wonder what it's about. Probably something dumb. Who wants to see a film anyway? They're always so dull and boring in school.

Mr. Kuo: O.K. We're ready to start. Oh—just a minute. I forgot to pull down the shades. (Students wait restlessly while Mr. Kuo pulls down the shades. One group starts giggling in the corner.)

Mr. Kuo: Hey, you guys. Keep quiet. O.K. Ellen, turn out the lights please. Here we go. (Film starts and students settle down. Suddenly the screen goes blank. Mr. Kuo stares at the projector and wonders what happened.)

Mrs. Colby: I believe the bulb has burned out. Do you have another one?

Mr. Kuo: I don't think so. Let me look. (Pause while students start whispering, poking each other, and laughing) I can't find one. Do you think they'd have one at the resource center?

Mrs. Colby: They probably do, but the librarian is out today and I doubt if the substitute would know where to find one.

Mr. Kuo: Pedro, would you go to the resource center for me and ask the substitute librarian if she can find a projector bulb? (Pedro starts off in search of a bulb. By now the class is throwing paper wads and paper airplanes. Some students are getting out of their seats. Carmelita trips over the projector cord and falls against the filing cabinet. She cuts her lip and it starts bleeding.)

Mr. Kuo (speaking in an excited, almost angry tone): All of you get back in your seats! Stop throwing things! Shut up! Pedro should be back soon.

Students: Oh, look! Carmelita's lip is bleeding!

Carmelita (wailing slightly as she looks at the bloodstained hand she has just removed from her mouth): My mouth is bleeding!

Mr. Kuo glances helplessly at Mrs. Colby, starts to say something then stops.

Mrs. Colby (speaking calmly and turning the lights back on): All of you get back to your seats now. Get out your math books and work on your assignment for tomorrow. (Students do as she says.)

Mrs. Colby: Let me see your lip, Carmelita. I believe it will be O.K. if you go to the girl's room and put a cold, wet paper towel over it until the bleeding stops. Kim, you go with her.

Pedro (just returning to the room): She looked for a bulb but couldn't find one. She says we'd better wait and show the film tomorrow when the regular librarian will be back.

Mr. Kuo: Thank you, Pedro. Class, I guess you might as well keep working on your math and we'll do social studies tomorrow when we can see the film.

1  Did Mr. Kuo succeed in his objective of introducing his unit on Scandinavia? Could he have introduced the unit anyway, even if he couldn't show the film?
2  Did Mr. Kuo ever make clear to the students his purpose in showing the film? If the film had been shown, do you think the students would have gained much from it? What could Mr. Kuo have done to create interest in the film and make sure the students learned all they could from it?
3  What could Mr. Kuo have done to prevent the class from becoming unruly?
4  How could Carmelita's accident have been prevented? How might Mr. Kuo have handled the incident?
5  What would you do to avoid making the same kinds of mistakes Mr. Kuo made?
6  Is there anything you think Mr. Kuo did correctly? If so, what?

## Case Study: Salvaging a Lesson.

Mr. Carson, the student teacher, is introducing a unit on Africa in social studies by showing his students a film on the region. He has reserved the film and equipment, set it up, and is ready to begin. Miss Rios is the media specialist.

Mr. Carson: This afternoon we are going to see a film. The film is about Africa, the unit we are going to begin studying today. Africa is the second largest continent and is made up of many different countries. As you watch the film, I want you to notice the different kinds of land regions you can find in Africa. Also, be sure to look for the natural resources that Africa has. Kim, will you please pull down the shades? I believe we're ready to start. (Film begins, but suddenly the screen goes blank.)

Students: Oh, no. What happened? Hey, it was just getting interesting.

Mr. Carson: I'm afraid the bulb has burned out. I tried to get a spare just in case, but there wasn't one. I'll try to get one by tomorrow.

Mike: Oh good. No film. Can we play a game?

Susan: Let's have free time.

Sally (jumping out of her seat): I think I know where there's an extra bulb. I'll go ask Miss Rios.

Mr. Carson: Never mind, Sally. I already checked with Miss Rios and she doesn't have one. We'll have to do something else instead.

Anthony: I want to get my math homework done. Is it O.K. if I do that?

Chris: No, let's play 20 questions.

Mr. Carson: Wait a minute, everybody. We can still begin learning about Africa today even if we can't see the film. We'll begin by finding Africa on the globe. Who can come up and show us where it is?

Sonya (raising her hand): I can see it from here. Let me show them.

Mr. Carson (after discussing the features of Africa on the globe and on a pull-down map): Africa has been in the news quite a bit lately and I've been clipping some items from the newspapers. I'm going to divide you into groups of four and let each group take one clipping. I want you to read your clipping and select someone from your group to report to the class about the article. Select another person to point to the country or region in Africa that is mentioned in your article. You may use either the map or the globe. I will give you a few minutes to do this work in your groups and then I will call on you to make your reports. Do you have any questions?

Jimmy: Who's going to be in my group?

Mr. Carson: I'll put you into groups just as soon as I'm sure you understand what to do.

Jake: What if we can't find our country on the map?

Mr. Carson: I'll help you. You may come up ahead of time to try to find it. Any other questions? (pause) I think we're ready to start now.

1 Suppose that Mr. Carson had not thought to use the map and globe and that he had not brought the clippings. What would have happened to his lesson?
2 What are some other ways that Mr. Carson might have introduced his unit without the film?
3 At what point was Mr. Carson about to lose control of the class? How did he manage to retain control?
4 Compare and contrast the lessons of Mr. Kuo and Mr. Carson according to the following criteria: preparation, class management, effectiveness of introducing a unit, and flexibility.

---

**Types of audiovisual media** Since the days of the cave dwellers, humans have communicated through audiovisual means. The human race has progressed from grunting sounds and crude drawings on rock walls to sophisticated electronic media. Various kinds of print materials and audiovisual media you can use for communicating ideas to your students are discussed in this section.

*Print materials*—Basal readers (series of graded reading instructional books) and content area textbooks provide structure and sequence in the school curriculum. They are the framework for learning experiences, but they should never be considered as the total instructional program. You will want to use trade books, or library books, to supplement the material in textbooks, and reference books to provide factual material related to specific areas of study. You may want to use magazines which focus on single topics of current interest for both informational and recreational reading. You may also want to begin a collection of leaflets and pamphlets. You may find some pictures and photographs to mount and cover with laminating film or clear contact paper to add to your collection of resource materials.

*Chalkboards*—The chalkboard is one of the most familiar visual devices in the classroom. Both students and teachers can use the chalkboard in a number of ways. As a change of pace, students enjoy going to the board individually or in groups to do their work. For teachers, the chalkboard is a readily available place to record information, place seatwork and homework assignments, and use in teaching lessons.

Although you are accustomed to seeing the chalkboard used in the classroom, you may not feel comfortable using it yourself. It is difficult to write a lot of material on the board while you are teaching, since you cannot watch the students when you are facing the board. If you have work to put on the board, do it the night before or early in the morning when you are not rushed. It is important to form your letters correctly so your writing will be a good model for the students to follow. You may need guidelines to keep your writing straight. You can soak chalk for 20 minutes in a mixture of three parts water and one part saturated sugar water to use for drawing lines along a straightedge as guides. These lines will not erase, but will wash off easily with water.

*Models, globes, and maps*—Models are three-dimensional replicas of actual objects which may be smaller (an airplane) or larger (the ear) than actual size. Globes are models of the earth, and maps are two-dimensional representations of the earth's geographic and/or political features. Both globes and maps are helpful in visualizing geographic relationships and understanding world affairs. Be sure they are current, because political boundaries change.

*Audio media*—You should use audio media when sound is of primary importance for learning or appreciation. You can use recordings of folk songs, important historical speeches, famous symphony concerts, or performances by military bands. You might want to play recordings of town meetings or forums to use as a basis for discussions of controversial issues. In many schools, students learn foreign languages in language labs that use audio media for instructional purposes. Dramatizations, documentaries, poetry readings, and great moments from history are also particularly well suited to audio presentations.

There are three major types of audio media: radio, phonograph, and audiotape recordings. Each has certain features that make it particularly appropriate for given situations. Radio is readily available and provides immediate communication on specific national or international affairs, such as a space launch. Many stations broadcast outstanding educational programs, but scheduling these programs into your instructional periods can be a problem. Phonographs have certain advantages over radios in that the same selection can be played more than once and whenever the time is right. They are not as versatile as audiotape recorders, however, for instructional purposes.

Audiotape recorders have many features that make them desirable for classroom use. Students can record themselves when they read orally or make speeches, play back the tape to listen for errors, and make efforts to improve. You can record classroom activities such as dramatizations, interviews, panel discussions, or musical programs, and play them back later. You could also record some stories or lessons for students to use individually or in groups at listening stations while you are working directly with other groups of students.

You may want to have your own audiotape recorder because there are so many good opportunities for using it during the school day. An audiotape recorder is fairly inexpensive, and tapes can be erased and re-used. Your school may have a tape library where you can find tapes for various purposes.

*Projected still pictures*—Four types of projected still pictures are generally available for classroom use: slides, filmstrips, overhead transparencies, and opaque projections. Slides can be selected and arranged to suit your purpose. After you assemble them, you can add a commentary tape with background sound effects. Instead of a prepared narrative, you may prefer to discuss the slides as you go, taking as much or as little time with each slide as you wish. Remote control projectors allow you to stand at the front of the class and point to details you want the students to notice.

Filmstrips may be used by individual students or with the entire class. You can use them with synchronized records or tapes, or you may prefer to read from the accompanying guide. When you use the filmstrips without synchronized sound, you can hold them on each frame for any length of time. You can also roll them forward or backward while the students discuss the filmstrip with you. If there are captions on the bottoms of the frame, you may want to cover them and discuss the pictures before revealing the captions.

The overhead projector is simple to operate, and can be used to project images on a screen in a normally lighted classroom. You can easily create your own transparencies by writing with a grease pencil or transparency marking pen on a clear sheet of acetate, or you can use commercially prepared transparencies designed for use with your textbook or units. If you have never used an overhead projector, become acquainted with it during your student teaching. Practice using it by yourself before using it with your class. Remember three important points: (1) check the placement and focus of the projector before the lesson starts; (2) know how to place the transparencies so the images are readable on the screen; and (3) identify items by pointing on the transparencies, not on the screen.

An opaque projector produces full-color images from materials that are not transparent, such as maps, mounted pictures, newspaper or magazine clippings, sheet music, or concrete materials. It can also be used to create enlargements; you project an image onto a large surface (such as newsprint or cardboard) and trace it. If you decide to use this projector, the classroom must be darkened in order to see the image clearly. Be sure to place the bulky machine so that it does not block anyone's view of the screen. You can move it forward to give a smaller image, or back to make a larger image. The bulb becomes very hot; it can easily overheat and actually destroy materials if you leave them in place too long. The fan may cause the paper to flutter, so you may need to hold it in place by mounting it on stiff cardboard.

*Films*—You can use films to create interest in a unit, to review and reinforce a subject under study, to provide a vicarious experience, or to initiate discussion. Some films are springboards for creative activities; others are straightforward presentations of subject matter through illustrated lectures. As processes are speeded up or slowed down on film, pupils can watch changes occur that would otherwise be unobservable.

*Television and videotape*—Two types of television programming are appropriate for educational purposes: instructional television, which is specifically intended for school use, and television of educational value, which is usually viewed at home.

Whether or not you make use of instructional television will probably be determined by your cooperating teacher and the availability of a television set. Unlike filmstrips and films, you cannot preview a television program, so you must study the manual to develop your lesson. Turn on your television set at least 15 minutes before the scheduled starting time to make sure it is operating correctly. Introduce vocabulary and concepts by writing them on the chalkboard and discussing them, and thoroughly prepare your students for what they will see. When the television lesson starts, encourage students to respond to the television teacher by participating actively in the lesson yourself. During the television lesson, take notes on points you want to discuss later and walk around among the students to make sure they are actively involved in the lesson. After the television lesson is over, don't reteach the lesson, but instead follow through with related activities.

You can assign the students to watch regular television programming. Documentaries, cultural programs, or series of educational significance are often shown during the evenings. Television guides are available for teachers for these types of programs. With the help of a guide, you can assign students to watch for certain points or ideas as they view the programs. The next day, you should follow up with a discussion or other experiences based on the programs.

Videotape recordings are similar to television programs, but have other features that make them especially useful in education. You can record television programs on videotape and play them back later. Be sure to observe the copyright laws concerning the period of time you are permitted to show videotapes of commercial programs, however. You can also record students' performances with portable videotape recorders and play them back for the students to see. The students can use these videotape recordings for self-analysis, especially in the areas of speech, drama, dance, and athletics.

*Computer Assisted Instruction (CAI)*—Computer literacy refers to knowledge of and experience with computers. It covers such areas as school lessons, problem solving, games, and awareness of the application of computer technology for future jobs and everyday living. In recent years, computer literacy has become part of the curriculum of many schools at all grade levels.

Schools use microcomputers for a variety of purposes. Computer literacy is the primary goal in many schools. Microcomputers provide enrichment in school subjects and offer challenges for bright students, and can also be used for remedial and compensatory purposes. Students can practice skills in mathematics and language arts by completing drill exercises; they can learn about social and economic situations by engaging in simulation activities. They can solve problems with microcomputers by writing their own programs or by using commercially prepared programs.

As a student teacher, you may find that computer assisted instruction is a part of the classes you are assigned to teach. You should have your cooperating teacher or the media specialist orient you to the particular computer used in your school. You will need to know how to load a commercial courseware package (the program that tells the computer what to do) and what the special keys on the computer keyboard mean. You also need to know what to do if a student "crashes" a program (causes it to cease to operate).

You should also know the proper way to handle and care for the courseware. If your system has a disk drive, you may find this information on the protective sleeve of the diskette. If your system uses a cassette drive, you should care for the cassettes the same way you care for the audio cassettes you use for recorded speech or music. Diskettes, cassettes, and plug-in modules must all be kept as clean as possible—dust-free and uncontaminated by food substances or drinks.

Be sure to read the documentation for each program your students are using. This will enable you to help students load programs, enter answers properly, and understand error messages. Some programs can be adjusted to the particular student; for example, response time or number of items can be varied. Usually, the accompanying documentation tells the teacher how to make these adjustments.

Some CAI programs have a computer managed instruction (CMI) component. These programs provide you with an analysis of student performances, may suggest further instructional needs, and may move the students through new instructional sequences without your direct intervention. Obviously, this component can be a valuable aid. If such a component is not included in the program, however, you may wish to check the results on the screen for each student before he or she ends the program.

## Community Resources

The community in which your school is located offers many opportunities for purposeful learning experiences. Through resource people and field trips, it provides links between the basic skills taught in the classroom and the application of these skills in the outside world. As a student teacher, your community involvement will be limited, but you can still utilize many resources if you begin early to explore the possibilities.

**Resource people**  A resource person can often attract students' attention better than the classroom teacher. Because of his or her direct experience with a topic, the presentation is usually more credible and more likely to make a lasting impression. You cannot be an expert in every field, so a visitor can supplement your knowledge. A resource person can be especially effective at the beginning of a unit to create interest, or near the end of a unit to reinforce and extend concepts.

The first step in using resource people is to consider who has expertise in the topics you plan to cover. Your personal friends may have hobbies or experiences that would make them valuable resource people. If you are student teaching in your hometown, you may already know people who could contribute to your unit. School personnel may discuss their work experiences or offer special knowledge. Your university employs specialists in many fields who may be willing to work with you. People from varied cultural, ethnic, and religious backgrounds may be available to share their heritage. Businesses and industries, banks, protective service agencies, public utilities, and government agencies at all levels often have representatives who go into the schools to provide information.

Resource people can be identified through various approaches. Your school may have a volunteer services program or a file with the names of resource people and their areas of expertise. Your cooperating teacher or other school personnel may be able to recommend a suitable resource person for your subject. Senior citizens can be recruited from retirement centers and church and community organizations. You may wish to survey your students to see if their parents or someone else they know can be helpful. A sample survey form is provided in Figure 1-5. If you become involved in the community, you may discover additional resource people. Before you take a survey, be sure to get permission from school authorities.

After you select someone with the appropriate specialized knowledge, you will have to contact him or her concerning the proposed school visit. Tactfully discuss the type of presentation, the need to adjust to the students' level, and the amount of time available. Discuss the students' background knowledge, attention span, and probable questions. The visitor may prefer to lecture, show slides, demonstrate a process, or talk informally. Be sure he or she understands the purpose of the visit and how it relates to what you are teaching.

You must also prepare students for resource visitors. They should be involved in the planning and may want to make lists of questions prior to visits. Students can issue invitations, arrange for any special equipment, meet guests upon their arrival, introduce them, and assist them in their presentations. Students should be encouraged to show their appreciation at the time of the visit and later in the form of thank-you letters. As the teacher, you must relate the presentations of resource people to your unit by preparing the students for visits and following them up with reinforcing activities.

Figure 1-5   Survey of Resource People

Date _____

Student's Name _____ Grade_____ Phone_____

Teacher's Name _____ School _____

Address of Student _____

Parent's Name _____

Address (if different) _____

Are you willing to volunteer your help in your son's or daughter's classroom?

_____

If so, what days and hours are most convenient? _____

Do you have any special talents, skills, or knowledge that you can share with

the class?_____   If so, what are they? _____

_____

Perhaps you know someone who would be able to contribute something worthwhile to the school in terms of ability. If so, please fill in the information below. (Use other side for additional suggestions.)

Name _____ Phone_____

_____

Address_____

Possible Contribution _____
Thank you for your cooperation!

Some business and civic leaders may not be willing to come to the school, but will grant interviews to students who come to see them. The experience of conducting an interview is worthwhile; however, careful and detailed arrangements need to be made prior to the interview. School personnel must approve the interview. Consent must also be given by the prospective interviewee and by the parents of the students participating in the interview. The students should draw up questions in advance, practice notetaking skills, and learn proper conduct in handling an interview. After the interview, students need to organize their notes and write summaries of the information to share with their classmates.

Students at the secondary level can become involved with resource people by taking surveys. The students need to identify an issue in which they are interested and design a simple questionnaire to give to people they know. Topics might include whether or not to build a new gymnasium, establish a teen center, or extend the city limits. Students can get additional information about their topics by searching through records and interviewing city employees. They can summarize their findings and draw conclusions that might have implications for community action. They can submit the results to the media for dissemination to the public.

**Field trips**  A field trip is an organized class excursion for the purpose of obtaining information through direct observation. A child's experiences with field trips usually begin with visits to places like the fire station and dairy farm. Some classes take end-of-year trips to a zoo or museum. Older students may "run" City Hall for one day of the year. Each student is appointed to a position and assumes the responsibilities of the person who occupies the corresponding position in city government. Participation in field experiences during their school years gives students many opportunities to understand how their community operates and to broaden their knowledge of specific subjects. Acquaintance with different occupations can also give them direction in choosing careers.

Although a field trip can be a valuable learning experience, it requires a great deal of planning; otherwise, it can be a fiasco. Students may become disorderly and disruptive, get injured, destroy property, and generally damage school-community relations. Unless you make careful preparations, students may not see the reason for the trip, and its educational value is therefore lost. The checklist in Figure 1-6 can help you plan a successful field trip.

Other problems beset the field trip from a different point of view. With gasoline costs rising and school budgets tightening, many school districts no longer provide free bus transportation for field trips. Increased concern about liability and lawsuits makes a teacher wary of the risks involved in taking students away from the school. In self-contained classrooms, scheduling a field trip is usually fairly simple because only one teacher is involved. It is far more difficult, however, to arrange trips in secondary schools because of the short class periods. Sometimes teachers of other subjects will cooperate to permit the absence of your students, but it may be necessary to plan trips at this level for after school or Saturdays.

Students who know what to expect are likely to learn more from a field trip than students who have no background information. The class should be involved in planning each trip. Even though you may have the idea in the back of your mind, you may want to let the students think the idea is theirs. For young children, a discussion about the subject and the proposed field trip may result in a set of questions on a language experience chart. These questions can be used as objectives for the trip. Older students can research the subject and develop individual lists of questions which may ultimately result in written reports.

Field trips are valuable only when they are an integral part of a total learning situation. You need to make adequate preparation

**Figure 1-6  Checklist for Field Trip**

1 _____ Permission to take a field trip has been granted by the school.
2 _____ Personnel at the destination have been contacted and a time has been set for the visit.
3 _____ Transportation arrangements have been made.
4 _____ If you are using private cars, insurance and liability regulations have been checked.
5 _____ An adequate number of adults have agreed to accompany the students.
6 _____ Proper arrangements have been made regarding the facilities at the destination: rest rooms, cafeteria, picnic tables, parking areas, size of observation areas.
7 _____ Lunch money and other fees have been collected (if applicable).
8 _____ Parental permission notes have been sent home.
9 _____ Parental permission notes have been returned.
10 _____ Students have been told how to behave and what to wear.
11 _____ Students have been told what to expect and have adequate background knowledge to understand what they will see.
12 _____ A list of questions has been prepared to set purposes for the visit.
13 _____ Tape recorders and note pads are available for recording specific information.
14 _____ Safety hazards, if any, have been noted and appropriate precautions taken.
15 _____ A first aid kit is available for emergencies.
16 _____ A signal (such as a whistle or raised arm) has been agreed upon for getting students' attention.
17 _____ Students have been paired and assigned buddies (if appropriate).
18 _____ Policy manual regarding field trips has been read and policies have been followed.

and reinforce the educational value of the field trip with a variety of follow-up activities. These activities often spill over into many areas of the curriculum—social studies, science, reading, language arts, art, and music.

One example of an integrated learning experience is the neighborhood field trip.[3] This trip can be taken within walking distance of the school and can provide students with experiences in observing, collecting data, and making inferences. Before setting out on the walking tour, students should be told what data to collect for later analysis. After returning to the classroom, they may work in teams of three to five students to share their data and draw conclusions from their observations. They may want to record some of the data in the form of bar graphs or pictographs. These are some questions the students can consider:

[3]Kenneth W. Kelsey, "A Neighborhood Field Trip," *Science and Children* (April 1979): 14—15.

1  Which houses do or do not have people inside them now? How do you know?
2  How many and what types of trees are growing in this block?
3  Which houses have pets and/or children? What makes you think so?
4  What kind of people live in each house? How do you know?
5  How many houses are constructed of brick, wood, stone, or something else?

### Examples of school-community experiences

1. A visit from an Antarctic scientist has become an annual tradition for children in an elementary school in Virginia. His presentation is part of a "Winter Holiday" theme and ties in with the SCIS Science Material. Children examine a stuffed penguin and look at pictures of his trips to Antarctica. In conjunction with his visit, they find Antarctica on maps and globes, read about Antarctica, and watch films of animals native to Antarctica.[4]

2. A retired bicycle repairman in Tennessee has worked with reluctant remedial students to create an interest in learning. All students in the school are encouraged to bring to school any bicycles that need repair. Under the direction of the repairman, the remedial students study repair manuals, mull over catalogs, place orders, and follow directions for repairing bicycles. Their interest in school and their achievement levels have soared.

3. Photography is the key ingredient in a community studies program for a class of junior high school students. The teacher is especially interested in photography and encourages her students to use their cameras to photograph community sites. At the same time, they collect historical photographs of the town. As they excitedly compare the old pictures with the new, they become aware of the many changes that have taken place in their community over the years.[5]

4. Second year chemistry students in a Pennsylvania high school are released from class two or three times a week to work in a host industry or medical center. The class is scheduled for the last period of the day, and students leave school at 1:30 to work until 5:00 in the community job. The students work in laboratories, where they use the latest techniques and equipment available.[6]

[4]Helenmarie Hofman, "Resource People," *Science and Children* (February 1978): 20–21.

[5]Casey Murrow, "The Classroom Goes to Town," *National Elementary Principal* (June 1979): 21–24.

[6]Thomas W. Clapper, "A School-Community Science Experience," *Journal of Chemical Education* (February 1980): 143–44.

You may find an opportunity to develop a plan for using resources creatively in your teaching situation. Talk it over with your cooperating teacher, then make it work!

## Discussion Questions

1   What should you do if you join the teachers in the faculty lounge and hear them discussing one of your students in a way you feel is unfair to the student? Should you get up quietly and leave, sit there quietly and not enter into the discussion, speak out and defend the student, or mention that you think it is wrong to talk about students that way?

2   Do you believe the school is responsible for providing education in values, sex, systems of government (including communism), morality, and religion? If so, how should these issues be handled? What would your approach be?

3   What are some things that cause stress? What are some ways you can reduce these stressors? Can you think of a time when you handled a stressful situation especially well?

4   What are some common areas of stress that you share with other student teachers? Can any changes be made in policies or assignments to reduce the stress?

5   Should you use a free, current, and interesting film from a company which uses the film to advertise its product? If you decide to use the film, what are some ways to handle the advertising message?

6   How can you use the resources in your community? What people, places, or agencies are available that relate to your subjects? How can you find out?

7   What do you do if one of your student's parents offers to share information with your class that you feel is inappropriate? How can you avoid offending the parent and the student? Is there another way you could use the parent's services?

8   What is the policy regarding field trips in your school? Are they permitted? How is transportation arranged? What regulations are in effect? Would a field trip be a good learning experience for your students?

## Selected References

Association of Teacher Educators. *Providing Legal Status for Student Teachers.* Reston, Va.: n. d. (36 pp. mimeographed)

Baker, Justine. *Microcomputers in the Classroom.* Bloomington, Ind. Phi Delta Kappa Educational Foundation, 1982.

Beyrer, Mary K., and Marlene Woodfill. "Ethics for the Eighties." *Health Education* 11 (March/April 1980): 9.

Borden, Christopher III. "Helping Print-oriented Teachers To Use Other Media." *Educational Technology* 18 (December 1978): 41–42.

Busse, Norman L. "Revealed: How Classroom Teachers Use Media." *Audiovisual Instruction* 21 (October 1976): 44–45.

Clapper, Thomas W. "A School-Community Science Experience." *Journal of Chemical Education* 57 (February 1980): 143–44.

Clark, Phillip. "Community Education and its Major Components." *The Education Digest* 43 (November 1979): 58–61.

Connors, Eugene T. *Student Discipline and the Law.* Bloomington, Ind.: Phi Delta Kappa Educational Foundation, 1979.

Davis, Charles C. "How to Cope with Stress in the Classroom." *Health Education* 8 (September/October 1977): 36–37.

Dunn, Rita S., and Robert W. Cole. "Inviting Malpractice through Mainstreaming." *Educational Leadership* 36 (February 1979): 304–6.

Evans, Christopher, et al. "Microcomputers in the Classroom." *Today's Education* 71 (April/May): 11–28.

Flygare, Thomas J. "Teacher's Private Lives and Legal Rights." *The Education Digest* 42 (February 1977): 26–28.

Gray, Lee J. "Slow Down: You Move Too Fast." *Teacher* 96 (April 1979): 52–53.

Hofman, Helenmarie. "Resource People." *Science and Children* 15 (February 1978): 20–21.

Hunter, Madeline. "Counterirritants to Teaching." *Instructor* 87 (August 1977): 122–25.

Kelsey, Kenneth W. "A Neighborhood Field Trip." *Science and Children* 16 (April 1979): 14–15.

Kemp, Jerrold E. *Planning and Producing Audiovisual Materials*, 4th ed. New York: Harper and Row, 1980.

LaMorte, Michael W. "What Is Your School Law IQ?" *Phi Delta Kappan* 57 (June 1976): 679–81.

Logan, John W. "The Gossiping Educators: A Problem in Professional Ethics." *Phi Delta Kappan* 60 (September 1979): 64.

Logan, John W. "I Could Have Told You Johnny Was A Problem, I Had Him Last Year." *Teacher* 96 (November 1978): 16–19.

Miklethun, Betsey A. "The Young Reach Out to the Old in Shaker Heights." *Today's Education* 70 (April/May 1981): 34E–35E.

Miller, J. Wesley. "The Ethics of Returning Papers to Students." *College English* 39 (January 1978): 606–7.

Miller, Jerome K. "Copyright Considerations in Teacher- and Student-Designed Learning Materials." *Social Education* 40 (May 1976): 282–83.

Miller, William C. *Dealing With Stress: A Challenge for Educators.* Bloomington, Ind.: Phi Delta Kappa Educational Foundation, 1979.

Moe, Dorothy. "Teacher Burnout: A Prescription." *Today's Education* 68 (November/December 1979): 35–36.

Murrow, Casey. "The Classroom Goes to Town." *National Elementary Principal* 58 (June 1979): 21–24.

Needle, Richard H., Tom Griffin, Roger Svendsen, and Coleen Berney. "Teacher Stress and Consequences." *The Journal of School Health* 50 (February 1980): 96–99.

Nolte, M. Chester. "The Legal Heat on Teachers—How to Avoid It." *Learning* 6 (February 1978): 86–93.

St. John, Walter D., and John Walden. "Keeping Student Confidences." *Phi Delta Kappan* 57 (June 1976): 682–84.

Schmid, William T. "The Teacher and the Media Specialist." *Media and Methods* 13 (October 1976): 22–24.

Selye, Hans. *Stress Without Distress.* Philadelphia: J. B. Lippincott, 1974.

Slater, Shirley. "Legal Aspects of Teaching." *Forecast for Home Economics* 25 (May/June 1980): 61–62.

Styles, Ken, and Gray Cavanaugh. "Stress in Teaching and How to Handle It." *English Journal* 66 (January 1977): 76–79.

Tractenberg, Paul L. "A Response to Dunn and Cole." *Educational Leadership* 36 (February 1979): 306–7.

Wegner, Hart. *Teaching with Film.* Bloomington, Ind.: Phi Delta Kappa Educational Foundation, 1977.

Winters, Kay, and Marta Felber. *The Teacher's Cope Book: How to End the Year Better Than You Started.* Belmont, Calif.: Pitman, 1980.

Woodbury, Marda. *Selecting Instructional Materials.* Bloomington, Ind.: Phi Delta Kappa Educational Foundation, 1978.

# 2
# *Human Relations*

Mrs. Sanchez is a cooperating teacher. Miss Mosley is her student teacher.

Mrs. Sanchez: Miss Mosley, there is going to be a special inservice education program at the teacher center Thursday evening at 8:00. Would you like to attend the session with me?

Miss Mosley: What is the topic?

Mrs. Sanchez: Our reading program. I know you aren't required to attend, but this is an excellent opportunity for you to learn about the materials you will be using for the remainder of the semester. I thought you would want to take advantage of it. I'll be glad to drive you over there, if you need transportation.

Miss Mosley: Yes, I would like to go. Thank you for inviting me.

At the end of the semester, Miss Mosley is pleased to see that Mrs. Sanchez has made the comment: "Interested in self-improvement of teaching skills."

1  Did Mrs. Sanchez have a good basis for her evaluative comment? Why or why not?
2  Do you show interest in self-improvement of teaching skills when opportunities are presented?

## Focus on Specific Relationships

An important part of the student teaching experience is developing appropriate relationships with a variety of people—students, college supervisors, cooperating teachers, other school personnel, other student teachers, and parents. Your interaction with these people can be a major factor in your overall success as a student teacher. Let us first look at each of these relationships separately.

## Students

The most important and most demanding set of relationships you must handle as a student teacher is the one with your students. It is they to whom you hope to impart the knowledge you have gleaned from your program of preparation. It is important to develop a positive and cooperative relationship with each student in the class. Some student teachers misunderstand the nature of this relationship. They want to be "buddies" with the students, because this seems the best way to be liked. Unfortunately, being liked is not sufficient for a student/teacher relationship. Respect is also important, as is recognition of the student teacher as an authority figure. The students' respect must be earned, and it takes time to earn it. It is not automatically accorded. Development of a "buddy" relationship can undermine the students' respect for you as an authority figure, and thus adversely affect classroom control. We will consider the topic of classroom control more thoroughly at a later time.

What, then, should your relationship with your students be? An appropriate relationship will require a great deal of perceptiveness and understanding on your part.

## General Guidelines

First, you must treat each student as a worthwhile individual. You must react positively to all students and show them you care about their progress and well-being. Something so simple as learning the students' names quickly can have a positive effect on your relationships with them. Noticing that a student was absent the day before and inquiring about her health or indicating that she was missed shows the student that you care. When students perform well, your approving comments help establish a positive relationship.

Nonverbal behavior can also promote good relationships with students. *Smile* at them often. Show them that you enjoy them. Let all the students know you are there to help them. *Listen* to them when they voice problems, and try to help each one. Let them know that you are on their side.

It is important to let the students know you respect them as individuals. You can do this by listening to their opinions and expressions of feelings and responding to them in a way that shows you have given careful thought to their ideas. Dismissing students' ideas as trivial or worthless will indicate that you feel they are unable to contribute effectively to the class. Such actions can cause students to withdraw from the learning environment rather than participate.

One important aspect of respecting students' individuality is to avoid labeling them according to racial, ethnic, socioeconomic, or sex stereotypes. Expectations should not be the same for all blacks, all whites, all Hispanics, all people of Polish extraction, all Jews, all poor people, all rich people, all boys, or all girls. Each of these groups has industrious individuals and others who are lazy, bright individuals and others who are dull, honest individuals and others who are dishonest, clean individuals and others who are not, athletic individuals and some who are not, and so on. Each member of a group should be looked upon as an individual with a variety of traits acquired through interaction with the environment. As a student teacher, you are an important part of that environment, and, therefore, you help to shape some of the traits your students develop. Don't be so narrow-minded as to expect all members of a group to be alike. Let us look at the case of Darren as an example.

## Case Study: Sex Stereotypes

Miss Chambers was a student teacher in a fifth grade class that was studying Mexico. She thought that staging a fiesta, which would give the children the opportunity to sample many Mexican foods, would be a good teaching device.

She told the boys to plan and construct a set to look like a festive Mexican home, while the girls located and prepared the foods to be tried. Darren, who was an excellent cook, wanted to prepare the tamales. Miss Chambers admonished him with the reply, "Cooking is women's work. You help the boys with the construction."

1  What is your analysis of Miss Chambers' reply to Darren?
2  What would you have said?
3  Do you suppose some of the girls might have enjoyed the construction project better than the cooking?
4  How would you have handled the entire project?

Sex stereotypes, such as the one Miss Chambers voiced, are unfortunately not uncommon. Certain activities, toys, and manners of speaking are arbitrarily attributed to boys and others to girls. A boy or girl who fails to fit the stereotype is treated as abnormal, instead of as an individual with a right to behave in a way that does not fit the stereotype. Teachers often discourage boys from crying, cooking, or sewing, saying that they are not appropriate activities for boys, just as other activities are considered inappropriate for girls.

Sexism is an issue you should be aware of when you choose materials and work with male and female students. It is a way of treating males and females differently solely on the basis of their sex. The practice of sexism can restrict what a person becomes by limiting choices of behavior and careers. Title IX of the Education Amendments Act of 1972 was enacted by Congress to prohibit discrimination against males or females in federally assisted education programs. Even though it is no longer legal to discriminate, many people continue to do so through their attitudes toward sex roles.

Consider your own feelings by answering the following questions. Are men or women more likely to cry? Should the wife or husband be the primary provider for a family? Are girls or boys likely to be better at each of the following: reading, math, science, cooking, industrial arts, or sewing? Who will cause the most discipline problems—boys or girls? If you have definite choices of one sex in each of your answers, you are probably reflecting the sex role stereotypes in our society.

The truth is, according to research, that there are very few innate differences between the sexes. Those differences that do appear to exist may be the result of different expectations for boys and girls as they grow up. You may be helping to cause the differences. Instead, you should help both boys and girls recognize the breadth of their behavioral and career choices. Girls should be encouraged to engage in athletic activities; boys should be allowed to try cooking and sewing as well as carpentry. You can talk about how men and women are beginning to explore nontraditional career choices, such as nursing for males and construction work for females. A girl who says she wants to become an airplane pilot should be given as much positive reinforcement as a boy who says the same thing.

Your language may unintentionally support sexist stereotypes. When you speak of the builders of our nation as forefathers, for example, it may seem to young children that women had no part. Use of the generic *he* may also cause young, and even adolescent, students to assume that only males are the topic of conversation. Use of terms such as *mailman* and *policeman* to refer to letter carriers and police officers seem to close these careers to females. Much of this language has probably been ingrained since childhood and may be difficult to avoid. Considering the possible effects of such usage on your students, however, you should attempt to eliminate it from your speech patterns.

Some people have grown up hearing language that is derogatory toward certain racial, ethnic, or socioeconomic groups. This language must also be eliminated from your vocabulary, or you can do real damage to some of your students' self-concepts.

Some of your students may speak little or no English, but speak another language, while you may not speak that other language. How can you relate positively to such a student? It takes persistence and effort, but you can have a positive impact. Include the student in classroom activities that require little language from the first moment he or she enters the class. At the elementary level, these activities may include playing action games at recess, drawing and painting, and viewing displays and demonstrations. At the secondary level, the activities may include almost all aspects of a physical education class or some vocational classes and viewing displays and demonstrations in other areas. You should attempt to communicate with the student through gestures, pictures, and any words you know from his or her language. You should assign the student a buddy to guide him or her to the cafeteria, rest rooms, and other classrooms, if the students change classes. If another student speaks the new student's language at all, he or she would be a good choice for this assignment. You should purchase a foreign language dictionary to refer to when trying to communicate with the student. If the student reads his or her own language fluently, you should provide a dictionary with English equivalents of familiar words. In the lower grades, you can construct a picture dictionary of English words for the student. You can also show the student pictures and objects and teach the English names for them, then let the student teach you the names in his or her native language. A student buddy can also participate in this activity. Whatever you do, even though attempting to communicate with this student may be frustrating, always be positive. Encourage other students to include the new student in their activities, explaining that they are already at home in this school and they can help the new student become comfortable by helping him or her learn the standard procedures and popular activities. Students often take behavioral cues from their teachers.

You can show respect for your students by allowing them to take on responsibilities. Giving students tasks for which they are responsible, no matter how small the tasks may be, shows that you trust them to fulfill the duties and recognize their capabilities to do so. This attitude can have an enormous effect upon the way a student responds to you. Let us look at the case of Randy as an example.

_____

## Case Study: Showing Respect for Students

Randy was a sixth grade student who had failed two previous grades. As a consequence, he was fourteen years old in a classroom with many eleven- and twelve-year-olds. He was larger than any of the other students and had different interests. To make matters worse, he was poor, and most of his clothing was worn and faded. The heels of his boots were run over, and his sleeves were a little too short for his arms. His general style of dress was reminiscent of a stereotypical motorcycle gang member on the late-night movies.

Randy was generally quiet and obedient in class, but rarely made any attempt to do his assignments. He displayed an extremely negative self-concept, informing the student teacher, Miss Davis, "I'm too dumb to do that," when she encouraged him to try some of the work.

Miss Davis tried very hard to treat Randy the same way she treated the other students. She called on him to respond in class and listened respectfully to his replies. She greeted him when he entered the classroom in the morning. She smiled and spoke when she passed him in the hall. She gave him much encouragement and assistance during directed study periods. Still, she felt she was making little headway. To be sure, he talked a *little* more in class than he had previously, and turned in a few more assignments, but Miss Davis still did not feel she had reached Randy.

One day, as Randy was leaving the classroom to go home for lunch, Miss Davis realized she had a letter that needed to be mailed and remembered that Randy passed by a mailbox on his way home. She called to him and asked him if he would do her a favor and mail the letter. Randy looked at her in disbelief. *Nobody* at school had ever trusted him to take responsibility for *anything*. He hesitated and said, "You want *me* to mail it?"

Miss Davis replied, "I would appreciate your doing it, if you don't mind."

Randy walked over and picked up the letter, glancing around to see if others had heard this exchange. "I'll be sure it gets mailed," he told Miss Davis rather loudly, and walked out of the room proudly holding the letter.

Upon returning to the room, the first thing he told Miss Davis was, "I mailed your letter." He said it with a smile of satisfaction.

Thereafter, Randy began to respond more and more to Miss Davis's encouragement to do assignments. He seemed to try much harder to do what she thought he could do. He did not become an overnight scholar, but he improved in all his work and once even scored a "100" in mathematics. And he continued to carry Miss Davis's letters with pride.

1  What is your analysis of the way Miss Davis handled Randy?
2  Would you have treated the situation differently in any way?

---

It is important to give attention to all students. Do not favor a few with your attention and ignore or avoid others. This may be difficult, for some students are not as appealing as others. Some dress carelessly or shabbily, fail to wash, or have belligerent attitudes. It is your challenge to be as accepting of and positive about the appropriate behaviors these students exhibit as you are of the neat, clean, and cooperative students. This does not mean you should accept behavior that deviates from school rules, but it does mean you should show acceptance of the individual, even when you show disapproval of his or her behavior. It also means you should find traits in each person to which you can react positively.

To have a good relationship with the students, absolute fairness is important. If you have a rule, enforce it equally for all students. Any hint that you have "teacher's pets" will cause poor relationships between you and the majority of the class.

Honesty is also important in your relationship with your students. Students quickly recognize insincerity and resent it.

In brief, to establish good relationships with students, treat them as worthwhile individuals, don't stereotype them, be positive toward them, treat them fairly, and let them know that you like them and are "on their side." (We will discuss this topic more fully in later chapters.)

# College Supervisors

Your relationship with your college supervisor is also important. He or she has the responsibility for overseeing and critiquing your work in the classroom. The college supervisor is there to help you throughout the student teaching experience, as well as to determine your grade at the end. Therefore, the college supervisor will be offering, either orally or in writing, suggestions for improving your teaching. These suggestions are intended to help you analyze what you are doing and make the most of your field experience. They are not meant as personal attacks upon your competence. Try to consider the suggestions objectively and ask questions about points that may be unclear, rather than react defensively and try to produce excuses for mistakes you may have made. If you show your college supervisor that you are open to suggestions and will make an effort to benefit from constructive criticism, your relationship is likely to be a good one.

Asking pertinent questions of your college supervisor shows a desire to improve and an interest in seeking new knowledge. These attributes are desirable in a student teacher and are likely to be appreciated. After observing your teaching, your college supervisor will probably hold a conference with you or with both you and your cooperating teacher. It is a good idea to take the written comments your college supervisor has made about your performance to these scheduled conferences. If conferences are not automatic, don't hesitate to request them if you feel the need for more feedback.

---

## Case Study: Fear of Exposure

Dale Martin was a secondary level student teacher, assigned to two classes of algebra, a class of plane geometry, and a class of trigonometry. His college supervisor had visited him several times, but all visits had been during one of his algebra classes. Dale felt very confident and comfortable teaching the algebra classes, and his comments from his college supervisor had all been positive. He was really struggling with the trigonometry class, however, and could sense that his cooperating teacher was displeased with his efforts. Dale confessed his concern to Alvin James, a student teacher in physical education.

Alvin suggested that Dale ask Mr. Walsky, their college supervisor, to make a point of sitting in on the trigonometry class on his next visit to the school, so that he could give Dale some feedback. Dale told Alvin that he thought he had better leave well enough alone—Mr. Walsky had only seen him in successful experiences. Perhaps if he saw the trigonometry class, Mr. Walsky's overall evaluation at the end of the quarter would be lower. Acting on this reasoning, Dale said nothing to Mr. Walsky.

1 How do you feel about Dale's situation?
2 What is your opinion of Alvin's advice?
3 What would you have done?
4 What is likely to be the result of Dale's decision?

When speaking with your college supervisor, it is important to be straightforward about your problems. He or she is the person best equipped to act as liaison between you and your cooperating teacher or other school personnel, if the need arises. Your honesty will make the supervisor's job easier and will probably ultimately improve your situation. Your openness about problems will also improve the rapport between you and the college supervisor.

The college supervisor is there to help you. Your openness, honesty, and willingness to accept suggestions will create a good relationship that makes it easier for the supervisor to help.

## Cooperating Teachers

A good relationship with your cooperating teacher is vital for achieving maximum benefit from the student teaching experience. Whereas your college supervisor may be in contact with you once or twice a week for a period or two, your cooperating teacher is with you every day. You and your cooperating teacher will be working together for the best interest of the students.

It is important to remember that the cooperating teacher has ultimate responsibility for the classroom to which you are assigned. He or she is legally responsible, and because of the responsibility, some cooperating teachers are more hesitant than others to relinquish control. The way you conduct yourself initially will have a strong influence upon how the cooperating teacher feels about leaving you in control. Taking an interest in everything that is going on in the classroom, asking questions about appropriate procedures and classroom rules, and making notes of information the cooperating teacher offers may be helpful. Being responsive to requests for assistance (putting up bulletin boards, grading test papers, etc.) will show the cooperating teacher that you are a willing worker.

Your appearance and manner are also important. Your cooperating teacher will feel more comfortable entrusting you with his or her charges if you dress appropriately (look more like a teacher than a student), speak correctly (use standard English), and exhibit self-confidence.

---

## Case Study: Appropriate Dress

Susan Granger was a secondary English student teacher. Her cooperating teacher was Mrs. Barfield, a fifty-year-old English teacher.

On the first day of student teaching, Susan reported to her assignment wearing a pair of jeans, a tee shirt, and a pair of tennis shoes. Mrs. Barfield made the mistake of asking Susan if she were a new student in the class before she had a chance to introduce herself. When she learned who Susan was, Mrs. Barfield said, "Ms. Granger, I believe you need to dress more appropriately for teaching in the future."

Susan, noticing that Mrs. Barfield was clad in casual slacks and shirt, was furious. Later that day she said to her roommate, "Who does she think she is, telling me what to wear. She had on pants herself."

1 What do you think about Mrs. Barfield's comment to Susan?
2 Was it justified?
3 Was there a difference in Mrs. Barfield's dressing as she did and Susan being dressed as she was? If so, what was the difference?
4 Might Susan's attire affect her relationship with Mrs. Barfield? Might it affect her relationship with her secondary students?

---

When you are given an actual teaching assignment, careful planning is likely to evoke a positive response from your cooperating teacher. Showing responsibility in small ways will encourage the cooperating teacher to give you larger responsibilities. (Chapter 3 has tips for good planning.)

Although you may be very eager to begin teaching, do not *demand* that your teacher let you start. Demonstrate your readiness, then *suggest* that you are ready. If this fails, you may wish to consult your college supervisor, who can act as a liaison.

You may find that your cooperating teacher does some things differently from the way you would do them and/or the way you have been taught. Do not criticize his or her methods; ask *why* he or she does things that way. Weigh the pros and cons of the teacher's method. If you feel it is not the best way, simply ask if you can try another way in which you have some background. Most cooperating teachers expect some experimentation and will allow this without your resorting to an attack on an existing procedure. This approach can certainly help your relationship with the teacher, and, upon examination, you may find things of value in the teacher's approach that you will wish to use also. Just because you have not been exposed to an idea or approach before does not mean it is not a good one.

Most programs have specified minimum requirements that student teachers are expected to meet. If you are willing to do only the *minimum* expected of you, your relationship with the cooperating teacher may be less than perfect. Dedicated educators do not settle for doing the least they can get by with doing.

Your cooperating teacher, like your college supervisor, will be giving you oral and/or written suggestions and constructive criticism. Accepting these comments as avenues to improvement will enhance the rapport between you and your cooperating teacher. If the teacher sees that you are attempting to put the suggestions to work, he or she will be more likely to have positive feelings toward you as a prospective member of the profession. Ignoring suggestions or indicating that you cannot or will not change will not promote a good relationship.

---

## Case Study: No Desire to Change

In his first conference with his cooperating teacher, Leon Garritt was told, "Mr. Garritt, you must watch your English when you are speaking to the class. I noticed you saying 'he don't' and 'I seen' several times during this single lesson."

Leon responded, "That's the way everybody talks back home. I've talked that way all my life. It's too late to change now. Besides, I'm going back home to teach. I want to sound like everyone else."

1  How do you think Leon's teacher responded to Leon's explanation?
2  Do you think Leon's reaction affected his relationship with the teacher? In what way?
3  How would you have responded if you had been Leon?
4  How would you have responded if you had been Leon's teacher?
5  Does where Leon plans to teach have any relevance to the issue at hand?

Taking the initiative and offering assistance before it is requested shows the teacher that you are ready to be a part of classroom activities. Waiting to be told every move to make is a sign of lack of maturity and confidence.

You can see that showing the cooperating teacher your preparedness, willingness, and ability to perform in the classroom can do much to enhance your relationship. Appropriate reactions to suggestions and criticism and willingness to work cooperatively are also important.

## Other School Personnel

In addition to your cooperating teacher, you need to develop good relationships with other school personnel, including other teachers, administrators, counselors, supervisors, secretaries, custodial staff, and cafeteria workers. From time to time, you will have occasion to interact with all of these people.

From the time you are first in the school, introduce yourself to the school personnel with whom you come in contact. Explain that you are a student teacher and may need their assistance in the future, so you are pleased to meet them. They will appreciate your acknowledgment that you may need their help and may seek opportunities to help you. Even if you do not need their help, just knowing them and knowing that they know who you are will make life in the school more comfortable.

---

### Case Study: Pleasantness Pays Off

Miss Garcia, a student teacher in first grade, had gone out of her way to meet and be pleasant to the school custodian, Mr. Nabors, who had a reputation among some of the teachers of being uncooperative. She had cause to be glad she had done so on the first day her cooperating teacher left her in charge of the class.

The children were moving down the hall toward their classroom following a milk break, when Mario became sick at his stomach. The children squealed and scattered as Mario's snack gushed onto the floor. Mario burst into tears.

Mr. Nabors, hearing the commotion, hurried over to help Miss Garcia. He saw that the remainder of the class lined up again and became quiet, while Miss Garcia calmed Mario. Then he assured Miss Garcia that he would take care of cleaning the hall immediately, while she continued with her normal procedures.

1 Do you think Miss Garcia's friendly approach to the custodian worked in her favor?

**2** In your opinion, is it possible that the custodian's reputation is unjust?

**3** How might the other teachers elicit more cooperation from him?

---

In brief, you should be pleasant to all school personnel and cooperate with them as necessary. Your friendliness and cooperation will be returned in kind.

## Other Student Teachers

There are probably other student teachers assigned to your school; if not, you have probably been assigned to a seminar with student teachers from other schools. These peers are facing the same challenges that you are, even though the different situations make each assignment unique. If you are willing to share your experiences openly with these peers, you may find that they can help you analyze and solve the problems you face. At the same time, solutions you have discovered yourself may benefit others in the group. Openness and willingness to cooperate can make your relationships with the other student teachers very rewarding.

*Sharing experiences with fellow student teachers can help you analyze and solve problems.*

Just because another student teacher is teaching in an elementary school and you are teaching in a secondary school, or because another teacher is a physical education teacher and you are a chemistry teacher, do not assume you cannot learn from each other. Regardless of level or subject area, many of the problems student teachers encounter, especially in the area of human relations, are similar.

---

### Case Study: Learning From Others

Troy was assigned to a secondary geography class for his student teaching experience. He had planned for and taught several lessons, but had had trouble estimating the amount of time his plans were going to take. As a result, he had twice run out of instructional material before the period ended. He hadn't known what to do, so he had just let the students have a study period each time. He mentioned his problem in his student teaching seminar.

Carol was teaching in a sixth grade self-contained classroom, but was expected to conduct certain classes during specified periods of the day. She had run into the same problem that Troy had. Her cooperating teacher had suggested planning several extra filler activities for each subject area in case her lessons did not take as much time as she expected. The practice had worked well for her. She mentioned several filler activities she had used for social studies, including blank outline maps to be filled in with data pertinent to the current topic, vocabulary card games, and construction of time lines. Troy adapted several of her ideas to meet the needs of his particular class and found that they worked well for him too. (See chapter 5 for suggestions for filler activities.)

1  Do elementary and secondary student teachers have many common concerns such as the one Troy and Carol shared?
2  What are some of the common concerns?

---

Treat your fellow student teachers with the same respect you show the other teachers with whom you have contact. Listen to what they have to say in your seminars, and share your knowledge with them. The relationships can be mutually beneficial.

## Parents

As a student teacher, you may or may not have a great deal of contact with parents. If such contact occurs, however, it is vitally important that you develop good relationships with parents.

One factor in effective interaction with parents is knowing about the community in which you are student teaching. Awareness of the types of businesses, industries, and recreational facilities in the community will give you some insight into the background from which the parents are speaking. Awareness of the general socioeconomic, racial, and ethnic balance of the community will also be helpful. Knowing that the people in the town are generally avid football fans and enthusiastically support the local high school team or that they work in the coal mines and may have associated health problems gives you a basis for interacting with community members with greater understanding and empathy. For this reason, it is a good idea to spend some time familiarizing yourself with the community and its people. Walk around the downtown area and observe the businesses and the people. Attend recreational activities, such as ball games, concerts, dances, and festivals, and note community interests. Drive around the residential section and observe the types of homes in which your students live. These experiences will help prepare you for encounters with parents.

Many parents are uncomfortable in the school environment, so when parents come to the school to discuss their child's progress, the teacher (or you as the student teacher) must make an effort to put them at ease. Open the conversation with a nonthreatening comment, perhaps about the weather or some recent local event. Then express your appreciation to the parent for taking the time to come to the school. It is difficult for many parents to schedule such visits, and your acknowledgment of this fact may put the parent more at ease. It is also best to begin the discussion of the student on a positive note. Almost all students have attributes that can be praised—a pleasant manner, creativity, talent in art or music, athletic ability, cooperativeness, or excellence in a particular academic area. Be honest with parents about problems, but do not be abrupt or unkind in your comments. Explain the procedures you plan to implement to correct the problem, and express anticipation of improvement. Try to end the interview with another positive note. Always stress your desire to help the child in any way you can and urge the parents to consult you if they have any concerns. Throughout the conference, remain pleasant, calm, and objective.

It is important that the parents perceive you as a competent professional who is truly concerned about their child. If you put your best foot forward in any encounter with parents, they are more likely to be supportive of what you attempt to do with the students.

Listen to what parents have to tell you about their children. They can often give you information that will help you understand the students' strengths and weaknesses and thus help you plan instruction that will be most beneficial to the students. Parents will also be favorably impressed with your willingness to listen to what they have to say.

If you meet parents outside the school setting, smile and speak to them. Do not bring up problems at chance meetings. These should be covered in carefully planned conferences.

---

### Case Study: Careless Comments Cause Problems

Mr. Meadows, a student teacher in the junior high school, saw the father of Joe Mills, one of his general science students, in the supermarket. Mr. Meadows walked over to Mr. Mills and said, "If Joe doesn't start coming to class more regularly, I will have to give him a failing grade. I think he cuts class to sneak off and smoke."

Mr. Mills was visibly upset. "Why haven't I been notified of this?" he demanded. "Why don't you keep parents adequately informed?" Then he turned and stalked away.

The next day, Mr. Meadows's cooperating teacher, Mrs. Daily, told him that Mr. Mills had called the principal and spoken angrily to him about the way the general science class was being handled. The principal demanded an explanation from Mrs. Daily. Now Mrs. Daily demanded an explanation from Mr. Meadows.

**1** What mistakes did Mr. Meadows make in his contact with Mr. Mills?
**2** What should he have done instead?
**3** What would you have done?

---

Parents are potential allies. If you make an effort to communicate with them appropriately, they can help you better understand your students. They have their children's best interests at heart and will respond favorably to you if they believe you do too.

## Discussion Questions

1 What conditions could cause you to have problems developing good relationships with your students? How might you work to overcome these difficulties?
2 Are there any special problems in developing good relationships with students of different racial or ethnic groups from yours? What are they? How can they be overcome?
3 How may the fact that the college supervisor is giving you a grade affect your relationship with him or her? Should this happen? Why or why not?

4 Why should you avoid criticism of your cooperating teacher's methods?

5 Why is it a good policy to develop positive relationships with many school personnel?

6 How can your relationships with other student teachers benefit your student teaching?

7 How could your poor relationships with parents inhibit a student's progress?

8 What will you do if:

(a) You are student teaching in second grade and an apparently bright and curious Vietnamese boy, who speaks no English, is in your class. Your cooperating teacher has ignored him, letting him entertain himself during lessons. The boy's father is an engineering student at the university who speaks broken English. The boy's mother is free during the day, but she speaks only a few words of English. No one in your school speaks any Vietnamese.

(b) You are student teaching in sixth grade and have a girl in your class who comes from an impoverished home which has no running water. The child's clothes are filthy, her face and hands are encrusted with grime, and she smells bad. The other children make fun of her and refuse to sit next to her.

(c) In the ninth grade history class where you are student teaching, there is a student named Pedro who speaks fluent Spanish, but refuses to try to learn more than the small amount of English he already knows. Many of the other students are Mexican-Americans like Pedro, but, unlike him, they are learning English rapidly. When it is time to give a test over the unit you have been studying, Pedro is the only one who has difficulty reading the questions. Do you translate into Spanish for him (assuming you can), read the questions to him in English, or let him do the best he can with the test on his own? What is the reason for your answer?

# Selected References

The ASCD Multicultural Education Commission. "Encouraging Multicultural Education," *Educational Leadership*, 34 (January, 1977): 288–91.

Banks, James. *Multiethnic Education: Practices and Promises.* Bloomington, Ind.: Phi Delta Kappa Educational Foundation, 1977.

Barnes, Willie J. "How to Improve Teacher Behavior in Multiethnic Classrooms," *Educational Leadership*, 34 (April, 1977): 511–15.

Bennett, Christine. "A Case for Pluralism in the Schools," *Phi Delta Kappan*, 62 (April, 1981): 589–91.

Carney, Janet. "The Language of Sexism: Sugar, Spice and Semantics," *Journal of Reading,* 21 (October, 1977): 51–56.

*Computerworld* staff writer. "Women Seen Suffering 'Subtle' Discrimination," *Computerworld* (June, 1979): 16.

Gough, Pauline. *Sexism: New Issue in American Education.* Bloomington, Ind.: Phi Delta Kappa Educational Foundation, 1976.

Graening, Joyce. "Sexism: Does the American School Structure and Curriculum Promote It?" *Kappa Delta Pi Record,* 17 (April 1981): 105–6.

Heathington, Betty S., ed. *Breaking Barriers: Overcoming Career Stereotyping in Early Childhood.* College Park, Md.: University of Maryland, 1981.

Johnson, James A., and Roger C. Anderson. *Secondary Student Teaching: Readings.* Glenview, Ill.: Scott, Foresman, 1971.

Johnson, James A., and Louis D. Deprin. *Elementary Student Teaching: Readings.* Glenview, Ill.: Scott, Foresman, 1971.

Morrison, James L., and Jerry M. Goldstein. "On Educational Inequality," *The Education Digest,* 42 (September, 1976): 31–33.

Nilsen, Alleen Pace, et al. *Sexism and Language.* Urbana, Ill.: NCTE, 1977.

Thomas, M. Donald. "The Limits of Pluralism," *Phi Delta Kappan,* 62 (April, 1981): 589–92.

"Toward a Nonsexist School." *American Education,* 13 (April 1977): 7–9.

# 3
## *Introduction to the Classroom*

Mr. Wiley is the cooperating teacher, Mr. Allen is his student teacher, and Mrs. Paris is the principal.

Mrs. Paris: Mr. Allen, I just received a call from Mr. Wiley. He is having car trouble and won't be able to get here on time. I realize you didn't expect to be in charge of the class this morning, but you have been observing for a week. You should be able to take care of the attendance and lunch records with no problem. He said the first two classes will be easy to handle, too. In one, you just have to give the test he left in his file cabinet, already duplicated. He should be here before the students finish the test. Good luck! Call on me if you have any problems.

Mr. Allen: Thank you, Mrs. Paris. I'll do my best. (Mrs. Paris exits. Mr. Allen goes to Mr. Wiley's desk and begins searching for his register. He finds it and looks at it in dismay. He can't remember how to fill it out. He *watched* Mr. Allen do it before, but he hadn't attended carefully enough. Embarrassed, he goes next door to ask another teacher, rather than sending a child to get the principal. In the meantime, the other children, left alone in the classroom, go wild. They run around the room, throw things, and yell. When Mr. Allen returns to the room with information about how to fill out his records, chaos reigns. "How does Mr. Wiley quiet them down?" he thinks in panic. "I have to do something quick.")

Mr. Allen (in a loud voice): Class! Be quiet! Return to your seats! (Mr. Allen's voice is hardly heard above the racket and has little effect. He suddenly remembers what he has seen Mr. Wiley do before, in a less chaotic situation. Mr. Allen quickly walks over and flips the classroom lights off, waits a few seconds, and flips them on again. The noise and movement slowly begin to abate. He flips the switch off and on again, and it becomes quieter still. Now his voice can be heard.)

Mr. Allen: Go to your seats and listen for your name as I call the roll. (To his surprise and relief, the students comply. The record keeping proceeds smoothly, and Mr. Allen feels more confident. Then he realizes he doesn't remember which class is first on Thursday mornings, since every day is not the same. Once again embarrassed, he turns to the students.)

Mr. Allen: What do we do first on Thursday mornings?

Chorus of answers: Spelling! Recess! (Mr. Allen knows recess isn't first, so he looks for the spelling book, wondering what activity to do on Thursday. Then he remembers the lesson planner Mr. Wiley keeps in his desk drawer. He finds the planner and verifies that the spelling lesson comes first. He also discovers that Mr. Wiley has planned a trial test for today. He saw Mr. Wiley give a trial test last week, but he doesn't remember the exact procedure. He leaps into the activity anyway, giving each word and a sentence with it as he vaguely remembers Mr. Wiley doing.)

Randy: You're supposed to say the word again after you give the sentence. That's the way Mr. Wiley does it.

Mr. Allen (frustrated and upset): Well, I'm doing it today, and I'll do it my way.

Rachel: What was the word again?

Mr. Allen: Clothes.

Randy: Mr. Wiley never repeats a word after we've passed it.

Rachel: Like you close a door?

Mr. Allen: Didn't you listen to my sentence, Rachel? Just do your best.

(The test proceeds along these lines until it is finished.)

Mr. Allen: Pass your papers to the front of the room.

Joe: But we grade our own trial tests so we'll learn the words better.

(Suddenly remembering that this is so, Mr. Allen decides to do it the way Mr. Wiley would. Half the papers have already been passed to the front.)

Mr. Allen: Okay. I'll let you check your own papers. Pass them back to their owners.

(Papers are passed back, amid much murmuring. Mr. Allen has to flip the lights again. While this is happening, Mr. Wiley walks in.)

Mr. Wiley: I'm sorry I'm late. I had car trouble. How did things go?

Mr. Allen: Okay.

Mr. Wiley: If you've finished that English test, that's perfect. We can go right on to math.

Mr. Allen: We didn't get to the English test yet. These are the spelling papers.

Mr. Wiley: You mean you took all this time on spelling! I'm going to have to help you budget your time better.

Mr. Allen (shamefacedly): Yes, sir.

1  Is there a difference in just watching and truly observing? What is it?

2  Had Mr. Allen been a good observer? Why do you say so?

3  Do you observe procedures carefully enough to be able to perform them alone, if necessary?

## Observing the Classroom Teacher

When you first begin student teaching, you will probably not be placed immediately in a direct teaching situation. On the contrary, you will probably be given a period of time to observe your cooperating teacher and perhaps other teachers in the school, to orient you to the teaching situation before you are in charge of one. It is important to try to derive maximum benefit from this observation time.

To benefit fully from your observation period, you need to realize that "observing" and "looking at" are not the same. Observation involves close attention to detail, analysis of what is happening, evaluation of what is happening, and assimilation of new ideas into your existing store of information.

In the opening vignette of this chapter, Mr. Allen had spent two weeks *looking at* what was going on in the classroom, not carefully *observing* it. Therefore, he did not gain the maximum benefit from his observation time. If *you* are to use your observation time to best advantage, you need to know *what* to look for and *how* to look at what you are observing.

When you enter the classroom for your first day of student teaching, your cooperating teacher will probably introduce you to the class and suggest that you spend the next few days observing to get the "feel" of the classroom and learn the general procedures of a typical day. The cooperating teacher may mention that you should become aware of the teaching and disciplinary techniques in use, with a view toward developing your own teaching approach. Whether or not this is mentioned, you should indeed be alert for these techniques, examining them analytically and critically, as you consider them for possible use when *you* are teaching.

Let us start at the beginning. Ask your cooperating teacher if there is a seating chart to use as you observe. If so, copy it, so you can take it home and study it at night. If there is none, try to make one out, with your teacher's help, before the next observation. Learning the students' names is extremely important for developing rapport with them and maintaining classroom control. At the secondary level, with several different sets of students' names to learn, it is extremely important to apply yourself immediately to the task. This is usually easier at the elementary level, although no less important.

Your cooperating teacher will probably first check attendance, and, at the elementary levels, collect lunch money. Don't just *look at* the process. Observe it. Notice how the teacher marks the register. Make notes, if necessary. If there is roll call, look at each student when his or her name is called. Try to fix the students in mind. Note features that will help you remember the students. You may miss a few on the first round, but study as many as you can; fill in others later in the day or on subsequent days of observations, adding to your notes each day. Study these notes after school, and try to set all your students in memory as quickly as possible.

Get a daily schedule from the cooperating teacher so you will be aware of the order of classes, times for breaks and special activities, and beginning and dismissal times. Secondary student teachers may find that each day's schedule is essentially the same, with the exception of variations for assembly schedules, test schedules, and other special events. Elementary student teachers may have a different schedule for each day of the week. Whichever is the case for you, familiarize yourself with the schedule as quickly as possible. Don't be left, as Mr. Allen was, wondering what comes next.

As your cooperating teacher begins to teach, once again, don't just be a *looker*, be an observer. To observe properly, you need to know *what* to look for. Here are a few things you should notice:

1. How does the teacher start the lesson? How does he tie it to previous learning? How does he arouse students' interest?

2. How does the teacher make the purpose and relevance of the lesson apparent? Direct teacher statements? Eliciting reactions from students? Other?

3. What procedures are incorporated into the body of the lesson? Lecture? Discussion? Audiovisual presentation? Demonstrations? Student activities?

4. What materials are used in the course of a lesson? Textbooks? Supplementary books? Films? Filmstrips? Audio cassettes? Video cassettes? Television? Records? Concrete objects? Illustrations? Models? Other?

5. What is the teacher's style of teaching? Direct? Indirect? Other? (See information on Flanders Interaction Analysis in chapter 9.)

6. Does the teacher show a broad knowledge of the subject area? Does he stick to the textbook or bring in information from other sources also? Does he relate the subject matter to other content the students have studied, or to current events, or to students' personal needs?

7. What provisions are made for individual differences? Small group work? Individual assignments? Differentiated reading materials? Other?

8. What disciplinary techniques does the teacher use? Light flipping? Penalty points? Deprivation of privileges? Other?

9. How do the teacher's personal qualities help advance the lesson? Is his dress appropriate, so that it does not distract from the subject matter? Is he free of distracting mannerisms? Does he use correct grammar? Is his voice volume and pitch appropriate?

10. How does the teacher end the lesson? Does he summarize the day's learning? What kind of homework assignments are made, if any?

11. What, if any, evaluation techniques does the teacher use in the course of the lesson? Oral questions? Written questions? Observation of students' verbal responses? Observation of students' application skills?

You can facilitate notetaking when you observe by making a separate page for each of the eleven observation areas.

Merely recording carefully the details of the lessons you observe will be beneficial, but it is not enough. At this point, you must analyze what you have seen and evaluate it critically. Below the notes you make on each observation area, write a brief analysis and evaluation, or do this mentally. Once again, some structure may help. Here are some questions you can ask yourself about each of the eleven observation areas.

Area 1: Did the students seem to grasp how the lesson tied to previous learning? Did the motivational activities seem to arouse students' interest successfully? If so, why do you think they did or did not accomplish their goal?

Area 2: Were the purpose and relevance of the lesson made clear to the students? Why or why not? How might they have been better clarified?

Area 3: Were the teacher's procedures effective for presenting the content? Might some other procedures have been more effective? Why do you think so?

Area 4: Were the lesson materials appropriate and effective? Would other materials have been more effective? Why do you think so?

Area 5: Was the teaching style effective with this particular group and for this particular lesson? Why do you think so? If the style was ineffective, what might have worked better?

Area 6: Did the teacher seem to have adequate knowledge of the subject matter? Was enough outside knowledge brought into the lesson? If not, what else should have been included? Was content effectively related to the students' lives? If not, how might this aspect of the lesson have been improved?

Area 7: Were adequate provisions made for individual differences? If so, how? If not, what steps might have been taken to improve the situation?

Area 8: Were disciplinary techniques appropriate and effective? Why do you think so? If they were inappropriate or ineffective, what techniques might have been better?

Area 9: Did the teacher's personal qualities advance the lesson effectively? Why do you think so? Might changes in this area be helpful to future lessons?

Area 10: Was the conclusion of the lesson effective? Why? If not, what might have been done to improve it?

Area 11: Were the teacher's evaluation techniques appropriate and effective? Why do you think so? If not, what techniques might have been better?

Even after this analysis and evaluation, you are not through with your observation. Now you must once again examine each observation area and ask yourself these questions: "How can I incor-

*Before you actually begin to teach, you will have a chance to observe your cooperating teacher. Take advantage of this time—observe carefully!*

porate this into my teaching? Will I want to use this technique, or an alternative I think would be better? How does what I have seen fit into what I have learned in my methods courses? Are there areas in which I need clarification?" If you answer "yes" to the last question, you should seek clarification immediately from your cooperating teacher, college supervisor, or college textbooks, or from all of these sources.

You should be observing more than lesson presentations. We have already pointed out the need to observe record-keeping processes, but there are many other areas you need to observe carefully: procedures for carrying out bus, lunchroom, hall, or play-ground duty, or any of the other duties teachers are frequently called upon to perform. Watch for time factors, control methods, procedures for handling special cases, and so on. Inquire about schoolwide rules, if you have not been supplied with a handbook outlining them. Take notes on what you see and hear so you can adhere strictly to school policy in the future.

Since teachers are also expected to attend faculty meetings, parent-teacher meetings, inservice sessions, and professional meetings, you would do well to attend these with your cooperating teacher for the purpose of observation. Your cooperating teacher may be asked to chaperone a school dance or take tickets for an extracurricular activity, such as a play, concert, dance, or athletic event. Observing these activities will help you better understand just what a job as a teacher entails.

Such small details as the method of dismissal in the afternoon are worthy of note. In many schools, not all students leave the room at the same time. If this is true in your school, make it a point to know who leaves when and why. In many schools, you also need to find out how hall passes are handled. Observe your teacher and ask questions about general procedures if they do not seem clear.

If you observe carefully, you won't end up like Mr. Allen, and you'll be more ready for teaching when your opportunity comes.

## Planning for Instruction

Without planning for instruction, your teaching experiences are likely to turn into disasters. Planning offers organization and direction to your teaching efforts. It can help you make sure you cover all important aspects of a lesson, while avoiding overemphasis on isolated points that interest you, but do not merit extensive coverage. It can save you from not having enough to do in a lesson, especially if you practice "overplanning." (By overplanning, we mean planning extra related and purposeful activities that you don't expect to have time for, but have ready in case the rest of the lesson progresses rapidly and time is available. See chapter 5 for some suggested "filler activities.") Planning can also help you avoid trying to cover too much material at one time. As you look at the complexity of the concepts you plan to present in a lesson format, you may find that you have isolated more material than the students can readily absorb at once and that certain complex concepts need much elaboration, rather than a hasty mention.

Good planning also enhances your poise and confidence and, as a result, class control will tend to be positively affected. Since class control is a major problem for student teachers, this advantage alone should encourage planning.

Written plans allow you to consult your cooperating teacher and college supervisor about the likelihood of a successful teaching experience. They can give you valuable feedback which may avert a teaching disaster brought on by inexperience. Some cooperating teachers and college supervisors *require* written plans. If yours don't, we highly recommend that you do them anyway, for your personal benefit. It will pay off.

When you are actually assigned to teach, it is vitally important that you plan for instruction, whether or not you actually write down the plans. Your instructional plans should always relate directly to the course of study for your class and should always build upon previous learnings.

One good way to ease into your teaching experience is to work jointly with your cooperating teacher in planning a lesson, watch your cooperating teacher teach the lesson in an early class, and then try it yourself in a later class. This gives you the benefit of seeing an experienced teacher move from plan to execution. Obviously, this procedure will only work in departmentalized settings where a teacher has several sections of the same course.

At first you will probably be assigned responsibility for single, isolated lessons. Later, as you progress, you will probably be assigned to teach entire units of instruction. These two planning tasks will be considered separately, in the order in which you are likely to encounter them, even though, obviously, lesson planning is an integral part of unit planning.

## Lesson Planning

Your lesson plans should be detailed enough that you or another person qualified to teach your grade or subject can teach from them with ease, yet brief enough that they do not become cumbersome. Usually, more detailed plans are needed at the beginning of your student teaching experience than at the end or after you become a regular classroom teacher. More detail gives an inexperienced person greater confidence and makes the inclusion of all important material more likely. Too much detail, however, can inhibit flexibility in a lesson. Do not, for example, plan to get one particular answer from students and build all your subsequent plans on this answer. That answer may not come. Plan to accommodate a variety of student responses.

What belongs in a good lesson plan? Opinions vary, and each teacher generally has to evolve a planning scheme that fits his or her personality. Certain ingredients appear almost universally, however, and you would do well to use these in initial planning activities.

1. Subject
2. Grade
3. Date (not always essential)
4. Time (useful for secondary teachers who teach more than one section of a subject and grade)
5. Objectives (be specific)
6. Content to be covered (be specific)
7. Materials needed
8. Activities and procedures with time allocations (keeps you from running out of time in the middle of something)
9. Alternative activities (in case a piece of audiovisual equipment won't work, a film doesn't arrive on time, or you overestimated how long other activities would take)
10. Method of evaluation (to determine if the students really learned the material)

11   Assignments (to provide practice on a taught skill, to prepare for a future lesson, or for some very specific purpose)

12   Self-evaluation (put this section in your written lesson plan, to be filled out after you teach the lesson)

13   Supervisory feedback (put this section in your written lesson plan, to be filled out after you have been critiqued by your cooperating teacher, your college supervisor, or both.)
[See Appendix C for sample lesson plans.]

When you write objectives for a specific lesson you have been asked to teach, be sure to study the overall objectives of the unit of which the lesson is a part, and check on the instruction that has previously taken place in that unit. Your chosen objectives should build upon previously taught material and lay a groundwork for future instruction, either by you or your cooperating teacher. Be specific in your objectives. Don't use a vague objective, such as "To help them understand verbs better"; instead, say "To help the students understand and apply the concept of subject-verb agreement" or in more behavioral terms, "In twenty consecutive trials the student will demonstrate accurate use of subject-verb agreement."

In the content section of your plan, list the major concepts you plan to cover. Don't just list "Causes of the Civil War"; list specific causes. Consult resources other than the textbook when planning this part of the lesson.

Make your materials list include *everything* you will need. If you need a visual aids pen and an acetate sheet for the overhead projector, list them. You can use this list to help you accumulate all necessary materials before the lesson begins, so you won't have to disrupt your lesson while you search the room for an appropriate pen for writing on transparencies.

Under the activities and procedures section, you may wish to list questions you plan to raise, motivational techniques you plan to use, what you plan to do, and what you are going to ask the students to do. Consult your college methods textbooks when you plan this part of your lesson. Vary activities. Students become bored with lessons that require one type of response. Plan to have students do some combination of listening, watching, reading, speaking, and writing in each lesson.

By estimating how much time each activity should take, you minimize the risk of finishing an hour lesson in twenty minutes or of getting only halfway through a thirty-minute lesson before the time has elapsed. At first, of course, your time estimates may not be extremely accurate, but the very act of keeping up with them in each lesson helps you learn how to judge time needs better. A common problem for student teachers is finishing all the planned material early and being forced to "wing it." This will not be a problem for you if you plan some good alternate activities to use in such an eventuality, or in case a projector bulb burns out and there is not another one in the school, or in case some other unforeseen difficulty occurs.

You should always consider how to determine whether or not your pupils have learned the lesson material. You can evaluate through oral or written questions, observation of pupil performance, or some other means, but you *must* evaluate. Planning future lessons depends upon whether or not students learned the material in the current one.

The assignments you give students for independent work should be carefully planned to meet a specific purpose. An assignment might be designed to offer further practice in a skill just taught, to help fix it in the students' minds. Another assignment might be designed to prepare the students for a future lesson. Any materials that students are assigned to read independently must be chosen carefully. They will be unable to complete independent assignments in materials that are too difficult for them to read, and for this reason, differentiated reading assignments may be necessary.

After you have taught the lesson, you should evaluate your effectiveness much as you evaluated lessons you observed others teach. When you recognize weaknesses, consider how you would teach the lesson differently if you taught it a second time. Those of you in departmentalized settings who are assigned to two sections of the same class may even have a chance to try out your ideas for improvement later in the day. If you do, remember to evaluate the second presentation also. When you receive feedback from your cooperating teacher and your college supervisor about your lesson, compare their comments to your self-evaluation. If you noticed the same things they did, your evaluation skills are probably good. If they mention many things you missed, you may need to work at evaluating your performance more critically and objectively.

## Unit Planning

After you have achieved some success at planning individual lessons, your cooperating teacher will probably move you into unit planning. Unit plans are coordinated sets of lessons built around central themes. In the elementary school, a unit plan frequently cuts across disciplines and includes activities in language arts, mathematics, social studies, science, art, music, and other areas. An example of this type of unit might be one on the Westward Movement. Although this unit has basically a social studies theme, the teacher can incorporate language arts instruction through reference reading, oral and written reports, and class discussions; mathematics instruction in figuring distances and calculating amounts of needed supplies and prices of supplies in those days (discovered from research) to discover the cost of a journey; science and health instruction through comparing disease remedies used then with those used today; art, in illustrating modes of transportation, clothing, or other features of the times, and constructing dioramas and models; music instruction through singing and playing songs of the time; and even home economics instruction, by making recipes of that era (which also requires mathematics skill) and performing sewing tasks appropriate to the times, such as quilting and making samplers. Secondary level units, especially in social studies classes and literature classes, may cut across disciplines, but this is not as common as at the elementary level. Most units at the secondary level and many at the elementary level are based upon major topics within single disciplines. A mathematics class, for example, may have a unit on measurement, incorporating a multitude of mathematical concepts and skills. You should review your methods textbooks for types of units appropriate to your grade and/or discipline.

*After you have learned how to plan individual lessons, you may be asked to plan a unit.*

Different situations require different types of units; that is, there is no one form for all units. Different reference books promote different formats, some of which are harder and some easier to use in a particular situation. You should examine these options and pick the one that best fits *your* situation.

Despite the variations in form suggested for unit preparation, there are certain important considerations you should not overlook when preparing any unit.

Make your unit plan fit into the class's overall course of study. If you are allowed to pick your own unit topic, examine the course of study and pick a topic that fits into the long-term plans for the class. Whether you pick the topic or your cooperating teacher does, check to see how your unit fits into the overall instructional plan. Locate the prior learnings upon which your unit can build. Check on the relationships between your unit and the previous and succeeding units. Decide what things you must include to ensure students' success in succeeding units.

Find out from your cooperating teacher the time allotment for your unit, and make your plans conform to this allotment. You will probably not be able to include every aspect of your chosen topic within the given time frame. You must decide, either independently or in conjunction with the students, which aspects to include.

Consider carefully the students who will be studying the unit. Find out their backgrounds of experience in relation to the topic, their general levels of achievement in school and/or in your subject area, their levels of interest in the unit topic, their reading levels, their attitudes toward school and the subject area or areas involved, their study habits and ability to work independently or engage in group work, and their special talents. Plan all your activities with these characteristics in mind. It may be useful to actually write down a profile of your class, including all these characteristics, to refer to as you develop objectives, teaching methods, activities, and evaluation methods.

Collect ideas for the unit from a variety of sources: students' textbooks, your college textbooks, professional journals, local resources (businesses and individuals), resource units on file in your school or college media center, and, of course, from your cooperating teacher. Make lists of helpful books, periodicals, audiovisual aids, and resource people for future reference. One caution is in order here: do not lecture straight from your old college notes. Remember that your students are not yet ready for material as advanced as the material in your college classes. Use the college notes as background material and work in information from them only as it is directly applicable and appropriate for your particular students.

Draft your objectives for the unit according to the content you want to cover and the students with whom you will be working. You may wish to refer to your methods textbooks to refresh your memory on writing clear objectives. Include both cognitive and affective objectives when appropriate.

Organize the procedures section of your unit plan to include the unit introduction, the body of the unit, and culminating activities. (a) The introductory part of the unit should connect this unit with prior learning or backgrounds of experience, diagnose the needs of the students and their strengths in this area of study (through pretests or informal discussions), and arouse interest in the topic and motivate students to study it. Methods and activities for this part of the unit should be of high interest; frequently, they should vary from usual classroom routine. (b) The body of the unit should address the teaching of each objective, matching teaching procedures and student activities, including assignments, to objectives. Include evaluative measures as needed. (c) Culminating activities for the unit should tie together all the previous learnings. Frequently, culminating activities include practical applications of the concepts acquired in the unit, interrelating the various concepts. Overall evaluative measures may be a part of the culminating activities.

Vary your planned activities. This will help keep the students' attention and can help your unit progress more smoothly, because certain activities suit certain types of learning better than others. Consider use of audiovisual aids, field trips, resource people, class discussions, library research activities, simulations and dramatizations, construction activities, oral and written reports, games, demonstrations, and creative applications. Be sure, however, that all activities relate directly to unit objectives.

## Case Study: Failure to Follow Through

Jerry Clement was planning a unit on law enforcement. Jerry's cooperating teacher, Mrs. Granger, knew an excellent resource person, Mr. McDonald, that Jerry might use in the course of his unit. She told Jerry about Mr. McDonald and, to her surprise, discovered that Jerry was a friend of Mr. McDonald's. She strongly suggested that Jerry ask Mr. McDonald to come to the class and share his knowledge with the students. Jerry seemed to think this was a good idea, but he never actually contacted Mr. McDonald. At the end of the term, Jerry was surprised that his cooperating teacher rated him lower than he would have liked on use of community resources.

1   Do you believe the use of a resource person would have enhanced Jerry's unit? Why or why not?
2   If you had been Jerry, what would you have done if you decided that having Mr. McDonald would not add substantially to your unit?

Decide on the different forms of evaluation you intend to use during the course of the unit, to be sure you haven't overrelied on a single type. Consider the use of formal and informal paper-and-pencil tests, oral or performance tests, observation of student performance in activities and discussions, evaluation of daily in-class and homework assignments, and individual pupil conferences, among other evaluation methods.

Estimate the time needed for the various instructional procedures and student activities and make tentative decisions about daily coverage. Make adjustments if your plans do not fit the allotted time.

Consult your cooperating teacher about the plan you have constructed. If it meets with the teacher's approval, you are ready to make detailed daily lesson plans based on your unit plan.

Here is a brief outline to apply to unit planning:

A. Topic and overall time allotment
B. Students' characteristics and background
C. Resources and materials
D. Unit objectives
E. Unit procedures
   1. Introduction
   2. Body
   3. Culminating activities
F. Evaluation

[See Appendix D for sample unit plans.]

If you remember that a unit of work is a series of interrelated lessons clustered around a central theme, then you will probably plan a good unit. Poor units are characterized by lack of continuity and interrelatedness and by irrelevant activities.

# Suggestions to Help You Be Successful

During your first days in the classroom, you may feel somewhat unsure of how to act or dress. Following these general tips will help alleviate some of your anxiety. Some have been mentioned earlier, but bear repeating here because of their importance to your success.

Be pleasant and polite toward everyone with whom you come in contact—students, parents, your cooperating teacher, other teachers, administrators, and support personnel. In your anxiety about the new situation, don't forget how to *smile*.

Be enthusiastic about the prospect of teaching. Show your cooperating teacher that you are energetic and willing, rather than lethargic and reluctant. Volunteer to help with tasks such as grading papers, giving individual assistance, and making instructional aids, as the opportunity arises. The more involved you become early, the more comfortable you will be when you begin teaching.

Be punctual. This indicates a professional attitude.

Dress as a teacher dresses. Don't wear faded jeans and sweatshirts. If you don't look like a teacher, the students won't treat you like one. This aspect becomes more and more important as grade level increases. It is easy for a secondary student teacher to look like "just one of the gang," but classroom management suffers when this happens. In most cases, you can take your cue from your cooperating teacher or other teachers in the school. Remember, however, that they are probably older than you and have already established their authority, whereas you are in the process of trying to establish yours.

Check with your cooperating teacher about school policies *before* a crisis occurs in which you need to know them.

Learn the students' names quickly. This helps you build rapport and maintain class control.

Always use good grammar. You are supposed to be a model for the students, so you must take care to meet this responsibility in speaking and writing.

Write legibly. You may be asked to construct worksheets or study guides for the students or write assignments on the chalkboard. Use the form of writing appropriate for your students (manuscript or cursive), and make sure you form the letters properly, that spacing and size of letters is appropriate, and that the overall product is legible. Once again, you are a model for the students.

Keep calm. Do not allow yourself temper outbursts in school, even if things are not going well.

Observe all school policies related to teachers, especially those about smoking, which is a trouble area for some student teachers.

Never criticize your cooperating teacher to another teacher or criticize other teachers in the school to each other. This is unprofessional behavior.

Learn the school's resources well before you are expected to take charge, so you will be able to locate the things you need when you need them.

Learn the daily routine thoroughly, so you can manage it smoothly when you take over responsibility.

Speak with pride about becoming a teacher. In these days of criticism of education, you should stand up for your chosen profession.

Later, when you begin teaching, you will need to remember the above tips, which apply to the entire student teaching setting, plus these additional ones, which apply to your direct teaching activities. Learn them so you can perform acceptably.

Be aware of the students' comfort. Adjust the temperature if the room is too hot or too cold. Adjust the blinds if there is a glare from the sunlight. See that there is adequate ventilation. Before, your cooperating teacher saw to these details; now they are your responsibility.

Don't lecture about something you have written or drawn on the board while standing in such a way that you block the students' view of the material.

Use your voice well when teaching. A droning monotone bores students. An overly loud voice may intimidate some students, especially younger ones. A too-quiet voice may not carry well enough to reach students at the back of the room.

Use only disciplinary methods sanctioned by your cooperating teacher. Avoid inappropriate practices such as punishing everyone for the misbehavior of a few and making unrealistic threats.

Don't call on the same students all the time. Distribute classroom participation as evenly as possible.

Vary activities to keep students' interest. Avoid leaning exclusively upon one teaching approach, such as the lecture method.

Plan each lesson thoroughly, no matter how well you think you know the material. Consider the level of the students and adjust your explanations and procedures accordingly. For example, a one-hour lecture is completely inappropriate for use with a second grade class.

Make clear and unambiguous assignments, and allow students the opportunity to ask for clarification if they need it.

Grade and return all assignments promptly. Students will learn more from assignments if they have immediate feedback.

Don't assign busywork. Make all assignments contribute to classroom goals.

If you take these suggestions seriously, you will greatly enhance your chances of success in student teaching.

## Discussion Questions

1   How can you make your observations of your cooperating teacher and/or other teachers most useful to you? Would keeping a log of "Ideas for Future Use" help?

2   Do all the teachers you have observed use the same teaching and disciplinary techniques? Why do you believe this might be so?

3   What are some different lesson plan forms you might use? What are advantages and disadvantages of each form?

4   Are units more effective in your teaching situation when they cut across disciplines or when they are chosen from content within a single discipline? Why do you think so? Is there a place for both types of units?

5  What areas of concern do you have about your initial experiences in the classroom? Were there areas of concern not mentioned in the "General Tips" given in this chapter?

# Selected References

Bluming, Mildred, and Myron Dembo. *Solving Teaching Problems.* Pacific Palisades, Calif.: Goodyear, 1973.

Brown, Thomas J., and Serafina Fiore Banich. *Student Teaching in an Elementary School.* New York: Harper & Row, 1962.

Callahan, Sterling G. *Successful Teaching in Secondary Schools.* Glenview, Ill.: Scott, Foresman, 1971.

DuBey, Robert E., et al. *A Performance-Based Guide to Student Teaching.* Danville, Ill.: Interstate, 1975.

Inlow, Gail M. *Maturity in High School Teaching.* Englewood Cliffs, N.J.: Prentice-Hall, 1970.

Johnson, James A., and Roger C. Anderson. *Secondary Student Teaching: Readings.* Glenview, Ill.: Scott, Foresman, 1971.

Johnson, James A., and Louis D. Deprin. *Elementary Student Teaching: Readings.* Glenview, Ill.: Scott, Foresman, 1971.

Popham, W. James, and Eva L. Baker. *Systematic Instruction.* Englewood Cliffs, N.J.: Prentice-Hall, 1970.

# 4
## *Discipline*

In science class, Mrs. Goldberg was doing a unit on reptiles and Miss Yeatch, the student teacher, was helping her. For the culminating activity, the children were to bring some specimens to class. Maria had brought an unusual lizard and Frank had brought a frog. Manuel had contributed a garter snake he had found near his house. These animals were placed in separate cages on a counter in the back of the room that the students called their "zoo." Most of the students were curious about the reptiles and liked watching them. A few boys and girls, however, seemed timid about approaching the cages and avoided looking in their direction. The day before the reptiles were to be taken home, Mrs. Goldberg was called to the office for an emergency meeting with a parent. Miss Yeatch was in charge.

Manuel (whispering to some friends in the back of the room): Hey, Mrs. Goldberg's gone. Have you noticed the way Benjy and Tony and Karen are scared to death of those animals? Let's give them a real good scare. When Miss Yeatch isn't looking, let's sneak over and let them out of their cages.

Rachel (also in a whisper): Yeah, let's each get one of the cages on a signal and let them all out at once.

Jake: What a blast! Let's do it!

Miss Yeatch (trying to introduce a lesson on pronouns): Quiet down in the back of the room. There's no need for any talking. Do you have your English books out yet? Turn to page 79.

Manuel, Rachel, Jake (mumbling): Yeah, sure, we're with you. (The three send secret messages to one another with their eyes, waiting for the right opportunity.)

Miss Yeatch: All of you get on with your work. Try to have this finished before Mrs. Goldberg returns. (She bends down to help a student who is having trouble with a sentence.)

Manuel, Rachel, Jake (in a mutual, excited whisper): Now! (They sneak quickly and quietly to the cages, unfasten the hooks and open the doors, and return to their seats. A few children who notice begin to giggle.)

Dottie: Oh my goodness! The frog's loose. He's hopping over to the window.

Allen: Look out. Here comes the snake!

Benjy: Oh no! I'm getting out of here! (He runs for the door and makes a quick exit down the hall.)

Miss Yeatch: What's happening? Oh no! Who let those animals out? Put them back. Manuel, get your snake back in its cage. Somebody catch that frog. (The lizard is hiding under a leaf; the snake is crawling toward a dark spot in the corner.)

By now, several of the children are screaming and standing on their desks. Miss Yeatch, who is terrified of snakes, is now speechless and can only stand rooted to the spot. Some of the children are grinning slyly at each other as they stand around the snake, watching it glide across the room.

Mrs. Goldberg (just returning to the room): What's going on in here? I heard the racket all the way down at the principal's office.

Miss Yeatch (in a weak voice): Somebody let the reptiles out.

Mrs. Goldberg (in a firm voice): All right. All of you return to your seats. Manuel, put the snake back and fasten the cage. Cathy, you catch the frog, and Mark, close the lizard's cage before it gets out too. Now get on with your work. I believe you're supposed to be studying pronouns.

1 Could Miss Yeatch have anticipated the problem? If so, how? Were there any preventive measures she might have taken?

2 What are some ways Miss Yeatch might have handled the situation when she first noticed the reptiles were out of the cages?

3 Can you think of a way Miss Yeatch could have regained control of the class before Mrs. Goldberg returned?

4 Do you think Mrs. Goldberg got the class under control when she returned and spoke to the students? Why or why not?

# Dilemmas in Discipline

Students occasionally misbehave in every classroom. How to deal with them can be a problem for you. Consider the following situations. None of the answers is necessarily the right one; in fact, you might be able to come up with a better solution. In some cases, you might choose more than one answer. Consider what the circumstances might be and the probable consequences of each alternative. After you read this chapter, reconsider your answers.

1 Billy sticks out his tongue at you and gives you a smart answer. What do you do?

(a) Paddle him.

(b) Tell him to shut up and sit down.

(c) Ignore his behavior this time.

(d) Speak to him calmly, explaining why you cannot tolerate this kind of behavior.

(e) Punish him by making him stay in at recess.

(f) Laugh at him. He really was sort of cute.

2 Chrissy throws an eraser at Tammy and hits her on the head. What do you do?

(a) Check to see if Tammy is hurt. If not, ignore the situation.

(b) Let Tammy throw an eraser at Chrissy and hit *her* on the head.

(c) Warn Chrissy that, if she does it again, she'll have to miss lunch for one week.

(d) Make an example of Chrissy. Scold her severely in front of the class and make her stand in the corner for an hour.

(e) Stop what you are doing. Quietly point out that throwing things can be dangerous and that this behavior is unacceptable.

(f) Go on with your lesson as if nothing happened.

3   At the precise moment of 10:07 (according to the clock on the wall) all students bend down to tie their shoes, even those who don't have shoe laces. What do you do?

(a) Ignore this event and go on with your lesson.

(b) Stop the lesson and demand to know who is responsible for instigating this diversion.

(c) Punish the entire class by making them write 100 times, "I will not tie my shoes during class."

(d) Deny the students an anticipated privilege.

(e) Pass the episode off with a humorous remark, such as "Next time you'd better wear self-tying shoe laces," then go on with your lesson.

(f) Lecture the class on the importance of paying attention and concentrating on the lesson.

4   Two students are talking and giggling in the back of the room while you are trying to conduct a discussion. What do you do?

(a) Move closer to the students, pause, and look at them significantly.

(b) Call on one of them to answer a question you have just asked.

(c) Stop and wait as long as necessary until everyone is quiet.

(d) Call them by name and ask them to pay attention.

(e) Say in a loud and angry voice, "Your talking is disturbing to the rest of the class. I want you to stop this minute. If I hear one more word out of either of you, I'll send you both to the office."

(f) Wait until after class, then talk to the students and explain that their talking was very disturbing.

5   Carol is eating potato chips during reading group. You ask her to stop and she defiantly tells you "No." What do you do?

(a) Try to take the bag away from her by force.

(b) Tell her that if she is going to eat potato chips in front of the other students, she will have to bring enough for everyone.

    (c) Tell her that if she'll put the potato chips away now, she can eat them during recess.

    (d) Ask her to return to her seat until she is finished.

    (e) Insist that she stop eating. Warn her that she will be punished if she does not stop right now. Continue until you win your point.

    (f) Drop the request for the moment. Get the children interested in an exciting part of the story, then quietly ask Carol to put the chips away for now.

6 Judy and Jerry are passing notes during math class. What do you do?

    (a) Pick up the notes from their desks and read them aloud to the class.

    (b) Pick up the notes from their desks, tear them into shreds, and drop them into the wastebasket.

    (c) In front of the class, say sarcastically, "Judy and Jerry seem to know all there is to know about math since they aren't paying attention." Then send them to the board and give them a difficult problem to work in front of the other students.

    (d) Assign Jerry and Judy ten extra problems for homework and threaten to do the same to anyone else who doesn't pay attention.

    (e) Walk toward their desks; look at them intently until they understand they are not to write notes any more; then continue your lesson.

    (f) Have them stay after school and pick up all the scraps of paper in the room.

To deal with situations such as these, you should begin by understanding what discipline is and what it is not. Discipline is controlled behavior. It is the ability to get attention when you need it. It does not call for an absolutely quiet and rigidly controlled class, although some degree of order is implied. There is often quiet, purposeful talking in a well-disciplined classroom, with students moving freely about as they work on projects.

Teachers often consider discipline their number one problem. Why is it so difficult to establish and maintain classroom control? The answer probably lies partly in the complexity of the causes. You must consider the students' personalities and backgrounds, the type of learning situation in which they are involved, and the distractions that may interfere with their concentration. Discipline is also difficult because, in most cases, you must decide what to do on the spot, and you cannot be sure of the consequences of your actions.

Even though effective classroom discipline may be difficult to achieve, you must have it to accomplish any of your objectives. Without it, too much time is wasted and too many students never get the message. Without it, students never learn to control their own behavior so as to become productive citizens later in life. Finally, without it, you will not survive. Teacher burnout is often the result of a breakdown in discipline.

## Causes of Discipline Problems

Who or what might cause discipline problems? Maybe society, maybe something in the classroom environment, maybe the students themselves—or maybe you! Let's look at some of the causes.

Society may need to shoulder part of the blame. At one time, teachers were highly respected and their word was law, but this situation is no longer true. Parents today seem to be more permissive toward their children and do not train them to practice self-discipline at home. Law enforcement agencies do not always support the schools in dealing with juvenile offenders. There is little you can do about society's changing attitudes toward the teaching profession, except to show through your actions that you are worthy of respect.

You *can* do something about your classroom environment, however. When there are so many other things to think about, it's easy to forget such apparently obvious factors as lighting, temperature control, room arrangement, and distracting elements. Analyze your classroom. Is there something in the room you could change that might reduce the number of discipline problems?

The students bring with them such a bewildering array of emotional, physical, and social problems that it's no wonder they sometimes misbehave. Sometimes you may be able to help them solve problems or accept what's troubling them. Sometimes just knowing that you care makes a difference to them. Students whose personal problems no longer interfere with their concentration are less likely to cause problems for you.

Without realizing it, you may be responsible for some of the discipline problems that arise. Can you answer all of these questions affirmatively?

1   Is my lesson well planned and purposeful?
2   Am I meeting the interests and needs of the students? Are they motivated to learn?
3   Are the students actively involved in learning?
4   Is the material at an appropriate level of difficulty and do I have reasonable expectations for each student?
5   Do the students understand exactly how I expect them to behave and know the consequences of misbehavior?
6   Am I fair and consistent with discipline and do I carry out my promises?

"Yes" to each of these questions will go a long way toward preventing discipline problems from developing.

Your situation as a student teacher is slightly different from that of the classroom teacher. No matter who is doing the teaching, the standards of discipline set by the regular teacher usually prevail. This condition can work to your advantage if your cooperating teacher is a good disciplinarian, or to your disadvantage if he or she is poor with discipline. The students realize that even if you're in charge of this lesson, they will ultimately have to answer to their regular teacher. You also have not had the experience of a regular teacher and must pay attention to many things that are routine for the experienced teacher. This predicament makes it difficult for you to notice all the small incidents that could lead to trouble in time to stop discipline problems from occurring. Finally, as a student teacher, you may overlook occasional infractions because you want the students to like you. When they find out they can get away with misbehaving, they will take advantage of you and your control will fly out the window.

# Prevention of Discipline Problems

Learning how to prevent discipline problems is one secret of classroom control. Some problems may develop anyway, but if you know when to anticipate trouble, you can prevent minor skirmishes from erupting into full-fledged battles.

## Student Relationships

Your relationship with the students is of primary importance. They are amazingly perceptive and can tell if you truly care about them and want to help. Try to learn something about their home environments, their special needs and problems, and what interests them. They will respect you if you patiently show them how to do something they want to learn. They will appreciate your recognition of their successes and achievements. You will win a loyal supporter if you find out that a student's mother is in the hospital and remember to ask about her progress. When you earn their support and respect, students are likely to cooperate with you in maintaining order in the classroom.

Verbal and nonverbal reinforcers are good ways to establish a warm relationship with your students. These are words and signals that influence their behavior. Verbal reinforcers can be comments such as "good work" and "nice going, Timmy." Light, kidding conversations before or after class, offers of help, and friendly greetings are good social reinforcers. Examples of nonverbal reinforcers are approving facial expressions and gestures. Use these reinforcers frequently during the school day.

*Students know when you truly care about them and want to help.*

Student self-control, or self-discipline, is the center of good classroom control. As long as the students rely on you to control their behavior, they are apt to lapse into poor behavior if you do not constantly direct their actions. Instead, teach them to be responsible for their own behavior. Self-control develops gradually, and your students probably have it in varying degrees, ranging all the way from the well-controlled individual to one who frequently seems totally out of control. If you can get your students to develop self-discipline, both you and the students are the winners. You will have fewer discipline problems and the students will acquire a skill they will need all their lives.

You can help students develop self-control in a variety of ways. Keep in mind that all students are not at the same level of self-discipline, and you will have to vary your strategies accordingly. Hold students responsible for performing classroom duties. Give them opportunities to be responsible for guiding someone else's progress by setting up a tutoring program. Encourage them to keep records of their own progress.

All students should be able to make some choices of their own—what books to read, interests to pursue, friends to be with, and behavior patterns to follow. They should know and be prepared to live with the consequences of their choices. They should be granted privileges as long as they honor them. If they abuse a privilege, it should be taken away.

Remember to start with small tasks and work up to larger ones as students demonstrate readiness to assume more responsibility. You can experiment with making long-term assignments occasionally, without checking daily, to see if students can direct their own activities. If assignments aren't completed on time, you may need to revert to daily evaluation. Among your teaching strategies, include independent activities such as projects and lab work, where students must carry an activity through to completion. If you show them that you believe they are capable of directing many of their own activities, they are likely to live up to your expectations.

Students feel responsible for their actions when they have a hand in planning activities and making their own rules for behavior. They realize that limits must be set for behavior, and they may understand what works better than you do. You will probably continue many of the policies already in effect in your classroom, but you might also work with the students to develop some rules of your own to take care of problems that seem to be arising. It is a good strategy for you and the students to agree on a signal to get instant attention, such as raising your hand, ringing a bell, or saying "Freeze!" After rules have been established, help your students evaluate their effectiveness. If a rule is frequently violated, perhaps the rule is unnecessary, or perhaps there is something else wrong with it. If a penalty seems unfair, perhaps there is a more appropriate consequence.

Your relationships with students are also important in other ways. Learn their names and use them as soon as you can. Use a seating chart or name tags to help you. Calling students by name gets their attention quickly. Expect them to say Mr., Mrs., or Miss before addressing you by name, to maintain a respectful relationship.

Observe the seating arrangement in your room to see if you might eliminate some centers of disturbance by relocating some students. Learn which students are likely to instigate trouble and watch them more closely. Even though you find yourself liking some students better than others, treat them all fairly and consistently. Don't let anyone accuse you of having "teacher's pets." Avoid confrontations with students in front of their peers. It's better to discuss problems rationally, later, during a one-to-one conference. Whenever you can, try to help students work out their problems without having to send them to an outside source.

It doesn't take students long to figure out what kind of disciplinarian you are. Some will deliberately test you to find out how far they can go. You need to be firm from the first day if you expect to have good classroom control.

## Presentation of Lessons

If you use the following suggestions, your lessons should give little cause for misbehavior. Make sure the classroom is as comfortable and free from distractions as you can make it. Get everyone's attention before you begin, and be sure that desks or tables are cleared of everything except what the students will need during the lesson. Be well prepared. Know your lesson well enough that you don't have to read from the manual while you teach. It's important to have good eye contact with the students during a lesson. Be ready to switch to another method if one strategy isn't working. Watch for students who may have trouble understanding the work and be ready to help them over their hurdles. Otherwise, their frustration can erupt in behavior problems.

Start and end your lessons promptly, and make transitions from one lesson to another quickly and smoothly. In discussion lessons, let only one student answer at a time to prevent a free-for-all calling out. Keep your lessons interesting and fast-paced. Be enthusiastic, and the students will catch your enthusiasm. Get the students actively involved in your lessons and keep them motivated. A highly motivated student seldom causes discipline problems. Have more than enough material for the entire class period. In case you still run short, keep ideas in mind for filling in the remaining minutes productively.

Give directions clearly and precisely. Reinforce important directions by writing them on the chalkboard. Be sure the students know what choices they have when they finish their work. If they don't know what to do next, they may become disruptive. Be patient with slow learners. If necessary, explain things more than once, so that everyone understands. Put things in simple words for young children.

Your teaching style makes a difference in how students respond to you. Move around the room, and use nonverbal communication to interact with various students as you teach. Call on students who seem inattentive to get them to stay with you. If a crisis occurs, keep your cool. Remain in charge of the situation and calmly decide what to do. Develop a sense of humor. Laugh with the students and occasionally at yourself. A good laugh reduces tension.

The volume of your voice can set the noise level of the class. If you raise your voice to be heard, the students will only get noisier. If you lower your voice, they will become quiet to hear what you have to say. Be sure, however, that you can be heard in the back of the room and that you speak distinctly.

## Reacting to Danger Signals

If you're alert to impending trouble, you can often stop problems just as they start. Boredom, daydreaming, restlessness, and long periods of inactivity breed discipline problems. Danger signals include a paper wad shot across the room, a half-smothered giggle, or a quick exchange of glances between students.

When you sense trouble brewing, nip it in the bud. Try these ideas:

1   Change your tactics fast. Switch to a different approach, read a story, play a rhythm game, or talk about an event in which students share an interest.

2   Use nonverbal communication to arrest the problem. Catch the instigator's eye and hold. Pause in midsentence and look intently at the potential troublemakers. Shake your head slowly to indicate disapproval.

3   Remind the students of a privilege or reward that will be the consequence of good behavior, while looking in the direction of the potential problem.

4   Move closer to the source of trouble. Indicate that you are aware of what's going on.

5   Speak softer and slower. You will get the students' attention for the moment, as they try to figure out why you shifted your speech.

6   Catch them off guard by saying something like, "I surely hope no one in here is thinking about throwing a pencil" or "Did I tell you what is going to happen this Friday?"

7   Use humor. Laugh off a minor incident instead of making a big deal of it. For example, to a student who has just thrown a paper airplane, say "Billy, I'll bet the Air Force could use you to help design airplanes. Now let's get back to work."

8   Call on the students you believe are about to cause a problem to answer a question. Or simply insert a student's name in midsentence to bring attention back to the lesson; for example, "The next question, Johnny, is number seven."

9   In response to an irritating noise, say, "Distracting noises interfere with what we need to accomplish in here. I guess we won't have time to play 'Twenty Questions'."

10  Confiscate distracting materials, especially toys or food, that are diverting students' attention.

# Models of Behavior

In recent years, many writers have proposed models of discipline. You may be able to draw from their ideas to solve discipline problems in your classroom. We will discuss five of these models briefly and illustrate their correct and incorrect use.

### Glasser

Let's look first at Glasser's reality therapy. In this approach, all students sit close to each other in a circle and participate in classroom meetings to examine problems and seek solutions. Students also participate in making reasonable rules for behavior which they are then expected to observe. The rules are flexible and may be changed as conditions change. Students are responsible for their own actions; they are free to make the choices that result in good or bad behavior. If they choose inappropriate behavior, however, the teacher accepts no excuses, and the student must observe the consequences. The teacher leads the student to evaluate the improper behavior and find a more acceptable choice. Student responsibility, helpfulness of the teacher, and a positive approach are key elements of the Glasser strategy. Punishment is no part of it.

## A Joint Endeavor

Miss LeCaro notices that Juan has not done his homework for the second night in a row. She questions him about it.

Miss LeCaro: Juan, where is your homework?

Juan: I don't know.

Miss LeCaro: What do you mean? You must have some idea where it is.

Juan: I guess I forgot it.

Miss LeCaro: Do you mean you forgot to bring it or you forgot to do it?

Juan: I didn't have time to do it. My mom expects me to take care of my brothers and sisters while she works at Dick's Diner.

Miss LeCaro: I'm sorry you have so much extra responsibility, Juan. It must be hard on you. But that still doesn't excuse you from doing your homework. What do you plan to do about the assignments you haven't turned in?

Juan: I'll try to do those tonight.

Miss LeCaro: What do you think will help you remember to do your school work each day?

Juan: I guess I'll remember if I do it as soon as I get home from school instead of waiting till I'm so tired that I fall asleep.

Miss LeCaro: That sounds like a good idea. Try that this afternoon. You know you need to turn in homework each day in order to keep up with the work we cover in class.

Miss LeCaro carried out Glasser's approach by continuing to question Juan until he admitted that he hadn't done his homework. She did not ask for or accept his excuse. She stressed that he must assume the responsibility for completing daily homework assignments. She did not punish him, but helped him evaluate his own behavior and plan a way to change it. The episode was quiet and orderly, and Juan developed a constructive plan for meeting the requirements.

## Teacher Imposed Discipline

Tony is behind in his reading workbook. He has been drawing pictures of army planes during his independent study time while Miss Olsen works with another reading group. One day Miss Olsen decides to check workbooks and discovers that Tony is twenty pages behind the rest of the class. She angrily confronts him.

Miss Olsen: Tony, what's the matter with you? What have you been doing when you were supposed to be working?

Tony: I guess I just didn't get all of those pages done.

Miss Olsen: Why not?

Tony: I don't know. I was too busy doing other things.

Miss Olsen: That's no excuse. I want you to stay in from recess every day until you get caught up.

This encounter results in Tony's feeling angry at Miss Olsen. He rushes through the work so he can go out to recess, and much of it is incorrect. Tony has been given no responsibility for changing his behavior in the future, and he is likely to resume his drawing instead of doing his work. Miss Olsen gave him no choices.

## Kounin

The ripple effect, according to Kounin, is the effect a disciplinary measure has on the rest of the class. When a teacher corrects one pupil, other students are influenced by the example that is set. You can make good use of this ripple effect if you know how. When you correct a student, clearly identify the student, what she is doing, and what she should be doing instead. Vague generalizations have little effect. For instance, say "Cathy, stop playing with those cards and finish your spelling paper." Simply saying "Class, get busy" makes little difference in students' behavior. Students learn how to behave by listening to your comments to other students. Correcting the behavior of classroom leaders instead of followers generally has a greater ripple effect. Rough physical treatment is generally ineffective since it usually makes the class uneasy and fearful.

Kounin also advocates smooth lesson transitions and effective teaching strategies as deterrents to behavior problems. Teachers must keep their lessons moving along without interrupting themselves with "dangles" (leaving a lesson hanging while tending to something else) and "flip flops" (changing back and forth from one subject to another). They must keep their students alert by calling on them randomly and occasionally calling for unison responses. They should become skilled at "overlapping," the ability to handle two or more students or groups at one time. Finally, they should be "withit" by using their sixth sense to react quickly and accurately to class disturbances.

___

## Withitness

Mr. Wiseman had taught algebra for fourteen years and knew pretty well what to expect of his students. They rarely tried to take advantage of him because it was said that he had eyes in the back of his head. One day he was writing an equation on the board for the students to work during class. The class was quiet as he began writing, but as he continued, he heard some whispers and movement in one corner of the room where Karen was usually the instigator of any trouble. As he turned around, Edna jumped up from her seat and demanded angrily, "All right, whoever has my calculator had better give it back." Two or three students got out of their seats to help her look for her calculator. Mr. Wiseman looked directly at Karen, who was secretly passing the calculator to Paul. Mr. Wiseman said, "Karen, return the calculator to Edna. Class, get to work on these problems." The students settled down to work.

___

Mr. Wiseman handled the situation well. He anticipated trouble when he first heard the whispering and turned quickly to nip it in the bud. By knowing his students, he was able to locate the source of the trouble, correct the problem, and get the students back on task with only a small interruption. The students respected him for knowing who the culprit was and dispensing with the problem quickly.

___

## Un-Withitness

In the class next door, Mr. Dole was preoccupied with assembling a science experiment, while the students waited with nothing to do. He heard some commotion in the classroom, but hoped it would subside without his intervention. He continued connecting the hose to the pump, but eventually the hubbub became so loud that he looked up. Mike and Bonnie were throwing an eraser to each other, and Alex was running between them trying to intercept it. Students were shouting encouragement and one or two others were moving into the game. Mr. Dole couldn't understand how things had gotten so out of hand in such a short time. He tried to yell over the noise, but only a few students heard his voice, and they ignored him. He frantically flipped the light switch, threatened the students with expulsion, and eventually got them back into their seats. He told Bonnie, Mike and Alex to go to the principal's office, even though they protested that it wasn't their idea to play Catch the Eraser. He told the rest of the class that there would be no experiment and that they should read Chapter Four for a test the next day.

Mr. Dole made a number of mistakes. He was unprepared when class started, and he left his students with nothing to do. He ignored the first signs of trouble when he could still have prevented a major disruption from occurring. He was unable to deal with more than one issue at a time. In his panic to restore order, he made a threat that he had no intention of carrying out. He wasn't sure who was really at fault, so he chose the three who were participating in the game and punished them by sending them to the office. In effect, he punished the rest of the class as well by assigning a test for the next day. The students were resentful and felt they had been unfairly treated.

## Redl and Wattenburg

Redl and Wattenburg examine group dynamics and their effect on behavior. They believe the behavior of individuals affects the group, and that group expectations sway individual behavior. Understanding the psychological forces underlying group behavior helps the teacher maintain classroom control.

Teachers can influence group behavior in four ways. In *supporting self-control,* a low-keyed approach, teachers help students to help themselves. *Situational assistance* requires the teacher to help the student regain self-control; an example is "hurdle help," or helping the student overcome a specific problem that is preventing learning. Another example is restructuring the situation when the present approach is not working. In *reality appraisal,* students are made aware of what behavior is acceptable and the consequences of breaking rules. Finally, the *pain–pleasure principle* provides for rewards to be given for good behavior and threats for unacceptable behavior. Punishment is used only as a last resort for those occasions when a student completely loses self-control.

## Restructuring the Situation

Mrs. Keen was teaching an American history lesson to her general curriculum students. It was the last period of the day, and the students were tired and restless. Mrs. Keen tried to involve her students in a discussion about the landing of the Pilgrims at Plymouth Rock. When she called on Kirk, usually a good student, he told her he hadn't heard the question. Randy didn't know the answer either, but whispered a few words to his neighbors that made them laugh. Mrs. Keen looked at Susan, who was watching Dennis try to balance his pencil on an eraser. Susan wouldn't know the answer either. As Mrs. Keen surveyed her class, she realized that no one seemed the least bit interested in what happened to the Pilgrims.

Mrs. Keen racked her brain for a way to get the students to respond. She suddenly thought of simulating this event, of having each person in the room become involved in the story by acting it out. She stopped her lesson, told the students that for the rest of the afternoon they were going to do something different, and began explaining the procedure. The class gradually got caught up in acting out the landing of the Pilgrims and their attempts to survive in a cold and primitive new world.

---

Mrs. Keen was perceptive enough to realize that if her students were to get anything out of the landing of the Pilgrims, she would have to change her tactics at once. Since her students appeared totally disinterested in the lesson, she tried to think of a way to get them all involved. Her change of pace worked, and she added simulation to her repertoire of teaching techniques.

---

## Maintaining the Status Quo

Mrs. Lee had planned her English lesson carefully. First she was going to tell her class about adjectives and how they are used. Then she planned to have them complete a worksheet on the use of adjectives.

Outside, there was a terrible storm with thunder and lightning. Some of the students were frightened, especially when one blinding flash of lightning was followed instantly by a loud crash of thunder. Mrs. Lee continued discussing adjectives, although she noticed that nearly all the children were pointing out the window at a tree that had been knocked down by the heavy winds. When Mrs. Lee had concluded her lesson, she asked the students if they had any questions about adjectives. They looked at her blankly, but said nothing. Mrs. Lee was disappointed to find that the children did not do well on the worksheet that followed her well-presented lesson.

---

Mrs. Lee was totally inflexible. She was unable to deviate from her lesson plan even when circumstances clearly called for a change. Instead of ignoring the storm, she could have talked about what causes thunder and lightning and allowed the children to observe what was happening. Afterward, she could have asked them to think of all the adjectives they could use to describe the storm. The lesson would then have been meaningful to the class.

## Canter and Canter

The Canters advocate assertive discipline as a means for establishing effective classroom control. Assertive discipline is based on the concept that teachers have the right to insist on appropriate behavior from students. From the beginning of the school year, teachers establish rules for behavior along with logical consequences for both proper and improper behavior. These expectations are communicated clearly to the students. Failure to behave well results in negative consequences such as losing privileges or preferred activities, remaining after school, being sent to the principal's office, or time out (isolation). Good behavior brings positive consequences such as material rewards, positive notes to parents, special privileges or awards, and personal attention from the teacher. Teachers can also elicit the support of parents and administrators.

## Playing It By The Rules

It was raining, and Mr. Arrow's students were staying inside for recess. They had requested free time and were well aware of the rules for behavior. Mr. Arrow had suggested that the students might like to go to the reading corner, play one of the games, or work on their mural. As Mr. Arrow was talking with a group of children, he noticed that Ken had snatched Dottie's lunch box and begun to run around the room with it. Dottie started to chase him, but soon realized she couldn't catch him. She whined, "Give me back my lunch box." Ken taunted, "You'll have to catch me first."

At that point, Mr. Arrow said firmly, "Ken, come here." When Ken reached him, Mr. Arrow continued, looking Ken directly in the eye. "Ken, I don't like what you have done. You know the rules in here. There is to be no running in the classroom. Also, you are not to take something that belongs to someone else. You have broken both of these rules. I want you to return Dottie's lunch box. Then I want you to sit in that chair by the counter until recess is over." Ken reluctantly did as Mr. Arrow told him.

Limits for behavior had been set early in the year in Mr. Arrow's class. The students were well aware of the limits and their consequences. Occasionally, a student slipped, and Mr. Arrow asserted himself, as in the case of Ken. He spoke to Ken firmly, maintained eye contact, explained the inappropriate behavior, and followed through with a reasonable consequence.

---

## Anything Goes

Mr. Wilson was a new teacher. He knew classroom control was important, but felt that it was even more important for the students to like him. In an effort to be a pal to his students, he overlooked many inconsequential incidents at the beginning of the year. One day, he realized that he had to enforce some rules of behavior or he would lose control of the class altogether. He told the students, "You'd better settle down now" and "Please get quiet." These requests didn't seem to make any difference.

The next time the noise level rose, Mr. Wilson threatened to send all the students to detention hall. They were confused by this unnatural behavior and responded with complaints of unfairness and pleas for another chance. Hating to lose the friendship of his students, Mr. Wilson gave in to their requests and withdrew his threat.

A similar situation occurred the next day, so Mr. Wilson told the students to put their heads down on their desks for ten minutes. After a minute or two, some students began looking up. They said they thought they'd been punished long enough, so Mr. Wilson let them keep their heads up.

---

Mr. Wilson's students took advantage of his nonassertiveness by kidding around in class and not accomplishing any work. His requests for good behavior were vague and unclear, so the students ignored him. They soon realized they could talk him out of any threats he made. They liked Mr. Wilson, but had little respect for him because of his inability to set and enforce limits for behavior.

## Behavior Modification

All discipline deals with modifying behavior in some way, but behavior modification is a specific model of discipline based on B.F. Skinner's ideas. The basic premise is that all behavior is shaped by what happens to the students following an action. In this model, reinforcement is used systematically to change student behavior. Students who perform well are given reinforcers, or rewards. The rewards may be words of approval, awards, grades, or even such tangible items as raisins or candy. Students who perform badly receive no reinforcers; their behavior is ignored. Some systems of reinforcement are quite complex, but the concept of rewarding good behavior and ignoring bad behavior can be observed in any classroom.

## Catch More Flies With Honey

Mr. Sahai had studied about behavior modification in his psychology class and decided to put it into action. He realized that his classroom control wasn't as good as it could be and thought that a system of reinforcement might help. He introduced the plan to his class, announcing that points would be awarded to the class for good behavior. He pointed to a poster showing the maximum number of points that could be earned for each function. For instance, if everyone was seated and ready to work when the bell rang for class to start, the class would earn ten points. If Mr. Sahai didn't have to correct anyone's behavior during an entire class period, the class would earn fifteen points. He continued with other examples, then explained that the number of points would be totaled at the end of each week. Then Mr. Sahai showed the class another chart indicating the number of points required to earn certain privileges.

The students were very responsive to this plan. They cared more about behaving well when they were rewarded for doing so. The only problem was that Jon kept calling out during class, and Mr. Sahai sometimes had to correct him. No points were earned during these classes. The other students decided to take matters into their own hands and make Jon stop interrupting. This peer pressure changed Jon's behavior so that the class was soon earning the full number of points.

Mr. Sahai's experiment with behavior modification was successful. He had carefully thought out his plan and made the rules clear to the class. He kept careful records and never forgot to let the students choose their reward. The students soon began to enjoy working for points that earned them rewards. They responded more actively in class, liked the quieter, more businesslike atmosphere, and respected Mr. Sahai for thinking of this plan. By exerting peer pressure, the students helped their teacher control the misbehavior of individual students.

## Catch Fewer Flies With Vinegar

Mr. Wynne decided it was time to crack down on his class. He was tired of the myriad interruptions and the inattentiveness of his students. He believed in giving them fair warning, so he told them that beginning Monday morning, he was going to expect them to behave themselves, or else!

The students came to school Monday in their usual carefree way, entirely forgetting Mr. Wynne's threat. Mr. Wynne remembered, however, and wasted no time in carrying out his intentions. "Bobby, stop talking and sit down," he snapped. Bobby looked bewildered. He was only talking to Terry while he put his jacket away. "Anyone who talks in here before the bell rings will have to come straight back to the room after lunch," Mr. Wynne said. The students looked at each other in confusion. Until now, they had always been permitted to talk before school started. Mr. Wynne continued, "We're going to run a tight ship from now on. I don't want to hear a sound in this room."

---

The students resented Mr. Wynne's treatment and thought he was being unfair. He had not even discussed with them the new rules of conduct he was imposing. Although they were afraid not to comply with his demands, the students no longer cared about the quality of the work they turned in to him. Mr. Wynne had tried to improve his classroom control through threats and punishments; in doing so, he had lost the willing cooperation and respect of his students.

## Appropriate Disciplinary Measures

As a student, you may have wondered why some teachers seemed to be aware of everything that went on in the classroom, even when they didn't appear to be looking. This is a knack good teachers develop, a sort of sixth sense that enables them to pick up the vibrations from their classes so they always know what's happening. You can acquire this ability if you develop a sensitivity to the sounds, movements, voices, and behavior patterns within your classroom.

Teachers "with eyes in the back of their heads" are usually good disciplinarians. In fact, it is difficult to observe the techniques they use because their methods are subtle and unobtrusive. A quiet nod, the mention of a student's name, or a warning glance usually suffices. Don't worry if you haven't yet mastered this technique—it often takes years of practice.

Even these master disciplinarians occasionally have problems that require more attention, as you probably will also. When problems do develop, you must consider several factors before taking action. It is important to keep in mind the purpose of discipline: to restore order by helping the student regain control of his behavior, not to seek revenge for violation of the rules. You should also consider the reason for misbehavior and the personal circumstances of the misbehaving student. Appropriate disciplinary measures vary according to the student's grade level, socioeconomic background, degree of motivation for learning, ability level, and personality. As you can see, there is no single solution for any problem.

Before deciding what to do, you must also consider your school's policy regarding discipline. Check with your cooperating teacher to find out what types of disciplinary action are permitted if a student misbehaves. Can you keep students after school, or do bus schedules prohibit this? Can you deny a student recess, or is a certain amount of free time compulsory? Is there a detention hall, and do you have the option of sending a student there? Is paddling permitted? Are hall passes required, and what is the penalty for failing to have one?

## Knowing Some Options

Tuck all of these considerations away somewhere in your mind so you can pull them out when a problem arises. You may sometimes reach the point that you must discipline a class or an individual

*Remember that the purpose of discipline is to restore order by helping the student regain control of his behavior.*

student. You may want to ask the advice of your cooperating teacher first, but there are some appropriate consequences for specific types of misbehavior.

1  If a student tries to be the class clown . . .
   (a)  Reverse roles. Ask the clown to teach and you take his or her place in class, imitating the way he or she acts.
   (b)  Give him or her an opportunity to put on an act for the class.
   (c)  Explain that there are times when that kind of behavior is appreciated, but it is not appropriate during class.
   (d)  Give the clown special assignments to show your confidence in his or her ability to assume responsibility.
   (e)  Praise the clown for completion of serious work while ignoring the clowning.
   (f)  If the behavior persists, isolate the clown temporarily.

2  If students talk at inappropriate times . . .
   (a)  Ignore the interruption if possible.
   (b)  Change the seating arrangement. Some students may encourage those who sit near them to talk during class.
   (c)  Give students a few minutes of free time to get talking out of their systems.
   (d)  Stop your lesson and wait until everything quiets down.
   (e)  Divide the class into groups. Reward the group that does the least amount of unnecessary talking.

3  If students litter or mess up things . . .
   (a)  Provide time for them to clean up their desks and work areas.
   (b)  Provide incentives for neat work.
   (c)  Brainstorm all the ways to make the room neater, cleaner, and more attractive.
   (d)  Let students be messy sometimes, then give them a chance to clean up.
   (e)  Confiscate articles left carelessly around the room. Return them at the end of the week.
   (f)  Use creative dramatics. Turn young children into vacuum cleaners and see how quickly they can run around and put everything in its place.

4  If students push, shove, and make noise when forming lines . . .
   (a)  Appoint a different leader each week.
   (b)  Dismiss one row or group at a time. Choose the best-behaved group first.

    (c)   Line up according to some plan, such as alphabetical order, height, or color of clothing.

    (d)   Have young children pretend to be Indians gliding quietly through the halls in soft moccasins.

5   If a student tattles . . .

    (a)   Explain that you don't want to hear personal information about another student (tattling), but only news of rules that have been broken or of someone who has been hurt (reporting).

    (b)   Ask the offender to write down the information for you to read at the end of the day, because you do not have time to listen. Writing should discourage the tattler.

    (c)   If there are several tattlers in your class, ask them to save all their tales to tell on Friday afternoon. By then, they will probably consider the matters too trivial to share.

    (d)   Role play a tattletale incident so students can understand why this behavior is undesirable.

6   If a student lies . . .

    (a)   Ignore this student if you know she or he is just fantasizing or exaggerating. To a young child, say "Oh, what a nice story."

    (b)   Praise this student whenever he or she tells the truth. Point out on these occasions how important it is to be able to trust another person.

    (c)   Have a one-to-one conference with a student who lies habitually to discuss the importance of being truthful.

    (d)   For serious and persistent lying, impose a penalty (such as demerits) that has been agreed upon by the class.

7   If students cheat . . .

    (a)   Rearrange the seats to separate those who "help" each other.

    (b)   Take the student's test away and retest the student at another time.

    (c)   Give open-book or essay tests.

    (d)   Use alternate forms of a test so students seated beside each other will be taking different tests.

    (e)   Move close to the student who is cheating. Whisper a comment such as, "I want to find out what *you* know. Please write your own answers."

8   If students fight . . .

    (a)   Stop the fight. It may be necessary to restrain the fighters physically.

    (b)   Encourage the fighters to make up, shake hands, and be friends.

(c)   Have each student write or tape record his or her side of the story.

(d)   Give students who repeatedly get into fights opportunities to fight with supervision. Let them Indian wrestle or use physical education equipment (boxing gloves, punching bags).

(e)   Discuss or role play situations that make students angry. Find solutions.

9   If a student steals . . .
(This is a touchy problem with many circumstances to consider!)

(a)   If you see a student take something that belongs in the classroom, such as a pen or a pair of scissors, discuss the matter with him or her privately. Ask that the student return the item.

(b)   If you think you know who is guilty of taking something that belongs to someone else, speak to that student privately. If the student admits taking the item, ask him or her to please return it. You might suggest that the student apologize for his or her behavior. If she or he doesn't admit taking anything, tactfully suggest that you look through her or his things together.

(c)   If you don't know who is guilty, you might hold a class meeting to discuss the problem.

(d)   Role playing may help students understand the problem and prevent future thefts.

(e)   If a student has admitted to taking something of value, the student should be asked to return it, replace it, pay for it, or work long enough to cover the expense of the stolen item.

(f)   If thievery persists, you will probably need to get outside help from the guidance counselor or parents (if you know the student's identity).

10   If a student is using drugs or alcohol . . .
Pass along this information to your cooperating teacher who, in turn, should notify school authorities and parents.

## Testing the Technique

Some common disciplinary practices are considered generally effective; some are considered good or bad depending on the circumstances; others are thought to be inappropriate.

### Effective techniques

*Reinforcers*—Both verbal and nonverbal reinforcers are effective for encouraging good behavior and discouraging improper conduct.

*Restitution*—A student who takes or destroys something should be expected to return or restore it. If this is impossible, the student should compensate for the loss in some other way.

*Role playing*—Students appreciate the feelings of other students and see incidents in a new light when they role play. (See chapter 6.)

*Contracts*—The use of contracts works well for intermediate and secondary level students. Contracts are agreements that deal with specified behaviors, tasks, responsibilities, and rewards. They give the effect of a legal commitment and are signed by both the teacher and the student.

*Group discussions*—Guided, open discussions are good ways to handle disputes and discipline problems. Students feel involved and responsible for carrying out their own recommendations.

*Gripe box*—A suggestion box or gripe box allows students to express their dissatisfactions. After reading the students' notes, you might want to make some changes.

*Nonverbal signals*—Effective use of nonverbal signals and body language is one of the best forms of discipline. Examples are a frown, a smile, a nod, movement toward a student, an intent look, a raised hand, and a wink.

*Time out*—Time out can be used to remove a student who is highly distracting to the rest of the class or who is acting in such a way that he or she could harm others. The teacher isolates the student from the rest of the class for five to ten minutes until he or she can regain control of his or her behavior. The isolation area should be secluded, quiet, and dull.

*Appeal to reason*—Explaining why good behavior is necessary often convinces students to act well. You might say, "Be careful with the equipment so we don't break anything" or "Work quickly so we'll have time to plan our party."

*Approval of behavior*—This method generally works well in the elementary school. The teacher notices students who are "ready to begin," "sitting up nicely," or "have their books open to the right page." Other students follow suit because they also want recognition.

*Grounding*—This technique is effective for the students who can't work well or cooperate at an interest center. The student must return to his seat to work until he is ready to rejoin the group.

*Matching the penalty to the offense*—A penalty should relate to the offense so the student can see the seriousness of it.

### Borderline Techniques

*Planned ignoring*—This may work for awhile. Sometimes if you ignore the problem, it will go away; other times, it only becomes worse, until you are forced to deal with it.

*Apologies*—If apologies are genuine, they are effective. If you force students to say words they don't mean, you are only teaching them to lie. Their apologies mean nothing.

*Removing students from the classroom*—Removal may seem the best procedure when a student is out of control; however, it is always better to try to settle the matter yourself. You and your cooperating teacher probably know the situation better than anyone else. If a student is sent from the room, someone should chaperone him or her to his or her destination. Arrangements should be made beforehand with the person to whom the student is being sent.

*Merits and demerits*—This system consists of awarding or taking away points for certain kinds of behavior. It generally works well if it is carefully structured, especially when it is used on a temporary basis. Students should eventually learn to control their own behavior, however, rather than rely on outside incentives. Also, the system can backfire if a student accumulates so many demerits that you can't collect all of them.

*Remaining after school*—Keeping a student after school, either in your own room or in detention hall, may have some value as a penalty for misbehavior. Unless some educational experience is planned for this time, however, this method will waste time for both you and the student. Remaining after school can also interfere with bus schedules or a worthwhile extracurricular activity.

*Withholding privileges*—A denied privilege is usually an effective penalty. It can have a negative effect, however, if a student is being denied something important for him. For instance, a hyperactive child who is denied recess probably needs this outlet for his surplus energy.

*Scolding*—An occasional reprimand is often necessary, but a bitter harangue has a negative effect on the whole class. Avoid nagging, constant faultfinding, and long discourses on behavior.

*Personal conferences*—A private, one-to-one conference often clears up problems. It helps the student and teacher understand each other. Privacy is necessary for a free exchange of views and for keeping a matter confidential. Conferences are ineffective when the teacher simply makes accusations and the student is unresponsive, and they can be destructive if they deteriorate into arguments.

### Ineffective Techniques

*Assigning additional class work or homework*—This practice generally results in the student's disliking the subject.

*Use of ridicule or sarcasm*—Students who are embarrassed or humiliated by their teachers may suffer serious psychological damage.

*Lowering grades*—Grades for academic achievement should not be affected by behavior.

*Dunce caps, holding books at arm's length, standing with your nose in a circle drawn on the board, writing sentences, and other such bugaboos*—These techniques belong back in the Dark

Ages. While they may deter students from certain kinds of behavior, they do nothing to rehabilitate the student or solve the problem.

*Threats*—It's usually better to act than to threaten. If you do make threats, be sure you are prepared to follow through. Generally, threats cause students to become upset and suspicious.

*Corporal punishment*—Corporal punishment rarely corrects a problem. Like threats, it usually has a negative effect on students and should be used only as a last resort, if ever. Improper use of corporal punishment can result in legal problems.

# Evaluating Five Case Studies

The following case studies are based on actual situations. Read them and evaluate the teacher's action in each case. Were other options available? How would you have handled these students?

## Case Study: The Last Straw

Jeff, a twelfth grade student, came from a low socioeconomic level home where he was taught the value of a good education. His parents were interested in his progress and encouraged him to do well.

In industrial arts class, Jeff was a reasonably good student, but he often caused minor disruptions. He would distract other students by sticking his foot out to trip them, making wisecracks, laughing raucously at nothing, and occasionally defying his teacher, Mr. Hamlin. Mr. Hamlin put up with his behavior for several weeks. He knew that Jeff was basically a good student and did not feel that Jeff's interruptions warranted a confrontation.

One morning, Jeff decided he would go to the cosmetology class to get a haircut during industrial arts. When he told Mr. Hamlin he was going, Mr. Hamlin refused to let him. Jeff told Mr. Hamlin to go to hell, and that he was going anyway. At this point, Mr. Hamlin realized he had been too lenient with Jeff. He knew something would have to be done or there would be a total breakdown in discipline in his class. Mr. Hamlin took Jeff to the office, where the principal suspended him for his defiant and discourteous behavior.

Following his suspension, Jeff returned to school with his father. During a conference with the guidance counselor, Mr. Carlin, the entire situation was reviewed and correct standards of behavior were discussed. A contract was drawn up which allowed Jeff to return to class as long as he acted like a gentleman. Mr. Carlin went over the contract with Jeff and his father in detail. If Jeff failed to live up to his commitment, he would be dropped from the class roll. Jeff seemed to hold no malice toward his teacher or the counselor and willingly agreed to sign the contract, along with his father and Mr. Carlin. The counselor also requested that Jeff apologize to Mr. Hamlin and the rest of the class, but only if he felt he owed them an apology.

Mr. Hamlin later reported that Jeff had been much less disruptive in class and that he was behaving more maturely.

## Case Study: Reaching a Truce

Ann is a large, unattractive eighth grader. She is rarely a discipline problem for her teachers, but has a record of tardiness and unexcused absences. Her home background is extremely poor and her father is unknown. Miss Horne is her guidance counselor.

Ann came to Miss Horne's attention because of her smoking in areas where smoking is prohibited. She had a smoking permit that her mother had signed, but she failed to restrict her smoking to areas designated for that purpose. Miss Horne forbade Ann to visit a particular rest room and threatened to send her home if she smoked in there. When Miss Horne found Ann smoking there again, she sent her home.

After Ann returned to school, she continued to smoke in forbidden areas. Miss Horne observed her on three occasions in a single day smoking in the rest room that was off limits to her. Ann denied that it was she, then said she had permission to smoke. Both of these statements were untrue. Miss Horne had written down the exact times she had seen Ann and the names of witnesses who were with her at the time. Ann was sent home again. She was warned that the next time she defied the rules, she would have to face the school board.

Ann has returned to school again on a probationary status. She realizes that Miss Horne means what she says and will follow through with her warnings. Ann has not been observed smoking again, but she still has a poor attitude toward school. She does speak to Miss Horne, however, and a temporary truce seems to have been established between them.

## Case Study: Moving Toward Acceptable Behavior

Jill is a fifth grader who lives with her mother and stepfather. She was abused by her father as a young child, and her stepfather has helped her make adjustments. Jill is much like her mother, and they do not get along well. Both parents are beginning to lose patience with her.

At the beginning of the year, Jill threw temper tantrums when things didn't go her way. She nearly went into convulsions sometimes and would have to be taken from the room. At other times, she was told to stand in the corner as punishment for her fits of temper. She hated standing in the corner, so the number of tantrums gradually decreased.

Jill was hostile toward the teacher, Mrs. Lynch, and the other children. She was loud and aggressive when she came to school in the morning. She called people names and frequently told lies. She was easily distracted and rushed through her work, not caring if it was done correctly. On the playground, she tried to get control of the ball and take it away from the other children. She had no remorse about hurting people, even when she caused them to bleed.

During the year, three things seemed to help Jill. First, Jill enjoyed getting the attention of the other students. She was beginning to discover that when she was nice to them, they would be friendly toward her. To win friends, she began to change her attention-getting strategies to more acceptable behavior patterns.

Jill's relationship with Mrs. Lynch also helped her. Mrs. Lynch and Jill talked frequently in private about why Jill acted as she did and how she might get along better with the other children. Jill began to trust Mrs. Lynch and stopped feeling that Mrs. Lynch was picking on her.

Jill was also helped by the school psychologist with whom she met each week. The psychologist required her to earn points for satisfactory achievement. Jill's teachers had to sign a paper each time she earned a point. Jill then took the paper to the psychologist, who granted her a privilege if she had earned at least sixteen points in a week.

Jill is still immature and demands attention in unacceptable ways, but her behavior is much better than it was at the beginning of the year.

---

## Case Study: Parental Restitution

Troy was a rather homely and unpopular fourth grader whose parents had a lot of money. His mother placed a great deal of importance on wealth and continually bragged about recent trips and acquisitions. It seemed to Troy that money could buy anything.

Troy wanted more than anything to be accepted by his friends. He decided to ask Sheila, the cutest girl in class, to "go with" him for ten dollars a week. This seemed like a lot of money to Sheila, but she was doubtful about the arrangement. She discussed Troy's proposition with her friends before deciding what to do. She really didn't want to be Troy's girl, even for ten dollars. She finally agreed, however, and Troy brought the ten dollars to school for her.

Until this time, Sheila had barely spoken to Troy, but now she occasionally sat with him during lunch and talked to him during the day. She allowed him to call her at night, but they never went any place together. This arrangement satisfied Troy. He boasted to his classmates about his new girl friend. They were properly impressed, and Troy gained status among his peers.

After two or three weeks, Troy's teacher, Mrs. Hobson, became suspicious. She had observed the new relationship between Troy and Sheila and thought it was unusual. One day she glimpsed Troy handing ten dollars to Sheila. She talked to the two quietly and found out about their arrangement.

Mrs. Hobson felt that the only thing to do was to bring both sets of parents to school and discuss the matter with them. During the conference, the parents agreed to talk to their children about ending the arrangement. Sheila's parents returned the money to Troy's parents and the matter ended. Troy and Sheila resumed their original relationship. Troy did not seem depressed over losing Sheila's attention.

---

## Case Study: Peer Pressure Does the Trick

Dan comes from a high socioeconomic level home and has the support of his family. Dan doesn't believe in law enforcement, school regulations, or God. He is an excellent student academically, but had begun using drugs as a high school sophomore.

As a junior, Dan became even more strongly hooked on drugs. His guidance counselor, Mrs. Tilton, was aware of Dan's dependence on drugs and talked to him about this problem on several occasions. Dan insisted that it was his right to use drugs and that no one could tell him what to do. He claimed that all the students used drugs, but Mrs. Tilton denied this. Mrs. Tilton warned him that drugs could eventually ruin him, but nothing she said made any difference. Dan continued to be cooperative and do well in his classes, but was beginning to go downhill by the end of the year.

Despite his heavy use of drugs, Dan won the history prize in his junior year. As he walked across the stage to receive his award, the students booed him. They had no respect for him because of his involvement with drugs.

For some reason, this rejection by his peers turned Dan around. He cared about his fellow students and their feelings toward him. He stopped using drugs and was elected president of the student body in his senior year. According to some, he was the best student body president the school had had. He went on to the local university, where he carries a double major and makes the Dean's List each semester.

---

## Discussion Questions

1 Which model of behavior do you think would have been effective in the vignette at the beginning of this chapter? Why?

2 Select one or two students who tend to be disruptive in class. Can you determine the reasons for their behavior? Is there anything you can do to change this disruptive behavior?

3 Analyze the five models of behavior. Which model, if any, does your cooperating teacher use? Which model do you prefer? Can you put together parts of the different models and come up with a plan you think would work for you? Can you identify some basic concepts that appear to be true of all five models?

4 Watch your cooperating teacher carefully. How does he or she control behavior? Do the teacher's signals, warnings, nonverbal messages, or other subtle measures prevent discipline problems from arising? Which techniques seem most successful? Do all students respond the same way?

5 Develop a plan for helping your students acquire self-discipline. What reasonable responsibilities can you give them? Can you vary the responsibilities to meet the capabilities of each student? How can you check students' progress toward developing self-discipline?

6 What kinds of verbal and nonverbal reinforcers do you use during the day? Do you reinforce each student's good behavior, or do you reserve reinforcers for just a few? How might you make better use of reinforcers to encourage good academic work and proper behavior?

## Selected References

Axelrod, S. *Behavior Modification for the Classroom Teacher.* New York: McGraw-Hill, 1977.

Canter, Lee, and Marlene Canter. *Assertive Discipline: A Take-Charge Approach for Today's Educator.* Seal Beach, Calif.: Canter and Associates, 1976.

Charles, C. M. *Building Classroom Discipline.* New York: Longman, 1981.

Collins, Myrtle T., and Dwane R. Collins. *Survival Kit for Teachers (And Parents).* Pacific Palisades, Calif.: Goodyear, 1975.

Faust, Naomi F. *Discipline and the Classroom Teacher.* Port Washington, N.Y.: Kennikat Press, 1977.

Glasser, William. *Schools Without Failure.* New York: Harper and Row, 1969.

Gnagey, William J. *Controlling Classroom Misbehavior.* Washington, D.C.: National Education Association, Association of Classroom Teachers, 1969.

Gnagey, William J. *Maintaining Discipline in Classroom Instruction.* New York: Macmillan, 1975.

House, Ernest R., and Stephen D. Lapan. *Survival in the Classroom.* Boston: Allyn and Bacon, 1978.

Johnson, Simon O. *Better Discipline: A Practical Approach.* Springfield, Ill.: Charles C. Thomas, 1980.

Jones, Frederic. "The Gentle Art of Classroom Discipline." *National Elementary Principal* 58 (June 1979): 26–32.

Kounin, Jacob. *Discipline and Group Management in Classrooms.* New York: Holt, Rinehart and Winston, 1970.

Long, James D., and Virginia H. Frye. *Making It Till Friday: A Guide to Successful Classroom Management.* Princeton, N.J.: Princeton Book Company, 1977.

Martin, Reed, and David Lauridsen. *Developing Student Discipline and Motivation.* Champaign, Ill.: Research Press, 1975.

Pearson, Craig. *Resolving Classroom Conflict.* Palo Alto, Calif.: Learning Handbooks, 1974.

Redl, Fritz, and William W. Wattenberg. *Mental Hygiene in Teaching.* New York: Harcourt, Brace and World, 1959.

Steinback, Susan Bray, and William Clarence Steinback. *Classroom Discipline.* Springfield, Ill.: Charles C. Thomas, 1977.

Tanner, Laurel N. *Classroom Discipline for Effective Teaching and Learning.* New York: Holt, Rinehart and Winston, 1978.

Volkmann, Christina S. *The Last Straw.* San Francisco: R. & E. Research Associates, 1978.

# 5
## Classroom Management

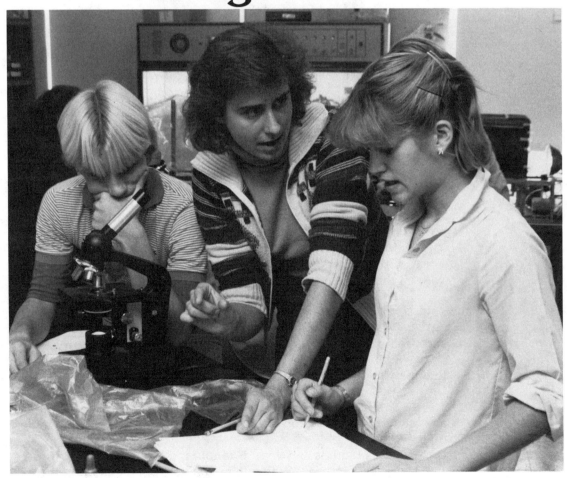

Miss Chervenak, a student teacher, has been successfully using the Newspaper in the Classroom program with her ninth grade students. As a culminating activity for the unit, she expects the students to publish a newspaper of their own. They have been divided into groups and are writing their paper.

Li-Jan: Miss Chervenak, what am I supposed to do?

Miss Chervenak: What is your job?

Li-Jan: I'm supposed to be the sports editor.

Tony: Miss Chervenak, where are we supposed to work?

Miss Chervenak: What is your group, Tony?

Tony: Feature stories.

Miss Chervenak: Well, try to find a place over by the bulletin board.

David: That's where you said *we* could work, Miss Chervenak.

Miss Chervenak: Well, find another place then, Tony. What is your group, David?

Li-Jan: Miss Chervenak—

Miss Chervenak: Just a minute, Li-Jan. What did you say, David?

David: We're writing the ads.

Miss Chervenak: Oh, that's right. Now, Li-Jan, what did you want?

Li-Jan: What is the sports editor supposed to do?

Miss Chervenak: Look at the sports section of the paper and see if you can figure out what's supposed to be in there.

Li-Jan: Who's supposed to be in my group? I can't find anyone to work with me.

Miss Chervenak: Let's see. I know I have that list here somewhere. It must be under these papers.

Linda: Miss Chervenak, Joe says he's in charge of the news stories but yesterday you said I could do that.

Miss Chervenak (to the whole class in a raised, agitated voice): Boys and girls. You must get quiet! We can't work in here with all that noise. Get busy now.

Li-Jan: Is it OK if I just write something about what our softball team did over the weekend?

Miss Chervenak: Yes, that'll be fine, Li-Jan. Just do that. I can't seem to find who the other members of your group are.

Phil and Steve: Miss Chervenak, you said we needed to go interview some other teachers. Is it OK if we do that now?

Miss Chervenak: I'm not sure.

Joe (approaching Miss Chervenak angrily): How come Linda says she's supposed to do news stories? I thought you told me to do that.

Linda (addressing Joe): She told me to do them!

Miss Chervenak: Why don't you two work together on them?

Joe (shuffling off and muttering under his breath): I can't stand that girl. She's a creep. She can do it by herself for all I care.

Phil and Steve: What about it? Can we go?

Miss Chervenak: Go where? Oh yes, I remember. Did you make appointments with anyone?

Phil and Steve: No, were we supposed to?

Miss Chervenak: Well, you really should.

Diane: It's almost time for my bus. Shall I get ready?

Miss Chervenak: I had no idea it was that late already. Yes, go get ready.

Miss Chervenak (addressing the class): Class! (no one hears) Class! (still no hears amidst the laughter, talking, and running around the room) Boys and girls!!! (now shouting to be heard) Clean up your work and get in your seats. The buses are coming.

The students finally hear her and begin to gather their things together. The buses arrive before they finish, and Miss Chervenak must straighten up the rest of the room herself. At this point, her cooperating teacher walks in and asks, "Well, how did everything go?"

Miss Chervenak (with a heavy sigh): I'll never try that again. These kids don't know how to work in groups.

1 Was Miss Chervenak's idea for a culminating activity a good one? How might it have been handled more successfully?

2 What mistakes did Miss Chervenak make in assigning group activities? How could she have prevented some of the problems from arising?

3 Why do you think Miss Chervenak ran out of time? What factors should be considered in scheduling activities such as this one to be sure there is enough time?

4 What could Miss Chervenak have done to get the children's attention instead of shouting at them? How could she have reduced the noise level while the boys and girls were working?

5 Do you agree with Miss Chervenak that these children can't work in groups? Do you think she was right to say she'll never try group work again?

---

# Support System for Teaching

Knowing your subject and how to teach it is important, but students won't learn if your plans go awry because of poor classroom management. What can you do about providing a classroom environment conducive to learning, scheduling activities within limited time frames, grouping students for different purposes, and keeping records for future reference? Unfortunately, there are no easy answers to these questions. Each situation is unique. You *can*, however, observe your cooperating teacher and read this chapter for some useful ideas on classroom management.

## Open versus Self-Contained Classrooms

Schools and individual teachers within the same school observe various degrees of formality in their approaches to learning. They may follow the open concept or unstructured approach, or they may be traditional and highly structured. The degree of formality in your school will affect the way you teach. The design of the building often, but not always, affects the school's philosophy toward openness. If you have been placed in a school consisting primarily of self-contained classrooms, you will probably follow a traditional or formal approach. On the other hand, if you are teaching in an open classroom building with large areas in which students move about freely, your school probably supports an informal, less structured approach. Many schools use a combination of both approaches; for instance, a self-contained classroom may have a work area, a reading corner, an abundance of resource materials, and interest centers.

In the self-contained or traditional classroom, learning is likely to be teacher-centered. Routines and schedules are adhered to strictly, and teaching is well organized and systematic. Teachers follow a curriculum guide and students use textbooks to learn their lessons. By the end of the year, students are expected to have achieved certain predetermined objectives.

There is a great deal more freedom and flexibility in open classrooms. The emphasis is on exploration, discovery, and spontaneity. Students may plan learning experiences with their teachers and take a more active part in classroom decision making. If students express interest in a particular aspect of a lesson, the teacher allows them to pursue that special interest rather than conforming rigidly to the lesson plan. Differences of opinion, sometimes resulting in arguments and conflicts, are permitted and even encouraged in the open classroom.

Both approaches to learning require a great deal of planning and classroom management. The rules are already established pretty clearly in the formal, self-contained classroom, and it will be your responsibility to enforce them. You will need to prepare your lesson plans carefully and keep the students on the subject during discussions. You should try to meet each objective and cover the material adequately. In the open classroom, where the students move and speak more freely, you will have to know how to help students resolve disagreements and conflicts. You should also set up situations and make resources available to stimulate the desire to learn. You must be sufficiently knowledgeable in your subject to expand on your lesson in response to the interest your students show. Develop an atmosphere of mutual trust and responsibility, and guard against permissiveness and chaos.

# Grouping

Most classes consist of students who differ greatly in backgrounds, personalities, attitudes, and intelligence. Ideally, to meet his or her special needs, you should teach each student individually. Practically, however, you should teach the whole class together, because it is more efficient to present a lesson only once. Grouping is an attempt to compromise between totally individualizing instruction and treating the entire class as a single unit. Individual differences are reduced to some extent by grouping, but many differences remain.

## Types of Grouping

By this time, you are probably well acquainted with your school. You may already know whether students are grouped homogeneously (according to ability) or heterogeneously (without regard to ability). Secondary schools may offer a multiple-track curriculum which groups students into a college preparatory, business, or general curriculum. There may also be special programs for groups of students with different needs. For instance, your school may group students who are learning English as a second language, who have been identified as potential dropouts, or who are recognized as gifted. Grouping patterns that cut across classrooms and grade levels are known as interclass groupings.

You will be concerned primarily with intraclass groupings (grouping within the classroom), however. Your cooperating teacher may already use small groups. As you teach, you may want to try grouping as a way to meet your objectives.

You can set up groups for different purposes. Most groups are established in an attempt to place students of similar achievement levels together. Groups are sometimes arranged for other subject-related purposes as well. Students having difficulty with a particular math skill may meet together two or three times to relearn the concept and do practice exercises. In social studies, students may work together in research groups. Science classes may be broken into groups to prepare an experiment that illustrates a certain concept. Physical education classes may be divided into homogeneous groups according to skill level, or into heterogeneous groups so that less able students can benefit from interaction with more proficient students. Groups may be short-term or long-term, depending on the length of time required to meet objectives.

You might want to try establishing friendship groups that allow friends to work together. Students in these groups are often highly motivated because they enjoy being with each other. You need to be careful of two things when allowing friendship groups. First, students may enjoy one another's company so much that they won't get any work done, so you will have to warn them that they can work with their friends only as long as they produce results. When they cease to work, the groups will be disbanded and other activities substituted. Second, there will probably be some students who do not seem to have any friends. You might tactfully approach one or two popular students about including these isolates in their groups.

Interest grouping is another kind of classroom organization you may wish to try. You might begin forming this type of group after you've gotten to know the students well enough to know their interests. You can also discover their interests by asking them to list three things they would like to know more about. After you have compiled the results of this informal survey, you can divide the class into several groups. If some students did not choose one of the topics selected for an interest group, allow them to join one of the other groups.

Since most groups are set up on the basis of achievement levels, low achieving students often develop poor self-concepts. They think of themselves and others in their group as "dummies." Ethnic groups tend to stay together and not mingle with other students. By forming project and interest groups, you encourage students of differing achievement levels and ethnic origins to work together, and students contribute according to their particular knowledge, skills, or talents.

*Reading groups will probably already be established when you take over teaching duties.*

## Implementation

Here is a situation you might meet in an elementary classroom. As you observe the class, you notice that the teacher does group for reading instruction in the morning; however, no other groups are held during the day. You notice that the children in the low group tend to goof off during the day and stick together during lunch and free time. Students in the high group seem to be cliquish and ignore the other students.

Another situation exists in a secondary classroom: as you observe the teacher leading the class discussion, you notice that the same six or eight students participate each day. The other students daydream, stare out the window, pass notes, and occasionally doze off.

Now let's see what might happen if you tried grouping the students in these two classes. In the elementary classroom, you set up interest groups that meet from 1:00 to 1:40 each day. It happens that three children from the low group, two from the middle group, and four from the high group have chosen dinosaurs as their topic. Their assignment is to create a room display and give a 20-minute presentation at the end of two weeks. Before they realize what's happening, the students are excitedly delving into books, working on drawings, sharing models from home, and planning their presentation. At least during this period, achievement levels are forgotten.

At the secondary level, you decide to abandon whole class discussion for the time being and break the class into four groups. You include in each group one or two leaders and five or six students who have not been participating actively in class. The assignment for each group is to decide which invention has had the greatest impact on the progress of the human race. Working secretly in their groups, the students investigate inventions, select the one they feel is most influential, and build a case to support their choice. Instead of only a small number of students participating, everyone is working creatively to prove to the rest of the class that their group's invention is most significant.

If you decide to create groups within your classroom, don't begin impulsively. Think your plan through carefully before you start. Try to make your groups a workable size, small enough that everyone must participate but large enough to develop a worthy project. Avoid putting in the same group students who cause trouble when they are together. Be sure resource materials—references and supplies—are available, and that students know how to use them.

Here are a few pointers to help you manage groups well. Set up guidelines so that students know their privileges and limitations. Make sure before starting that all the students understand exactly what they are to do. Allow them freedom to talk quietly and move around the room. If possible, let them go to the library for additional information. Suggest that each group appoint a leader who will more or less be responsible for the group's activities. Experiment with the length of time; allow enough to get something accomplished but not so much that students lose interest and stray off task. Give each group space to carry out its activity without interfering with the other students. Be available to offer ideas. Miss Chervenak should have observed some of these pointers!

Reading groups are probably the most common form of grouping, and they operate somewhat differently from interest or project groups. Reading groups are composed of students who read at approximately the same level. The groups are teacher-guided and generally follow an established procedure. There are usually two, three, or four groups in a class, depending on the range of levels within that class. If you are an elementary major, you may begin your field experiences by teaching a reading group. You will quickly become accustomed to the way the group operates by observing your cooperating teacher and studying the basal reader manual.

The procedure and the students who make up the group are probably already established when you arrive, but here are some techniques that will help the group operate smoothly. If you have any choice, sit in a corner of the room facing the group, with the rest of the class beyond the group. This forces the children in the group to watch you instead of their classmates, and you can see both your group and the rest of the class. Sit next to a chalkboard or an easel with a chart tablet so you can write important words or examples as you say them. Unless it is a dire emergency, don't allow children from the rest of the class to interrupt you during a group lesson. Have all the materials you will need during the lesson ready before you start. Don't let children bring anything with them to the group except what they will need. Toys and food should be strictly forbidden.

Observe your students carefully during the reading groups to see if they are comfortable in their group or if they might perform better with another group. As a general rule, if pupils miss more than one word out of twenty, they should move to an easier level. If they always finish first and know all the answers, they might work better at a higher level. Grouping should always be flexible, to allow for variations in students' learning rates, so don't hesitate to suggest a move to your cooperating teacher if you think a change is warranted.

Grouping provides variety in the school program and serves many purposes. You will not always want to have students work in groups, however. Some activities are best done with the whole class, while others are best accomplished individually. Good activities for the entire class include listening to a resource visitor, being introduced to a unit, seeing a film, participating in a discussion, watching a demonstration, and taking a field trip. Individual work may be best for remediating skills or writing research reports. One program that provides for individualized reading is called Sustained Silent Reading (SSR). In this program, students, teachers, and the entire school

*Listening to a resource person is usually a whole class activity.*

staff read materials of their choice during an agreed-upon 15- or 20-minute period each school day.

During the day, you will probably want to spend some time with whole class instruction, some time with small groups, and the remainder of the time individualizing instruction. A day in an elementary classroom may proceed this way. You make announcements and explain assignments to the whole class. Then groups of children come to you for reading instruction while others work independently at their seats. After reading groups, the whole class goes to the gym for physical education. When they return to the classroom, you instruct the whole class in adding fractions. After lunch, some children work in project groups to compile booklets on the solar system, while others work individually at learning centers. During this time, you are holding individual conferences with children who need to do make-up work. At the end of the day, you meet with the whole class again to give a trial spelling test and, finally, to review what has happened during the day.

A secondary class might also involve whole-class, group, and individual activities. Usually, you will want to meet with the entire class at the beginning of the period to review old material, introduce new information, and give directions. You should also pull the whole class together again near the end of the period to evaluate progress, make further assignments, and clear up any confusion. During the remainder of the class time, students might work together on group projects, such as making mock investments in the stock market, tracing the development of amphibians for a class presentation, or writing a play about good citizenship. They could work in pairs as they review for a test or proofread each other's creative writing. They might also do assignments or research independently.

# Scheduling

The use of time enters into nearly every phase of your teaching. It has a lot to do with how much you accomplish, how well you hold the interest of your students, and how you feel as you proceed through the day. Good time management will make teaching a lot easier, as well as more effective, than if you rush helter-skelter through the day.

## Flexibility within a Routine

Routine and flexibility seem to be contradictory ideas, but you need some of each to build a balanced program. You will probably begin teaching by following the schedule already set by your cooperating teacher. A well-planned routine helps you cover everything you are supposed to accomplish, fosters good classroom control because students feel secure when they know what to expect next, and is comfortable, because you don't have to wonder all day long what to do next.

Don't be a slave to your schedule, however. The schedule is for your convenience; don't let it become an obstruction to learning. Sometimes you will need more time than what is scheduled to develop a concept fully. You may want to use audiovisual media, invite a resource person, or take a short field trip. You may get into an activity and realize that some really creative experiences are taking place. Whenever possible, allow these learning experiences to continue, even if it means extending them beyond the scheduled time limit.

One way to have flexible scheduling within a fixed schedule at the elementary level is to plan on a weekly instead of a daily basis. Perhaps you will spend 20 minutes extra on math today because you are working with manipulative materials and cut 20 minutes out of language arts. You can pay back this time later in the week.

Some schools provide for flexibility through modular scheduling. Modules are uniform blocks of time arranged to meet instructional needs. For instance, a field trip would require several connected modules, whereas reviewing a test might require only one module. Check with your cooperating teacher to see if your school uses this plan or a similar one.

Some students report to supportive classes. A handful may go to remedial reading from 10:05 to 10:40 three times a week; another group may go to the gifted class from 1:15 to 2:15 every Friday. Don't plan an activity for the whole class when some students will be elsewhere.

Your school may support a Youth Participation program, through which young people engage in service or learning activities that are not a regular part of the school curriculum. Students involved in Youth Participation programs have served as teachers, medical assistants, mechanics, journalists, and tour guides. Although many of these programs are beneficial, finding flexible ways to schedule them is a problem. Some school systems have found solutions in these ways:

1  Enrichment and creative activity periods
2  Elective or noncredit courses
3  Scheduling of two classes with consecutive double periods once a week
4  Use of before and after school hours, weekends, and summer programs
5  Released time one day a week for a period of time.

## Using Time Efficiently

Your time, both in and out of the classroom, is precious. You'll get more done in the classroom if you use your time well, and you'll have more free time out of the classroom if you plan efficiently.

Evenings and weekends are not entirely your own during student teaching. You may be working with your cooperating teacher on the yearbook, sharing late afternoon bus duty, or coaching the football team well into the evening. Sometimes you will have a parent-teacher conference after school or a meeting in the evening. Planning and record keeping also take a great deal of time. For these and other reasons, many universities do not permit student teachers to take additional courses. If you have held a part-time job during your college years, you may have to quit or reduce your hours. Avoid committing too much time to extracurricular or social activities. Full-time student teaching is generally much more demanding on your time than 15 or 18 hours of course work.

Planning will probably take more time than you expect. Many of the procedures that have become habit for experienced teachers will require detailed planning for you. Whenever possible, make use of planning time during school. Don't depend on this time, however, as unexpected interruptions frequently occur during any school day.

Good organization will enable you to plan thoroughly for your lessons and still have time for yourself. Plan well ahead. Order or reserve materials in advance. If you will need to make several games or posters, buy all the materials at once. A single trip to the library can serve many purposes if you get resource material you will need over a period of time. Instead of spending hours searching through curriculum guides for ideas, sit down and think hard for a few minutes. Your own idea is often as good as or better than one you find in another source. Combine social activities with school functions—take your date, a friend, or your family with you on a Sunday afternoon hike while you collect specimens for a terrarium.

You should use time efficiently in the classroom, also. The most effective teachers are those who spend most of their time giving direct instruction to students and waste little time with disruptions and periods of confusion. These teachers give presentations, explanations, and reinforcement to students to help them learn. They encourage students to spend time on assignments, because the more time students spend on academic tasks, the more likely they are to learn.

Here are some tips for keeping things moving in the classroom. Have learning centers ready for action, fully equipped and neatly arranged. Put markers in your books so you can turn quickly to the right page. Be sure all the resource materials you will need for the day are readily available, including supplies you will ask students to distribute. Erase the chalkboards as soon as you finish one lesson so you will be ready for the next. Have everything ready for the next day's lessons before you go home in the afternoon. If you are an early riser, however, you may prefer to come early and get things ready in the morning.

Your expectations of your students have a lot to do with efficiency. Do the students take five minutes to change from one lesson to another as they yawn, stretch, sharpen pencils, drop books, and make remarks to each other, or do they quietly put away one book and get out another? Do you have to repeat instructions three or four times before everyone knows what to do, or do they listen the first time? When you ask them to line up or get into groups, do they make a mad dash, or sit and stare in confusion, or do they do what you expect of them? When it's time for class to start, are they still roaming around the room, or do they know to get into their seats?

These negative behaviors are big time wasters. You can avoid these and other problems, however, by setting realistic expectations for your students and holding them responsible. If it takes too long for students to change from one book to another, practice doing this one day. Have a race against time to see if they can make the change in 45 seconds, 30 seconds, or less. They won't always work this quickly, but knowing what they *can* do should speed things up.

It's important to train students to listen well the first time you say something. Not only is repeating yourself a time waster, it also teaches students that they don't really have to listen the first or second time; they know you'll keep repeating what you want them to hear. You can break this habit by warning them that from now on you will say something only once. Get their attention, speak clearly, and don't repeat yourself. Some students may do the wrong assignments or miss out altogether on an activity, but if you really mean it, most of them will eventually learn to hear you the first time.

If the students don't know what to do when you tell them to line up or get into groups, the fault is probably yours. This was undoubtedly the case with Miss Chervenak. Have you told them what you expect? Are your directions clear? You may have to practice doing this one day so you won't waste time on other occasions. Students must also realize that, at a certain signal, they are expected to get into their seats and be ready to begin. You might warn them that failure to do this may result in losing an equal amount of time from an activity they value.

Establishing routine procedures saves time during the day. Assign responsibilities to different students and be sure they can carry them out efficiently. Minimize interruptions by letting students know in advance what you expect. For example, students won't need to raise their hands and interrupt the lesson if they already know what they are permitted to do. With young children, establish regular times for using the lavatory. After that, if a child really has to go, allow him or her to go alone without asking permission. Encourage students to sharpen pencils before school starts, but if a point breaks, allow a student to sharpen the pencil again without first asking you. If students interrupt discussion with an irrelevant story, ask them to tell you later. Saying this allows you to continue the lesson and satisfies the student by letting him or her know you will listen later.

While it's true that some students need more individual attention than others, you must be careful to attend to all students' needs. Guard against spending so much time with an individual student that you neglect the rest of your class. Perhaps you can help a particularly needy student by arranging peer tutoring, working with the student before or after school, or conferring with a parent to get assistance at home.

If you are planning to introduce a new approach, do it gradually. It can be chaotic to plunge the entire class at once into something they've never done before. For example, if you want to try individualized reading, begin with your top group. Explain exactly what they are to do and work out the problems before introducing the program to the other groups. This procedure avoids wasting class time during an adjustment period.

No class must always operate on schedule, however. Sometimes something funny happens, and everyone needs to take time for a good laugh. You may lose some time from a scheduled activity by taking advantage of a "teachable moment," but this time is well spent. For instance, when the first snow falls, let the students go to the window and watch. Then share a poem or a song about snow, or talk about how snowflakes form and note their delicate beauty. After a particularly tense test-taking session, students may need time to relax. Remember—schedules do keep things moving along, but they are not cast in concrete.

## Filler Activities

Even the most experienced teacher cannot predict exactly how long a lesson will take. As a relatively inexperienced teacher, you will often find yourself running out of time—or having time left over. When you realize your lesson will end five or ten minutes before the class is over, you should have some ideas in the back of your mind. The best filler activities are those that directly relate to your lesson or unit. For instance, if you are teaching a unit on energy, the students could brainstorm several ways to conserve or produce energy. Try to plan one or more filler activities for each lesson in case you have too much time. These are some general activities that could be adapted to specific subject matter areas or used for other occasions:

1  Read or tell a story—good at any age level.
2  Put a long word on the board and see how many words students can make from it (Thanksgiving, revolutionary).
3  Play "Twenty Questions." Students try to guess what you're thinking by asking questions that can be answered only by yes or no.
4  Get a paperback book of brainteasers, riddles, and puzzles, and ask the class for answers.
5  Ask students to do mental addition or subtraction.
6  Let students play storybook charades by acting out favorite stories.
7  Introduce a new vocabulary word that has an interesting meaning or origin. This can be a "Word of the Week" activity.
8  Sing a folksong or round with the class.
9  Let students dictate headlines about current news stories for you to write on the board.
10  Write a cinquain, a simple five-line poem. First line is the title (topic); second line is two descriptive words; third line is three action words; fourth line is a descriptive phrase; fifth line is a repeat of the title or a synonym for it.
11  Name a topic and see how many facts the students can tell you about it.
12  Scramble the letters in a word and see how many words they can make from it (opts, mtae).

13  Let students pantomime their favorite sport or hobby and have the class guess what they are doing.

14  Start a story with a one-line introduction and have each student add a line to the story. (A good starter: "It was cold and dark and dreary and suddenly I heard a noise.")

15  Have a question box and let a student pick a question. It could be serious (What can we do for senior citizens?) or silly (Why would a grasshopper make a good pet?). Students answer the question.

16  Role play a recent classroom conflict.

17  Build word families from such phonograms as -it, -at, -ill. (Example: -an, can, fan, ran, pan, Stan, than, bran)

18  Play "Gossip." Whisper a sentence to one student, who whispers it to the next, and so on. Compare the original sentence with the final result.

19  Look for geometric shapes in the classroom. (Example: chalkboards as rectangles and pencils as cylinders)

20  Give students, one at a time, a series of directions to follow and see if they can remember to do everything in the correct sequence.

21  Write the months of the year on the board. Poll the class to find out how many students' birthdays fall in each month.

22  Rearrange the seating in the classroom.

23  Divide the class in half to create two teams. Name a country and let a student from each team try to locate it on a world map within ten seconds.

24  Make a list of all the things to do on a rainy day.

25  Brainstorm solutions to a problem. (See chapter 6 for suggested topics.)

You can also use these ways to fill a few extra minutes.

1  Review assignments.

2  Discuss plans for an upcoming event.

3  Let students have free reading time, finish their class work, do their homework, or clean out their desks.

# Record Keeping

Every teacher has the responsibility of keeping records. The amount and type of record keeping varies from one school system to another, and your cooperating teacher will show you what records your school requires. When you are responsible for keeping records, record the information promptly so you don't forget to do it later. Keeping accurate records is an important aspect of professionalism.

## Personal Record Keeping

As part of your student teaching assignment, you may be asked to keep a diary or log of your daily experiences. If it is required, your university supervisor will give you directions for doing this. Even if it is not a requirement, you may want to keep track of the lessons you teach and your feelings about teaching. You can also write down some of the funny things the students say or insights about teaching you don't want to forget. Looking back at the end of your experience, you will probably notice how your attitudes changed and your confidence grew as the weeks passed.

## School Records

The attendance register is one of the most important records. Class roll must be taken daily or every period of the day, and all absences and cases of tardiness recorded. These records are used for various purposes, including computing average daily attendance for state funding. The state allocates a certain amount of money for each child counted in the average daily attendance record. Records are sometimes used in court cases to verify a student's presence in school on a particular day. This information is summarized at the end of every month. Even though these records may be handled by a computer or by office personnel, you should learn how to do them yourself.

You will have to keep other records when you are teaching. Many schools require each teacher to turn in a milk money or lunch money report every morning. Some schools have fund raising activities that require a great deal of bookkeeping, and you will have to keep an accurate account of the money collected and each student's sales record. If you (through your cooperating teacher) sponsor an extracurricular activity, you may be responsible for keeping membership and financial records. You also need to keep records of students with special programs or problems, such as those who are excused from physical education or who go to special classes at specific times during the day. Additional records are required for students in federally funded programs.

As a student teacher, you may have very little responsibility for ordering books and supplies or keeping inventory. It would be a good idea to learn these procedures anyway, so you will know what to do when you are in your own classroom. Supplies, such as paper and chalk, should be ordered well in advance to avoid running out. You will probably be limited as to how many supplies you can order, so don't waste anything. Become familiar with school supply catalogs so you know what materials are available, their prices, and how to order them. Learn how to requisition new materials that can be ordered when funds are available. It is difficult for school systems to reimburse you for money you have already spent for school supplies.

You will also have to keep records related to your teaching. You will need a daily lesson plan book to record brief outlines of your lessons and page numbers of material you expect to cover in each class. You can never be sure exactly how far you will get in your lesson, so you will probably have to modify these plans slightly from day to day. You will also need to make up a broad course or unit outline as a framework for daily plans. If you schedule a field trip in connection with a lesson, you will be responsible for keeping records of parent permission notes and any money you collect. If you use audiovisual media, you may need to fill out request forms. You might give the school media specialist a list of topics you will be covering and request help in locating appropriate books and materials. At the conclusion of a unit, you might want to write up your culminating activity and invite the local newspapers to cover the story.

## Reporting Students' Progress

Keeping track of students' progress is one of the most important forms of record keeping. You should keep records of daily quizzes and completed workbook pages, as well as scores of major tests. Your cooperating teacher probably has a grade book with the scores of each student before you arrived.

Some teachers keep tests in folders at school so they have a record of each pupil's progress throughout the year. Teachers who feel parents should be kept aware of their child's performance may send tests home. If you decide to send papers home but are not sure all the students are showing them to their parents, ask them to have a parent sign their test papers and return them to you.

Reporting to parents is usually done through report cards, although it is sometimes done with descriptive letters or orally, at parent-teacher conferences. Your cooperating teacher may ask you to assist in assigning grades on report cards or to assume the full responsibility for grades during the period you do most of the teaching. In either case, be sure you thoroughly understand the school's grading system. Most schools give grades according to achievement, but some give marks for attitude and effort and some grade on the basis of student ability. Most report cards have a place for comments which you may or may not wish to use. Putting grades on report cards requires some hard decision making. If the responsibility is yours, be sure to have good records of student work on which to base decisions.

You may want to send notes to parents of students who have behaved or achieved unusually well. Notes of this type are always welcome and help build positive relationships among the student, parents, school, and you. These notes will be especially appreciated by students who rarely receive praise and are often in trouble. If you make a practice of sending favorable comments home, the students are likely to do better work for you.

## Case Study: No Records for Support

Miss Patel is the student teacher. She has been concerned about Vinetta's behavior recently. She doesn't do her homework and doesn't seem to be doing good work in class. Miss Patel decides to ask Vinetta's mother, Mrs. Kolsky, to come for a conference. Mr. Kehl is the cooperating teacher.

Miss Patel: Good afternoon, Mrs. Kolsky. I'm glad you were able to come talk with me about Vinetta. I'm Miss Patel, Vinetta's student teacher.

Mrs. Kolsky: Yes. Naturally I hope Vinetta is getting along all right.

Miss Patel: That's just it, Mrs. Kolsky. Vinetta doesn't seem to be doing as well as she could be.

Mrs. Kolsky: Why not? What's wrong? Is there a problem?

Miss Patel: She isn't doing her homework, and she isn't doing very well in her class work, either.

Mrs. Kolsky: Well, this is the first I've known anything about homework. And what do you mean she isn't doing well in her class work?

Miss Patel: I've been sending homework home each night, but Vinetta never has hers done. As far as class work is concerned, she just doesn't seem to be doing her best work any more.

Mrs. Kolsky: May I see her grades on her class work?

Miss Patel: I'm afraid I don't have any records of her grades. I've given some quizzes, but I've let the students take them home with them. I can remember, though, that she didn't do very well. Didn't she bring her tests home?

Mrs. Kolsky: No, she hasn't brought any of them home. It seems to me you don't really know what you're talking about. You say she isn't doing well, but you can't show me any grades. When I ask you what she isn't doing well in, you don't seem to have any definite answers. I don't think there's anything wrong with Vinetta at all. I think you just don't have your facts straight. I'd better talk to Mr. Kehl.

1   Was it a good idea for Miss Patel to have a conference with Vinetta's mother if she felt Vinetta could be doing better work?
2   What went wrong with Miss Patel's conference?
3   What could she have done to back up her statements to Mrs. Kolsky?
4   Is there any way to make sure parents know their child

has homework assignments? How can you be sure parents actually see the test papers you return?

---

You may want to obtain information about a student through an anecdotal report—an objective, detailed account of a pupil's behavior. During your period of observation, you have an excellent opportunity to study a student's behavior. Your reasons for selecting particular students may vary. You may choose a student who is different in some way, perhaps because of achievement level, relationships with other children, or ethnic origin. You may want to observe a student who is being recommended for an award or one who is being considered for disciplinary action. You may want to collect data on a student whose parents are concerned about his or her progress, or you may select any student simply to learn about typical behavior patterns.

Be accurate and objective in recording your observations. Don't let your feelings affect what you select to record or how you write your observations. Write the date and time of your observation, and try to include everything that happens, both good and bad. It is better if the student doesn't realize what you are doing, so that he or she will continue to act naturally.

Your classroom organization determines to some extent how you keep records. If you use an individualized or independent study plan, you will probably need a manila folder in which to record each student's program and progress. Your class may use a systems-management program that has a checklist of concepts or skills to be mastered. In this plan, quizzes are given frequently to make certain a student has reached an acceptable level of mastery before moving on to the next skill. If your class uses learning centers most of the day, your cooperating teacher has probably already set up a way to check each student's work at the different centers. In science classes, you may need to keep progress charts on lab projects.

Records of students' progress sometimes motivate them to do better work. They may want to chart their spelling test scores and see if they can improve their records. You might want to average the scores from weekly math quizzes and make a class chart comparing the scores from different weeks. Students can also be motivated to do more recreational reading by using devices to record the number and sometimes the types of books they read.

All the records a school has on a student are generally kept in a cumulative record file in the school office. This file contains records of health, attendance, comments by school personnel, and standardized intelligence and achievement test scores. As a student teacher, you will probably be allowed to see this information, but remember that it is confidential.

## Case Study: To Look or Not to Look

Three student teachers, Miss Luke, Mr. Feinstein, and Mrs. Tsai, are talking while waiting for their student teaching seminar to begin. They have been student teaching for four weeks.

Miss Luke: Do you know what cumulative records are?

Mr. Feinstein: I think they are some records in the office files that nobody ever looks at.

Mrs. Tsai: They *are* files that are kept in the office, but I've looked at the ones on my students. My cooperating teacher took me right down on the first day I got my classes and told me where they were and that he expected me to read them all the first week. Some of them are really eye-openers, I'll tell you!

Miss Luke: What do you mean?

Mrs. Tsai: I really learned a lot about my students, and I knew just how to treat them right from the beginning. Linda's file said that one time they caught her stealing a transistor radio, so I don't trust her for a minute. Any time anything disappears, I feel sure Linda had something to do with it. And Tad. They said all through the grades that Tad has been a discipline problem, and they're surely right. He's always causing trouble.

Mr. Feinstein: I'm not sure it's right to read all that personal information about your students. Doesn't that influence how you feel about them?

Mrs. Tsai: Sure, it influences how I feel. But this way I know right away all I need to know about the students instead of waiting until the end of the semester to find out.

Miss Luke: I'm not going to look at my students' cumulative records. I want to make up my own mind about them and not go by what other teachers have said.

Mr. Feinstein: But suppose there's something really important in there? Something we *should* know about? Maybe one of the students had psychological testing or something and the psychologist made recommendations about how he learns best. Wouldn't that be helpful?

Mrs. Tsai: Definitely! It said in one of my records that Chad's parents had been divorced a couple of years ago and he had a real emotional problem with that. The teacher suggested that we all be patient with him and consider his feelings.

Mr. Feinstein: I'm just not sure if it's a good idea to read all those records. It still might do more harm than good.

1  How do you feel about reading your students' cumulative records? If you feel you should read them, should you look at them as soon as you meet the students or at some later time?

**2** How could the information in cumulative records be helpful? How could it be misused?

**3** What is the purpose of keeping cumulative records?

**4** Do you think Mrs. Tsai is able to treat Linda and Tad objectively? Would she have arrived at the same conclusions about these two students if she hadn't read their files? Do students tend to live up to our expectations of them?

**5** Who is allowed to read cumulative records? Do you know what the law says about this?

---

In regard to examining students' cumulative records, it is good policy to give yourself enough time to evaluate the students for yourself, then look at the records to learn more about them. When you read the files, keep in mind that test scores do not always accurately reflect a student's capability. Also, be sure to look for factual information and specific situations. Avoid being swayed by unsupported generalizations and statements of opinion previous teachers may have made. Using cumulative records wisely can help you understand your students better and plan appropriate learning activities for those with special needs.

Since passage of the Family Educational Rights and Privacy Act of 1974 (PL 93–380), control of student records has changed. Now, students over 18 years old or parents of students under 18 may examine these records—they have access to all teacher comments, test scores, and special reports in the file. On the other hand, the law forbids anyone except those directly involved in the student's education to see the records without written consent.

# Classroom Environment

As a student teacher, you will take some responsibility for the appearance and comfort of your classroom from the early days of your experience. By the time you take over full teaching responsibilities, the appearance and comfort of the classroom will, in most cases, be completely your responsibility. Naturally, in many matters you will follow the procedures established by your cooperating teacher. In some areas, however, you may want to try variations, with the teacher's approval.

## Neatness and Cleanliness

Although in years past teachers were expected to sweep and mop their classrooms, chances are good that you will not be expected to perform these duties. Most schools hire maintenance personnel to care for such matters. These people generally work before or after school hours to clean classrooms, although some schools have maintenance personnel on duty during the school day. In some schools, you may be expected to handle emergency situations (paint, ink, or sand spills, etc.) yourself, so you should know where cleaning materials are located. In other schools, you may not be expected to do the cleaning; instead, you simply need to know how to summon the custodian for assistance. Where custodians perform these duties during class hours, it is especially important to develop a good relationship with them. Let them know that you value their help and that their work contributes to your effectiveness. Even if the custodians work only after hours, showing appreciation for a well-cleaned room is likely to pay dividends in the care your room receives.

Cooperation with these support personnel is also important. You may be asked to have students put their chairs on their desks so it will be easier to clean the floors. Be sure to comply with such a request.

A neat room requires floors free of paper and other trash and supplies put away instead of left out where they were last used. Make students responsible for keeping the floor clear of trash and putting away supplies, and make sure they fulfill these responsibilities. Be sure there are designated places for storing all supplies, and that these places are easily accessible. This kind of planning greatly enhances the functionality of a classroom. It is more pleasant for both teacher and students to work in a neat and clean classroom.

## Control of Temperature, Ventilation, and Lighting

Proper temperature, ventilation, and lighting in a classroom promote comfort and ability to concentrate. Students are easily distracted when a classroom is too hot, too cold, or too stuffy, or when the lighting is too dim or there is a glare on work surfaces. They focus on their discomfort rather than their assignments. They may become drowsy from excess heat or insufficient ventilation or develop headaches and eyestrain from inappropriate lighting. It is your responsibility to adjust these factors or to see that they are adjusted by the proper person. If your room has an uncomfortable temperature or poor ventilation, you may need to adjust thermostats, windows, or vents, or you may need to summon the custodian to make appropriate adjustments. Be sure to follow the school's regulations. If you are not supposed to change the thermostat setting, don't do it, but if it needs doing, see that the person designated to take care of such matters makes the adjustment before valuable class time is wasted. You can handle lighting problems yourself by turning on more lights, adjusting seating arrangements, and adjusting blinds or curtains to provide enough light without glare.

## Case Study: Not Attuned to the Students

Ms. Jordan, a cold-natured student teacher, entered her empty classroom at 7:45 one morning, took off her coat, shivered, and turned up the room's thermostat. This was the first day she had full responsibility for the classroom, and she didn't want to be uncomfortable all day. At 8:00, the students poured into the room. The body heat of thirty extra people, plus the higher thermostat setting, resulted in a very warm room. Ms. Jordan, who enjoyed the warmth, at first failed to notice how lethargic the class seemed as she began her first complete day of teaching. As time passed, however, the signs were unmistakeable. Students were inattentive, and many seemed to be drowsy.

"What is the matter with you?" Ms. Jordan snapped irritably. "Did you all stay up all night watching television?"

"No! No!" came a chorus of answers.

"Then what is wrong?" Ms. Jordan asked again.

A boy in the back of the room finally replied, "It's too hot in here to work."

"That's ridiculous!" Ms. Jordan responded. "I'm perfectly comfortable. Now pay attention."

It was Ms. Jordan who was not paying attention. She was seeing the signs of an overheated room but doing nothing about them. Furthermore, she failed to pay attention to the fact that, because of her cold-naturedness, she could be comfortable when the students were not, despite a direct verbal cue. Don't be a teacher like Ms. Jordan.

1  Are you extremely hot-natured or cold-natured? How may this affect your ability to keep your classroom at a comfortable temperature for your students?
2  What clues in the students' behavior may help you determine if the classroom is comfortable for them?

## Bulletin Boards/Displays

Bulletin boards and displays can add much to the attractiveness of a classroom; however, they should not be limited to this function. The best bulletin boards and displays are both attractive and informative. They add color and interest to the room while conveying useful information in a content area or while providing motivation to study a particular topic.

All bulletin boards and displays must be carefully constructed to maintain their effectiveness. Inaccurate data, material inappropriate for the age group, sloppy drawing and lettering, or faded or torn background material on bulletin boards and displays make them undesirable rather than helpful additions to the classroom. Even carefully executed displays lose their effectiveness if they are left up too long. Thanksgiving turkeys are out of place in January, even if the display has an excellent instructional focus.

You can make effective bulletin boards and displays for your classroom by following a few simple guidelines.

1  Choose material appropriate to your students' learning and maturity levels.
2  Make sure all the information is accurate.
3  Choose a central theme for a focus.
4  Organize the materials carefully to show their relationship to the central theme.
5  Choose a pleasing color scheme.
6  Do not use faded or torn background material.
7  Use a variety of materials, such as construction paper, crepe paper, yarn, cloth, and cardboard to give the displays texture. Consider use of three-dimensional effects.
8  Change your bulletin boards and displays regularly. They become faded as time passes and cease to generate interest. Never leave seasonal displays up past their time of relevance.
9  Make some bulletin boards manipulative. Students at lower grade levels particularly enjoy such boards. Examples are matching synonyms with yarn strips, opening cardboard doors for answers to riddles, etc.

Bulletin boards and displays can be great learning experiences, because they help make concepts more concrete. They can sometimes provide even more learning opportunities if you let the students construct the displays themselves or assist you in the construction. It is certainly easier to keep fresh displays in the classroom when you have student assistance.

Bulletin boards and displays should occasionally include examples of students' work. Don't succumb to the temptation of putting up only the best work. Put up any work of which an individual can be proud, even if it lacks the precision of more advanced students' offerings. On the other hand, do not display especially poor work in an effort to embarrass a student into doing better. This practice is psychologically unsound. Do not display a student's work if the reason for the display is negative rather than positive.

Use bulletin boards and displays as teaching tools that enhance the attractiveness of your classroom. Keep a file of ideas for good ones as you observe your cooperating teacher and other teachers and as you read professional materials. This file will prove valuable when you have your own classroom.

## Learning Centers

Learning centers are areas of the classroom set aside for development and practice of specific skills. You can develop learning centers for any grade level or content area. They usually consist of a skill objective, materials that have been collected to help students meet that objective, task cards or assignment sheets explaining what students are supposed to do in the centers, and a means of evaluating the completed work. Students are frequently assigned to center work on the basis of diagnostic tests the teacher administers. Posttests may be provided at the center to determine whether students have acquired the indicated skill.

Learning centers may be designed to introduce new skills, offer practice in skills already taught, or provide students with motivation for studying a particular topic. The particular objective of a specific center should be made clear to the students who are expected to use it. If you help them see the importance of completing the center activities, the activities will have more value for them.

You must assemble the necessary materials for meeting the objective of a center and arrange them so that they are accessible. You may need to label some materials as to purpose, but not all of them.

You must prepare the task cards or assignment sheets with directions for the center activities carefully. They may need an accompanying cassette tape for younger children or older students with reading disabilities. You can include tasks at different levels of difficulty and code them so you can differentiate assignments. If you include more than one task in a center, each should be labeled clearly and located in a separate part of the center.

Whenever possible, center activities should be self-checking. In many cases, answer sheets will suffice. Some work may not lend itself to self-checking. In these cases, you should collect the work, evaluate it, and return it to the students as promptly as possible.

Some routines related to center use should be made clear from the outset. Students need to know when they can use the centers, the number of people allowed to use a center simultaneously, how to care for materials, when assignments from centers are due, what personal codes they must use to choose activities, and what they should do when center activities are completed.

You may have one or many centers set up in your room at a time. They can be set up on tables, in large containers such as refrigerator boxes, on the floor or carpet, in corners, behind bookshelves, or behind folding screens. Your ingenuity is the only limiting factor.

An elementary level learning center might be based on a skill objective like this one: The student will be able to answer multiplication problems containing the multiplier 9 and multiplicands from 1 through 12 with 100 percent accuracy. Materials for developing this skill might include multiplication study sheets containing the appropriate multiplication facts and multiplication skill tapes to which the child listens and responds, checking his or her answers with answers supplied on the tape later. Obviously, a tape recorder would have to be located at the center for playing the tapes, and it would be best to have headphones so the center activity does not disturb the rest of the class. The task card for the center would direct students to study the facts, using the multiplication study sheet, then listen to the multiplication skill tapes, respond as directed on the tapes, and then check their answers.

A secondary center might have as an objective: The student will be able to complete analogies with one missing element with 90 percent accuracy. A microcomputer program to offer instruction on what analogies are and practice in completing them might be the material chosen for this center. Naturally, a microcomputer compatible with the designated program would have to be provided. A duplicated test on analogies could be available as an evaluation technique. The task card would give directions for loading the program and interacting with it, as well as instructions to complete the test located in the center and turn it in to the teacher.

Learning centers have been prevalent at the elementary level for a long time, but, in recent years, applications have been made with excellent results at the secondary level. Don't write off the idea without trying it. You may be amazed at the results.

## Seating Arrangements

Few classrooms today have stationary furniture. The moveable furniture in your classroom represents another responsibility—proper arrangement of this furniture for instructional purposes. You may want one arrangement for whole-class instruction, another for small-group instruction, and still another when students are working on individual projects. Moveable furniture makes this flexibility possible. An instructional group that requires a chalkboard can cluster around the chalkboard for that lesson, then disperse when another learning activity begins. Chairs can be turned to face a film shown on a side wall, a follow-up discussion using a chalkboard on a different side wall, and a demonstration at the front of the room, all within the space of a single class.

With all this mobility, there are other considerations about seating which you must not overlook. Students with certain handicaps must be seated in the most advantageous positions possible. For example, students who have hearing difficulties should usually be seated near you; those who are nearsighted may need to be seated close to boardwork, displays, and demonstrations; and so on. Potentially disruptive students should also be seated where they are less likely to cause trouble. This may mean seating them near you or making sure certain students do not sit beside each other.

## Case Study: Arbitrary Seating Arrangements

When Miss Gomez first came into the seventh-grade business mathematics class in which she was assigned to student teach, the students seemed to be arranged in no logical order. One day, Susie Carter would sit in the front row; the next day, she might sit near the back bulletin board. Furthermore, Susie and several other students seemed to change seats frequently in the middle of class. Miss Gomez felt she would find that distracting when she was teaching.

When Miss Gomez took over the class, she announced that the seating would be alphabetical for the rest of the year. When Susie raised her hand to protest, Miss Gomez said, "There will be no discussion of this matter. Take your assigned seat as I indicate it."

Susie was seated near the back of the room. When Miss Gomez wrote the assignment for the next day on the board, Susie stood up to move to the front of the room as she had been accustomed to doing.

Miss Gomez said abruptly, "Susie, didn't I make it clear that you must stay in your assigned seat?"

Susie replied, "I can't see the board from this seat. Our regular teacher let me sit in the room wherever I needed to so I could see. Whoever was in a seat I needed was supposed to swap until I could get the information I needed. I didn't mean to cause problems."

Miss Gomez was embarrassed. She didn't know what to do. She seemed to have backed herself into an uncomfortable corner.

1  What would you have done at this point?
2  What should Miss Gomez have done to prevent this from happening?
3  Could anyone other than Miss Gomez have helped to avoid this problem? If so, who?

Another concern for teachers, particularly of younger children, is making sure each child has a chair and desk of suitable size. Small children should not be allowed to choose large desks just because they are attracted to them. They will be in a strained position most of the time if they do. For the same reason, larger children should not have desks too small for them. The children in a single grade will vary greatly in size, and one desk size will not be suitable for all of them. If necessary, swap with other teachers to get a desk appropriate for each student.

The days of nothing but straight lines, exclusively alphabetical seating, and desks bolted to the floor seem to be behind us. The future for teachers and students is much more flexible. Use this flexibility for your benefit and that of your students.

## Discussion Questions

1  Observe the groups that have been set up in your class. Can you see the reason for each type of grouping? Do you think it would be helpful to have additional groups? How might grouping be used to better advantage? If there are no groups now, can you see any reasons for forming them? If so, how would you do this?

2  Do you see any indications of student discouragement because of their group placement? If so, how could you try to correct this situation?

3  Investigate your school's grouping patterns. Are classes homogeneously or heterogeneously grouped? Do some students move from one class to another for instruction? Do low achievers meet together? Is there a program for gifted students? Are there other ways interclass grouping takes place in your school?

4  Did you waste any time today during your classes? What did you spend time doing that wasn't really important to achieving your goals?

5  Can you think of a better way to organize your class periods or your day? What factors should you consider if you decide to use a different schedule?

6  Why is it extremely important for teachers to be accurate and objective in the material they include in a student's cumulative record? What might happen if a teacher makes careless, negative generalizations about a student?

7  What special reports and records does your school require? What is your responsibility for keeping these records?

8  What is the school's grading system? Is there any provision for giving information to a student's parents about effort, attitude, or interest? Is it important for parents to know this information?

9  How can a neat and clean classroom be an asset to your teaching?

10  Why is control of the classroom's temperature, ventilation, and lighting an important responsibility?

11 Could there be situations in which you might not have control of temperature and ventilation? Why might this happen?

12 Do all bulletin boards and displays serve the same purpose? What purposes do they serve?

13 How often should bulletin boards and displays be changed? Why do you think so?

14 What are some bulletin board or display ideas for your grade or content area?

15 How can learning centers enhance instruction in your classroom?

16 How can classroom seating arrangements be used to best advantage?

17 Is your classroom open or self-contained? What is some evidence of structure or flexibility in your classroom?

## Selected References

Beach, Don M. *Reaching Teenagers: Learning Centers for the Secondary Classroom.* Santa Monica, Calif.: Goodyear, 1977.

Bennie, Francis. *Learning Centers: Development and Operation.* Englewood Cliffs, N. J.: Educational Technology Publications, 1977.

Blake, Howard E. *Creating a Learning-Centered Classroom.* New York: Hart, 1976.

Bluming, Mildred, and Myron Dembo. *Solving Teaching Problems.* Pacific Palisades, Calif.: Goodyear, 1973.

Brown, Thomas J., and Serafina Fiore Banich. *Guiding a Student Teacher.* New York: Harper and Row, 1962.

Burns, Paul C., and Betty D. Roe. *Reading Activities for Today's Elementary Schools.* Chicago: Rand McNally, 1979.

Callahan, Sterling G. *Successful Teaching in Secondary Schools; A Guide for Student and In-Service Teachers.* Glenview, Ill.: Scott, Foresman, 1971.

Cotler, Harold C. *Encyclopedia Deskbook of Teaching Ideas and Classroom Activities.* West Nyack, N. Y.: Parker, 1977.

Crabtree, June. *Learning Center Ideas.* Cincinnati, Ohio: Standard, 1977.

Crow, Lester D., and Alice Crow. *The Student Teacher in the Elementary School.* New York: David McKay, 1965.

Crow, Lester D., and Alice Crow. *The Student Teacher in the Secondary School.* New York: David McKay, 1964.

Davidson, Tom. *Learning Center Book.* Santa Monica, Calif.: Goodyear, 1976.

Drayer, Adam M. *Problems in Middle and High School Teaching.* Boston: Allyn and Bacon, 1979.

Dubey, Robert E., et al. *A Performance-based Guide to Student Teaching.* Danville, Ill.: Interstate, 1975.

Harmer, Earl W., Jr. *Instructional Strategies for Student Teachers.* Belmont, Calif.: Wadsworth, 1969.

Hoover, Kenneth H. and Paul M. Hollingsworth. *Learning and Teaching in the Elementary School.* Boston: Allyn and Bacon, 1970.

Horn, George F. *Bulletin Boards.* Reinhold, 1962.

Hornick, Joanne. *Elementary Creative Bulletin Boards.* New York: Scholastic Book Services, 1969.

Inlow, Gail M. *Maturity in High School Teaching.* Englewood Cliffs, N. J.: Prentice-Hall, 1970.

Johnson, Hiram, et al. *Learning Center Ideabook: Activities for the Elementary and Middle Grades.* Boston: Allyn and Bacon, 1977.

Johnson, James A., and Louis D. Deprin. *Elementary Student Teaching: Readings.* Glenview, Ill.: Scott, Foresman, 1971.

Kohl, Herbert R. *The Open Classroom.* New York: Vintage Books, 1969.

Kozoll, Charles E. *Time Management for Educators.* Bloomington, Ind.: Phi Delta Kappa Educational Foundation, 1982.

Ptreshene, Susan S. *A Complete Guide to Learning Centers.* Palo Alto, Calif.: Pendrogen House, 1977.

Schine, Joan G., and Diane Harrington. *Youth Participation for Early Adolescents: Learning and Serving in the Community.* Bloomington, Ind.: Phi Delta Kappa Educational Foundation, 1982.

Singer, Robert N., and Walter Dick. *Teaching Physical Education: A Systems Approach.* Boston: Houghton Mifflin, 1974.

Thompson, James J. *Instructional Communication.* New York: American Book, 1969.

Worell, Judith, and C. Michael Nelson. *Managing Instructional Problems.* New York: McGraw-Hill, 1974.

# 6
# *Teaching Strategies*

Ralph is a ninth grader reading at a fourth grade level in Mrs. Kelsey's remedial reading class. During the year, Mrs. Kelsey and Mr. Sunas, the intern, tried to encourage Ralph to read by finding him easy materials and offering rewards for progress. Ralph didn't respond and showed no interest in reading. Mr. Sunas was determined to find some way to reach Ralph before the end of the year. One morning Ralph came to school unusually tired.

Mr. Sunas: What's the matter, Ralph? You seem so tired today. Did you have a rough weekend?

Ralph: We was out planting soybeans all weekend, Mr. Sunas. I'm beat.

Mr. Sunas: I don't know much about growing soybeans, Ralph. Tell me about it.

Ralph: Gosh, there's so much to tell. I don't know where to begin. My folks've been raising soybeans for as far back as I can remember.

Mr. Sunas: Is that what you plan to do, too?

Ralph: You bet! I want to grow the very best soybeans in these here parts. That's why I'm just waiting to be 16 so I can drop out of school. I want to get out and work with the soybeans and not just sit here all day doing nothing.

Mr. Sunas: Ralph, if you really want to be the best producer of soybeans in the area, how are you going to go about it?

Ralph: I don't know—guess I'll just do what my dad and his folks have always done.

Mr. Sunas: But Ralph, the Agricultural Experiment Station is developing more efficient ways of raising soybeans all the time. There's a lot to know about disease control, fertilizers, soil conservation, and marketing. I'll bring you some information about it.

Ralph: Naw, don't bother. I don't want to read nothing about it.

Mr. Sunas (a few days later): I found some pamphlets on how to raise soybeans. I thought you might want to look at them.

Ralph: Maybe later. (Ralph yawns, leans back in his chair, and stares out the window.)

Mr. Sunas (20 minutes later): Ralph, have you looked at those pamphlets yet?

Ralph: No, not yet. (He picks up his pencil and starts doodling on a scrap of paper.)

Mr. Sunas (10 minutes later): Did you have any trouble with blister beetles last year? I hear they're supposed to be bad again this year.

Ralph: Yeah. They really gave us problems last year. (pause) Why? Does it say something about them in here?

Mr. Sunas: Yes. It tells you what to do to prevent having so many and how to control the ones you do have.

Ralph: No foolin'? I bet my dad would really like to know about this.

Mr. Sunas: Why don't you read about it for the rest of the period? I'll help you with the words you don't know.

Ralph: Hey, here's a picture of one of them beetles. This is really neat. What's this say here, Mr. Sunas? I really need to know this stuff.

---

Florinda was a bright, eager child who came to first grade already knowing how to read. At age three, she was reading signs on franchises along the highway, and at age four, she was picking words out of the storybooks her father read to her. By the time she was five, she could read simple books by herself. Mrs. Cho, Florinda's teacher, had 29 students in first grade that year and had her hands full working with a large number of immature children. She realized Florinda knew how to read, but she certainly couldn't take the time to work with her on a different level. Florinda was placed in a readiness group, then in a preprimer group.

Florinda (one morning before school starts): Look, Mrs. Cho, this is the book my daddy read me last night—*Where The Wild Things Are!* It's so exciting, and I can read it all by myself.

Mrs. Cho: That's fine, Florinda. It *is* a good book. Now put it away. It will be time for reading group soon.

Florinda: But Mrs. Cho, those stories in reading group are too easy. I already know all the words. They're no fun to read.

Mrs. Cho: I'm sorry, Florinda, but you'll just have to read what the other boys and girls are reading. I don't have time to listen to you read your books.

Florinda: Well, O.K.

Mrs. Cho (observing Florinda reading her book during class time later that morning): Florinda, I told you to put that book away. This isn't the time to read. You have four ditto sheets to do.

Florinda: But I don't want to do them. They're dumb.

Mrs. Cho: Give me your book, Florinda. Do your work like the other boys and girls. I don't want you causing any trouble.

1   What motivational techniques were mentioned in the vignette about Ralph? Which one seemed to be successful? Why do you think it worked?

2   Was Ralph internally motivated? If so, why didn't he respond positively to the school situation? How are both intrinsic and extrinsic motivation a part of the story about Ralph?

3   Does Ralph's interest in the blister beetle mean that he is now motivated to learn? Is there a danger that his interest in learning will pass? How could his interest be extended until it becomes part of his internal motivation?

4  How could Ralph's interest in soybeans be used to increase his achievement in other areas, such as math and science?

5  What was Mrs. Cho doing to Florinda's internal motivation? What might happen to Florinda as a result of her teacher's attitude? What are some choices Mrs. Cho had for keeping alive Florinda's interest in reading?

6  How did these two teachers differ in dealing with their students' needs and interests? What long-term effects do you think their different strategies had on their students?

## Helping Them Learn

Now the groundwork has been laid. You know about lesson plans and discipline, as well as your resources, co-workers, and students. It's time to start teaching. In this chapter, you'll find some traditional approaches to teaching along with some creative activities. You'll also find some ways to motivate students and help them learn effectively. Student teaching is a good time to experiment with new ideas and find out what works for you.

Remember that you cannot teach your students all there is to know. Such a feat would be impossible in view of the current knowledge explosion. What is important is that, through your teaching, you help students discover how to learn. Provide them with skills for solving problems and teach them to think for themselves.

## Motivation

One of your greatest challenges as a teacher will be to motivate your students. All learning is motivated in one way or another. Highly motivated pupils almost teach themselves in their eagerness to learn. Poorly motivated students are unlikely to learn much of anything, no matter how well you teach.

Before learning some strategies for motivating your students, you need to understand what motivation is. Motivation for learning in school is what "gives direction and intensity to students' behavior. . . ."[1] It influences how well students learn.

### Intrinsic Versus Extrinsic Motivation

Motivation comes both from the student's inner self and from external forces. Internal or intrinsic motivation arises out of a student's needs, personality, attitudes, and values. Students who are inter-

[1]Jack Frymier, *Motivation and Learning in School* (Bloomington, Ind.: Phi Delta Kappa Educational Foundation, 1974), 7.

nally motivated are driven by the need to be popular, the desire to excel, or the fear of failure. Intrinsic motivation is generally long lasting; it is a part of the individual that drives him toward his goals. Successful experiences tend to increase a student's internal drives, but repeated failures may eventually destroy inner motivation.

Intrinsic motivation is part of a student's basic personality and changes very slowly, if at all. This means you will have little opportunity to change the underlying motivational patterns of students in the short time you will work with them. By stimulating their curiosity and building on their interests, however, you can lay the foundation for lasting internal changes.

External or extrinsic motivation originates in the learning environment and causes the student to want to do certain things. As the teacher, you may want to employ various types of external motivation to modify student behavior. Be aware, however, that this type of motivation is usually short-term and may disappear when the student reaches the immediate goal.

You can use incentives as extrinsic motivators to make students want to work or behave better. Rewards are generally more effective incentives than punishments. Positive incentives that you may find useful are free time, extended recess periods, recognition on the classroom bulletin board, or prizes and awards. Students can also be motivated by earning good grades and seeing their names on the honor roll.

Keep in mind that external incentives are only artificial ways of getting students to try harder. They should never become the major reason for doing school work, or students will value the reward more than the learning. Most learning tasks don't require incentives. Students should develop self-discipline to get their work done. If you decide to use incentives, learn which types work best for your students; then use them sparingly and for only short periods of time.

Be careful about giving awards or prizes as incentives for top achievers. These students are usually internally motivated anyway, and poor achievers become even more frustrated when competing against them. One way to overcome this problem is by having students compete against their own records instead of trying to be the best in the class. For instance, students can keep charts of their daily or weekly grades and try to show improvement. Another way to avoid the problem is to have one group or class compete against another group or class. Students work together to win a reward, and all students have a chance to win. Recognition can also be given for increased effort and for improvement in attitude.

## Who Is Motivated?

You will be able to observe different levels of motivation among your students. Those who seem poorly motivated will need more patience and skill to get them interested. If you aren't sure which students are well motivated and which are not, use the following lists of questions as you observe students. The more "yes" answers you get on the first list, the more positively motivated the student. On the second list, a large number of "yes" answers indicates a poorly motivated student.

**Highly Motivated Students**   Does the student:

—— 1   Appear to use good study skills?
—— 2   Read or seek information during free time?
—— 3   Ask questions in class?
—— 4   Listen attentively?
—— 5   Express curiosity and interest when given new ideas?
—— 6   Take a lively part in class discussion?
—— 7   Do extra work beyond regular class assignments?
—— 8   Think independently instead of following the crowd?
—— 9   Persist in solving problems until reaching a solution?
——10   Send off for information?

**Poorly Motivated Students**   Does the student:

—— 1   Seem inattentive and appear to daydream a lot?
—— 2   Give up on a test or just guess at answers?
—— 3   Try to avoid participating in class activities?
—— 4   Cause disruptions by distracting other students?
—— 5   Waste time?
—— 6   Not do homework or other assignments?
—— 7   Jump to conclusions instead of thinking something through?
—— 8   Seem bored and uninterested most of the time?
—— 9   Seem unable to work independently?
——10   Read assigned pages without understanding what has been read?

## Setting Goals

All your students need approval, acceptance, and achievement. Most of them also have special interests, such as taking care of a new puppy or rebuilding a car engine. These needs and interests become the basis for setting goals. If you can develop a relationship between their goals and your instructional program, they will be motivated to learn. That is what Mr. Sunas tried to do with Ralph.

You can set goals for your pupils, but if you expect them to work toward them, they must accept them as their own. They should see that *your* instructional goals will help them achieve something *they* want; otherwise, they will not be motivated to do their best work.

One eighth grade teacher was frustrated because, even though her students could pass tests on the correct use of English, as soon as they were outside the classroom, they used poor grammar. She realized they didn't see any point in speaking Standard English. One day she asked them, "Can you think of any reasons for needing to speak correct English?" Finally, one student said, "Well, I guess so. I plan to earn money next summer by selling books. If I can't speak right, no one will buy books from me." Another student said, "When I go to church, sometimes they call on me to make a prayer. I get embarrassed in front of the preacher if I make a mistake in English."

Using their interests in establishing goals is a good way to motivate students. You can learn about their interests by taking a simple written or oral survey. You may have a problem if the interests in your class vary widely, but students' interests usually tend to cluster around a few general topics. Once you identify these, you can begin to relate instructional objectives to them. If you find this difficult, build on their interests until you make a connection with what you need to teach. For instance, if several students are interested in race cars, let them: (1) read books about race cars; (2) solve math problems that involve the speed of race cars; (3) do research reports on the history of race cars; and (4) investigate the construction of race car engines. Common interests, such as holidays or community and school events, also make good focal points for setting instructional goals.

Students must also view goals as reasonable and attainable. Unreasonably long assignments will only frustrate them and discourage most of them from trying. If you want to assign work that will take a period of time to complete, break it down into small steps. For instance, research reports can be broken down like this: (1) select a topic, (2) read about it in different sources, (3) take notes and turn in note cards, (4) outline the report, (5) make a rough draft, and (6) write the final report. Goals do not seem so difficult to reach when they become a series of small related tasks.

## Motivational Strategies

You may want to use some of these specific suggestions for motivating students.

1   Keep records of progress, books reviewed, or tasks completed, so students can see what they have accomplished.
2   Encourage students to identify their own problems, then help them solve them creatively.
3   Use variety and occasional surprise in your lessons. Vary teaching strategies so students will be eager to see what you do next.

4   Work in some riddles and jokes. It takes intelligence to appreciate humor, and you will keep the students interested.

5   Arouse their curiosity. Bring a praying mantis to school and don't say anything. Let them observe and ask questions.

6   Vary the activities. Follow a quiet study session with a song or physical activity.

7   Have plenty of scrap materials, games, audiovisual media, and manipulative devices. Use them in your lessons and let students use them for independent learning.

8   Be enthusiastic. Enthusiasm is contagious, and your students will catch it.

9   Create failure-proof situations for slow learners and poorly motivated students. Offer challenges to highly motivated students.

10  Use educational games, concrete objects, and audiovisual media to create interest.

11  Write brief messages to students when you return their papers instead of assigning only a letter grade.

12  Videotape a special presentation, debate, panel discussion, or activity.

13  Set up a mailbox or communications bulletin board for each class so you and the students can exchange messages.

14  Use a popular song (choose carefully!) as a basis for a lesson in language arts. Look for new vocabulary words, synonyms, antonyms, rhyming words, alliteration, and special meanings.

15  Instead of the textbook, teach from the newspaper. It can be used for any content area.

16  In a foreign language class, translate the school menu each day from English to the foreign language. Play "Password" in the foreign language.

17  Encourage home economics students to prepare projects for competitions, such as county fairs.

18  Compute averages, figure percentages, and make graphs in math class from data the students collect. Sample topics are height of students, size of rooms, students on the honor roll, male and female faculty members, etc.

19  Let students set up and carry out experiments in science class. Be sure they can explain what is happening and why.

20  In social studies class, assign different groups of students to present daily news broadcasts.

# Classroom Techniques

There are many techniques available for helping students learn. Some are more appropriate for slow learners than for bright students, for younger children than for older students, or for some subject areas than for others. As a student teacher, you should try a variety of techniques to find out which ones work best for you.

## Lecture

"Good morning, class. Today I will be telling you about. . . ."
And so the familiar lecture technique begins. The teacher does the telling and the students listen.

Lectures can be divided into two types: formal and informal. You can probably recall some of your college professors who delivered highly structured, carefully worded, inflexible, and uninterrupted lectures. The formal lecture is generally inappropriate for public school teaching, except occasionally for classes of college-bound students who are good listeners. On the other hand, informal lectures are often effective for getting information across. An informal lecture is usually brief and often involves use of audiovisual materials along with minimal student participation.

You will probably want to do some lecturing in your teaching because it is often the most direct and efficient way to convey the message. Lecture is particularly appropriate for history and literature classes and can also be used to explain an experiment in science. Brief, informal lectures can provide background information when you introduce a new topic, or summarize what has happened during a learning experience.

When you prepare to lecture, keep certain points in mind. Remember that elementary children and slow learners have short attention spans and cannot listen very long. Even older, bright students probably won't want to listen for more than about 20 minutes without a change of pace. Get to know your students well enough so that you can adapt your lecture to their interests and needs and relate it to their background experiences. Then prepare and organize your material carefully so you can make a concise, easy-to-understand presentation.

Delivery makes the difference between a boring and a stimulating lecture. Keep your voice pitched low, use expression, and make sure every student can hear you. Maintain eye contact and occasionally interject a student's name to recapture the attention of a student who appears to be drifting away from you. Speak in Standard English and use vocabulary words each student understands.

You can use several techniques to hold students' interest as you lecture. Begin by making sure that students remove everything from their desks so they will not be distracted. Introduce your topic in such a way that you arouse curiosity. Use audiovisual materials or demonstrations to supplement the lecture. Emphasize major points by writing them on the chalkboard and encourage secondary students to take notes. Occasionally ask a question to get students involved and to check on how well they are listening to your presentation.

Although lecture is often a quick way to transmit information, it has many dangers. It does not allow for student creativity or problem solving, nor can students practice applying the knowledge that is being passed along to them. During this one-way communication process, many teachers get carried away with their own speech making while students sit passively and daydream.

## Discussion

Guided discussion is also a teacher-centered technique, but it affords greater opportunities for students to participate than does lecture. Students can exchange ideas and consider the pros and cons of issues. Guided discussion is a natural and informal way for students to communicate their thoughts.

By engaging students in guided discussions, you can help them achieve many worthwhile goals. They learn to see different points of view and to keep their minds open. They begin to think critically about important issues and to question whatever they are told or see in print. They develop speaking and listening skills by reacting to what their classmates say. They also develop tolerance for other people's ideas when they hear different opinions expressed.

If you want to conduct a guided discussion in your class, first decide whether you want a whole-class discussion or several small group discussions. In the latter case, you will need to divide your class into three or four groups and appoint a leader for each group. You should move from one group to the next, checking to see that students are making relevant comments. Small groups should meet for 20 to 30 minutes, after which the leader can summarize the group's ideas for the rest of the class. Students who are afraid to speak out in front of the entire class are usually willing to participate in small group discussions.

In a discussion with the whole class, you have several responsibilities as the discussion leader. Choose a controversial topic familiar to your students so they can discuss it intelligently. Create a supportive atmosphere where students are not afraid to say what is on their minds, but control the discussion so it doesn't deteriorate into pointless conversation. Encourage widespread participation by asking questions directed toward students of different ability levels. Conclude the discussion by summarizing the points that were made and suggesting a solution that seems acceptable to most of the class.

A good topic for discussion might be "What sources of energy should we pursue for future development?" Possible answers include solar, nuclear, geothermal, synthetic fuel, wind, and biological sources. You could consider these sources in terms of their cost to develop, the length of time before they would be available for independent use, their impact on the environment, and their safety. The whole class could consider these issues, or you could divide the class into groups with each group discussing one source and making recommendations as to its feasibility.

During a guided discussion or other type of lesson, students may raise questions you can't answer. Rather than take a chance and give a wrong answer, admit that you don't know the answer. Then, depending on the situation, you can look it up in a reference source immediately, tell the students you will try to find the answer, or suggest that they find the answer and discuss it in class the next day. Of course you should know your lesson, but no one knows all the answers all the time.

Panel discussions and debates are variations of the discussion approach. In panel discussions, students prepare in advance to discuss issues related to a specific topic in front of the class. One student usually serves as chairperson and directs the discussion. Debates are similar to panel discussions, but call for two teams of students to present opposing sides of a topic. With both procedures, make sure the participants understand the ground rules and are well prepared. At the conclusion of the activity, ask the rest of the class to respond to the presentation.

## Demonstration

Another teacher-centered instructional activity is demonstration. With this technique, students learn by watching as well as by listening. You can use demonstrations in every part of the curriculum and at any age level. In the elementary grades, you might need to show some children how to tie their shoes or show a baseball player how to pitch a ball. At the secondary level, you can demonstrate how to make a soufflé in home economics or show the correct position for the fingers on the keys of a typewriter in typing class. If you teach science classes, you will have many opportunities to demonstrate scientific processes by performing experiments yourself or helping students set them up.

Demonstrations have a special attraction for students. They create a feeling of anticipation. Students welcome the change from routine lessons and give their full attention to what you are doing.

In preparing for a demonstration, make sure it relates clearly to your objectives. Try to keep it simple and to the point—it's a mistake to try to teach too many concepts in a single demonstration. If your demonstration could cause injury, be sure to take safety precautions. Then practice it several times until you are sure nothing can go wrong.

Now you are ready to present the demonstration to your class. Collect all the materials you need and provide a good viewing area for the students. Prepare them for what you will be doing so they will know what to expect. During the demonstration, you can ask questions or point out what is taking place. Afterward, review what happened and why it happened as it did. If something went wrong, ask the students if they can tell you why.

## Guided Study Activities

Get an assignment, study the text, discuss the material, memorize the important facts, and take a test. You know the routine. It is not much fun, but is sometimes useful for helping students acquire specific knowledge in a short time.

*Constructing models is one type of guided study activity on which children can work individually or in groups.*

**Supervised study** As the teacher, you may want to supervise occasional study sessions in which students are responsible for mastering content you have assigned. Be sure to make reasonable assignments that all students can complete successsfully if they apply themselves to the task. You may have to individualize some assignments according to students' different ability levels. You should walk around among the students while they study, stopping occasionally to answer questions, offer suggestions, and head them in the right direction. Your guidance during a supervised study session can help students learn to use study time efficiently when they are on their own.

Supervised study during class time is a useful teaching technique if you are introducing a new subject or type of assignment. You are there to offer encouragement and make sure students are getting off on the right foot. It is also valuable if the assignment requires the use of resources in the classroom or the school library.

Because of its limitations, you should use this approach infrequently. It can easily become boring and routine, seldom involves the student in creative or critical thinking, and may seem unrelated to real-life situations. This procedure has little power to motivate the slow learner, and the bright student learns not for the purpose of gaining information, but for the reward of a good grade.

**Drill** Nine times two is 18; nine times three is 27; nine times four is 36. On and on, over and over. This is known as drill, or organized practice. Is it really necessary? Why do we do it?

Drill can be a valuable instructional technique when it is based on solid understanding of a concept. It provides practice through repetition to the point of overlearning. In such areas as math, spelling, grammar, and motor development, repeated practice is helpful for mastering skills.

Although drill is often boring, it doesn't have to be. Here are some ways to keep drill from becoming tedious. Think up games for practicing skills. Keep drill periods short—don't go beyond the time when it ceases to hold the students' attention. Vary the amount and kind of drill according to students' needs. Slow learners generally need more repetition than fast learners. Make sure students see the reason for complete mastery of the concept. Let students keep individual charts to record their progress. Intersperse drill with other types of instruction to avoid monotony.

**Review** Review is similar to drill. It is based on previously learned concepts and makes use of recall. While drill simply provides practice in skills, however, review explores students' attitudes, understandings, and appreciations. Review is essentially a group process which extends initial learnings by bringing out relationships and applications of the topic. Use review before tests and whenever you want to pull together the major concepts you have been teaching.

**Project**    Another type of guided study activity is the project technique. In this approach, students have more freedom to direct their own activities and can become more actively involved in the learning process. Usually several groups work simultaneously on different but related projects. Groups may conduct research, construct models, or solve problems, then prepare a report to present to the class. Your role as the teacher is to support, encourage, and assist as groups work toward completing their projects. Quite often, course content is not covered as thoroughly in this approach, so you will need to fill in the gaps with other techniques.

**Homework**    "Can't tonight. I've got tons of homework to do." Sound familiar? Educators dispute the value of homework; it may or may not do any good. Therefore, think carefully before you make a homework assignment and be sure it is realistic as well as purposeful.

Your cooperating teacher's policy on homework will probably influence the homework assignments you give. Chances are, though, that you will assign some homework during your student teaching experience, so here are some things to keep in mind. Take time to explain your assigments thoroughly—don't wait until the bell rings. You may want to write the assignment on the board and discuss it at the beginning of class, or you may choose to save the last five or ten minutes of class time to let students begin their assignment, so you can clear up any confusion. Always help them see the connection between what they are studying in class and the homework they are expected to do.

To avoid a mutiny, keep these points in mind as you assign homework. Don't make unusually long or pointless assignments. Avoid assigning homework on nights the students have special events. Try to give major assignments several days in advance so students can plan their study time around other obligations. Vary the type of assignments. Don't always assign a certain number of math problems or a certain number of questions to answer from the text. Ask students to investigate, discover, interview, work on projects, do programmed text assignments, or solve problems dealing with real-life situations. With young children, it is probably inadvisable to make any skill/drill homework assignments.

Remember that some students have little time or opportunity to do homework. They may have jobs or chores to do after school. The home may be so crowded and have such poor study facilities that doing homework is impossible. Have realistic expectations for these students.

## Questioning

Questions are a part of almost any teaching strategy: informal lecture, discussion, demonstration, and others. Sometimes, however, questioning is the focal point of the lesson; the teaching strategy may then be called reflective thinking or discovery inquiry. Through skillful questioning, the teacher leads students to reflect upon things they already know and to discover new ideas.

Suppose you want to try your skill at leading a question session. How would you start? First, choose an appropriate topic. It should be one your students already know something about, that is important and interesting to them, and that is within their level of understanding. Get their attention before you begin, then ask your questions clearly. Ask each question once, so they will know they must listen carefully. Once the session begins, keep to the subject and don't get too far off the track. Try to include all the students in the questioning, even those who don't volunteer.

It is not easy to ask good questions. Write down in advance some questions designed to achieve certain purposes. Phrase them simply and clearly so students will know exactly what you want. Don't be afraid to include a question for which you don't know the answer—you and the students can seek it together. As the session progresses, you may find yourself discarding your prepared list and asking spontaneous questions that arise from student responses.

The types of questions you ask determine the kind of thinking your students will learn to do. Include a wide variety of question types, stressing critical-creative thinking and avoiding yes or no answers. Table 6-1 lists purposes for various types of questions

**TABLE 6-1 Questions and How to Begin Them**

| PURPOSE | QUESTIONS |
| --- | --- |
| If you want to: | Ask questions that begin with: |
| Assess knowledge | Define, Describe, Tell, List, Who, When, Where, Identify |
| Check understanding | Compare, Contrast, Explain the relationships, How do you know |
| Help analyze problems | How, Why, What procedures, What causes, What steps in the process |
| Lead students to explore values | Why do you feel, What is important, Why do you prefer |
| Promote creative thinking | How else, What if, Just suppose, Create a new, Design an original |
| Help evaluate situations | Judge the following, Select, Evaluate the result, Rate as to good or bad |
| Show how to apply knowledge | Demonstrate, Show how to solve, Construct, Use the information to |

and words to use to begin appropriate questions that meet these purposes.

Asking questions is only half the process; the other half is knowing how to respond. Give your students plenty of time to answer—at least three seconds or more. Wait-time encourages more students to consider the answer, to grope and ponder, and to think through the question. Don't rush on after an answer has been given, but leave the door open for other students to express their views. Extend a thought by asking "Are you sure?" and "How do you know?" Be willing to accept reasonable answers even if they don't agree with your interpretations.

One aim of a good questioning session is to let students ask questions of you and of each other. Foster this purpose by setting an accepting, noncritical classroom atmosphere in which honest questions, no matter how silly they seem, are welcome. Students may ask you something you don't know. Don't be afraid to admit that you don't know the answer, but encourage them to join you in finding the answer. A really productive questioning session involves a lively exchange of ideas in an effort to reach a logical and satisfying conclusion.

You can use questions to promote convergent or divergent thinking. When things converge, they come to a point. When they diverge, they go off in many directions. A convergent question is narrowly focused and usually has a single correct answer. An exam-

*Divergent questions encourage reflection and discovery.*

ple of a convergent question is "Who was the first president of the United States?" If you use many convergent questions, you will be checking knowledge of facts, but you will not be helping your students think creatively or critically.

Divergent questions, on the other hand, challenge students to think of many possible solutions. These questions are the type used in reflective thinking or discovery inquiry. A good divergent question is "How many ways can we think of to help make our community more attractive?" You may want to begin a questioning session with divergent questions, then move toward more convergent questions as students approach a decision or reach a conclusion.

You should also be familiar with deductive and inductive teaching. Both types are useful, but a great deal of teaching is deductive. You can probably remember that many of your teachers told you rules and even made you memorize them. Then you applied them, probably by completing workbook pages and ditto sheets. Most of the time, you didn't have a chance to discover for yourself, and therefore you have probably forgotten much of what you were taught. Here is an example of a deductive lesson on syllabication.

**Deductive lesson: Syllabication**   Say: "Today we are going to learn a new rule for dividing words into syllables. The rule states that whenever a word has two consonants with a vowel on either side, you divide the word between the two consonants. Here is an example. In the word *comfort*, we divide the word between the *m* and the *f*. Now I want you to divide the words on this worksheet into syllables."

---

WORKSHEET
Divide the following words into syllables:
butter     after     problem     hammer     sermon

---

Say: "When you finish your worksheet, be sure you can say the rule that tells you how to divide these words into syllables."

Inductive teaching calls for an inquiring mind and leads students to make their own discoveries. It is based on the use of examples. By asking students questions about the examples, or helping them form their own questions, you can guide them toward a solution. The discovery inquiry approach challenges students to think for themselves and pull together clues for discovering the answer. Students internalize what they discover for themselves; it becomes a part of them, and they aren't likely to forget it. An example of an inductive lesson is given below. By using your ingenuity, you will be able to come up with other examples of inductive lessons that are pertinent for your class.

**Inductive lesson: Syllabication** Say: "Sometimes we need to divide words into syllables. How do we know where to divide them? Look at these examples on the board."

but/ter     af/ter     prob/lem     ham/mer     ser/mon

"How many syllables are in each word?"

"What do you think the slash mark means?"

"What do you notice about the position of the slash mark in each word in relation to consonants and vowels?"

"Does it make any difference whether the two consonants in the middle of the word are alike or different?"

"Can you give me a rule that tells where to divide words into syllables? Using this rule, can you divide these words into syllables?"

suppose     sister     content     channel     blunder

## Programmed Instruction

Programmed instruction is implemented through many types and combinations of media. It may be administered through workbooks, teaching machines, or computers. (See chapter 1 for information on computer-assisted instruction.) Programs are usually *linear* or *branching.* Linear programs consist of a series of small steps in the development of a skill or concept, with frequent provisions for student responses. They are easy to use and provide good practice in areas such as spelling and word recognition, math problems, and literal translations of foreign words. They allow for only one "right" answer, however, and do not provide for creative thinking.

Branching programs are much more complex. Students answer multiple-choice questions, and each answer determines what question they see next. If the student answers incorrectly, he or she leaves the main line of the program and is branched to a track where the concept is retaught. When the student is able to answer the questions on the branched track correctly, he or she returns to the main line to continue the work. With branching programs, a student selects answers and moves to the next step based upon his or her answer.

The effectiveness of programmed instruction depends on how you use it. You should not grade programmed materials, but use them simply for providing practice in skills that will be tested later. Don't expect programmed instruction to be the total instructional program; it should be used along with other learning activities. While students are engaged in programmed learning, you need to check their progress and help them with any difficulties they may be having.

### The Case Method

The case method is suitable for training young people to analyze real-life situations. Case study allows students to extend and apply information from their textbooks. To discuss the issues of each case, they also must pull together knowledge from different subject areas. The case method encourages them to think critically and acquaints them with problem-solving techniques.

Cases are built around conflict situations. They describe actual problems and supply facts related to the situations. Some cases may be open-ended, with no solution given; others may be closed, with one solution or several alternate solutions. The incident case, a short, three- to five-paragraph description of a situation, is more appropriate for young students than the more complex case studies used at the college level. Some of the vignettes and case studies in this book could be used as incident cases. The case method is appropriate for almost any subject area, but is particularly effective in history, economics, sociology, psychology, and business courses.

If you want to try the case method with your students, first select a fairly simple situation that will interest them, such as the development of a well-known fast-food franchise or the promotion of a famous rock star. Then learn all you can about the subject. Draw up a set of questions that will lead students to define the problem, analyze different aspects of the problem, reach one or more possible solutions, and evaluate the possible consequences of their conclusions. You can start with a simple case that can be completed in one class period, then work up to a more complicated case that could last for several days.

As the teacher, you must play an active role in presenting and developing an incident case. Lively discussion is the key to learning through this method. You must be knowledgeable about all aspects of the subject so you can supply additional information as the students begin asking questions about the case. After students have arrived at a tentative solution, you may need to offer alternate proposals to stimulate further critical analysis of the problem. You should guide the class in making decisions based on facts rather than personal prejudices or hunches. Finally, you will need to help the students evaluate their decision and look at its long-range implications.

## Creative Activities

A great deal of school work is based on learning the one correct answer to a question. Dates, facts, names, and places are presented to the student, who must learn them and give them back on tests. Often, a young child's creative urge dies soon after he or she enters school, and learning becomes dull and routine.

Divergent thinking is closely related to creativity. It requires a student to seek many different solutions and try new ideas. You can encourage students to think divergently or creatively by praising their creative efforts. Establish a classroom atmosphere where students can experiment, discover, and create. Give them materials to work with and time to solve problems in their own way.

Many types of creative activities encourage divergent thinking. Using these activities accomplishes two purposes: (1) your lessons will be livelier and more interesting, and (2) your students will begin using their imaginations and creativity while they are learning. Four types of creative activities are brainstorming, simulation, role playing, and creative dramatics.

## Brainstorming

Brainstorming can be used to develop creative thinking at any grade level. Students are given a real or imaginary problem and asked to think of as many ways as they can to solve it. You will probably have to direct the activity yourself the first time you try it, but later a student can lead it.

Here's how it works. First, identify a *specific* problem, one that is limited in scope. Then divide the class into groups of six to ten students. Appoint a recorder for each group to write down the ideas. Brainstorming sessions are brief and are usually most productive in the morning. You may want to ask students to meet again the following day for additional "afterthoughts" and to select those ideas that are worth following up.

Students must understand how the session will be conducted before they start brainstorming. Tell them to think of as many ideas as they can, the wilder the better. They should build on the ideas of others, combining and modifying what other students suggest. They can offer only one idea at a time and speak only one at a time. Most important of all, there must be no criticism of any ideas during the session. You may ask anyone who criticizes or ridicules someone's idea to leave the group, because such criticism destroys creative thinking.

You may want to use brainstorming to solve real problems, or you may want to use fantasy situations simply to promote creative thinking. Here are suggestions for both types of brainstorming sessons.

Realistic situations:

1  How can we raise enough money to take a trip to the Space Center?
2  What are some things we can do to make our classroom more attractive?

3  How can we become more considerate of Jorge? (Conduct session on a day when Jorge, a handicapped student, is absent.)

4  How can we show our appreciation to the parents who have given us parties and helped in our classroom during the year?

5  How can we prevent a group of ninth grade bullies from picking on the seventh graders?

Fantasy situations:

1  What would happen if we learned to create energy from sand?

2  In what ways are a steam engine and a chain saw alike?

3  How many ways are there to kill a mosquito?

4  How many ways could you change a bicycle to make it more fun to ride?

5  What would be different if you woke up one morning and discovered that it was a hundred years from now?

## Simulation

An interesting way to involve your students in real-life situations is through simulation activities. In simulation, a realistic situation is created in which students play various roles or act out scientific processes. It is a "learning by doing" activity. By acting out a situation, students come to understand what processes are involved and how problems are solved.

Simulation offers many advantages over textbook learning, but it has disadvantages, too. You will find that most students are enthusiastic about participating in simulation and are highly motivated to learn all they can about the roles they are playing. They are using high-level communication skills and thinking creatively. They need freedom to move around and negotiate with each other, though, so your classroom may become noisy and disorderly at times. Some students may remain on the fringe of the activity and not get the full benefit of the experience. The entire simulation can be a waste of time unless the experience and the follow-up discussion are skillfully directed.

If you decide to try simulation, your first problem will be to locate an activity appropriate for the students' age level, the time available, and the lesson topic. Many commercial games are available, or you can plan an activity yourself. You need to become thoroughly familiar with the activity, preferably by trying it out first with some of your friends. When you present it to the class, give the directions simply and clearly. At the close of the activity, be prepared to lead a discussion based on the students' experiences. During this discussion,

**Figure 6-1   Site Location Simulation**

The Speedwheel Bicycle Manufacturing Co. wants to build a new plant. Members of the Site Selection Committee are meeting to select a desirable location. They are considering four sites. As members of the Committee, discuss the advantages and disadvantages of each location and reach a decision.

| Criteria | City A | City B | City C | City D |
|---|---|---|---|---|
| General Information | Population 90,000 Industrial part of a megalopolis | Population 450,000 State capital | Population 2,800 Isolated rural town | Population 25,000 Center of a generally rural area |
| Transportation Facilities | On major tidal river, major rail lines, near large metropolitan airport, on N–S interstate | On major railroad and interstate routes River running through city | On old E–W highway and railroad spur line Limited air service 30 miles away | On major N–S interstate and railroad freight line Local small airport |
| Tax Situation | Extremely high taxes on individuals and industry | No state income tax Low municipal rates Adequate for services | High progressive state income tax Heavy industrial taxes | Low tax rates No state income tax Inadequate for service |
| Labor Force | Heavily unionized Poor productivity Highly skilled Adequate supply | Unskilled or semiskilled Chiefly nonunion Short supply | Heavily unionized with coal mining background Unskilled to highly skilled Adequate supply | Large supply of unskilled and semiskilled Unions active |
| Utilities | Electricity, water adequate; low supply of gas; all expensive | Low rates Abundant supplies | Adequate supplies High rates | Low-priced electricity Adequate supplies of natural gas and water |
| Plant Sites Available | Existing old factory sites available No open land | Six well-developed industrial parks Land reasonably priced | Hilly forestland available No industrial park Expensive | Two industrial parks Reasonably priced |
| City Management | Expects kickbacks from industry | Generally favorable to recruiting industry | Inactive in industrial recruiting | Selective recruiting of industry |

Figure 6-1   Site Location Simulation (continued)

| Criteria | City A | City B | City C | City D |
|---|---|---|---|---|
| School System | Meets state standards Old buildings and outdated facilities | Quality varies, but generally adequate | Good quality education Limited facilities | Good quality but low funding |
| Cultural Activities | None in city but full range available in adjacent cities | New Arts Center Symphony Orchestra Several universities | Nothing local Concert series and extension courses 30 miles away | University town Small orchestra Well-developed arts programs |
| Parks and Recreation | Organized sports No local parks 80 miles from ocean | Several city parks Lakes nearby | Good hunting, fishing Ski resort nearby | Lakes, waterfalls, and parks within an hour's drive, but not much locally |

encourage students to express different points of view and explain their reasoning. Simulation may be followed with related assignments to reinforce and extend the learning experience.

Controversial subjects are often the subject of simulation games. Conducting a political campaign followed by a mock election is an excellent way for students to understand political maneuvering and strategic campaigning, especially during an election year. Other simulations deal with zoning decisions, race relations, profits and losses, and ecology. Students discover why people hold certain values and attitudes as they play out the roles they have assumed.

These are possible simulation activities:

1   You are a tiny seed planted in the ground. The sun is shining and makes you feel warm. Now the rain comes and helps you to grow. You become a small plant and push through the earth. You grow taller and stronger. The wind blows gently and you move. A small bud forms on your stem. Slowly the bud opens, and you are a beautiful flower.

2   Five of you are being sent to an uninhabited island for two years to pass a survival test. You are allowed to take ten things (not to exceed $100 in value) with you, besides the clothes you are wearing. What will you take? Why?

3   A spaceship lands in your neighborhood. Three Crimson Creatures emerge and let you know they want to stay in

your community. Some concerned citizens call a meeting. Those at the meeting are the PTA president, a television agent, an environmentalist, a medical doctor, a civil rights representative, and a journalist. You must decide if the creatures can stay. If the answer is no, how will you persuade them to leave?

4   The city council is meeting to decide whether or not to legalize gambling to bring in more revenue. Members of the council include a minister, a businessman connected with organized crime, a motel developer, an unemployed construction worker, an independently wealthy playboy, a young mother, a school teacher, a banker, and a farmer. Discuss your feelings about the proposal and reach a decision.

5   A site location simulation is described in Figure 6-1.

## Role Playing

Role playing is closely related to simulation. During role playing, a student assumes the role of another person in order to understand the other's feelings and attitudes. Role playing that involves several people is sometimes called sociodrama. Role playing can develop communication skills, creative thinking processes, and clarification of values.

In directing role playing situations, you should observe certain guidelines. Encourage the players to speak distinctly and make their actions clear to the audience. Remind students who are not participating to be good listeners and not interrupt or carry on side conversations. When you choose students to play certain parts, assign them to play roles that are unlike their own personalities; for instance, let the well-mannered student be the class bully.

Usually, in role playing situations, two or more characters become involved in a conflict. There should be plenty of action and dialogue. The characters are led to a point where they must choose from among several possible courses of action. After students play the situation, you should discuss what took place and whether or not the problem was solved.

Role playing helps students see emotional situations clearly and objectively. In playing out a situation, they experience the emotions connected with it. Good subjects for role playing include conflicts on the playground, family disagreements, misuse of drugs, disobedience to rules, and peer relationships.

You can develop role playing situations from real life or create imaginary circumstances. Here are some suggestions.

*Nick doesn't do his share:* Mrs. Miller's ninth grade class has been studying different systems of government. As their final project, the students have been divided into groups to make presentations.

All students in each group will receive the same grade. Janie, Roger, Mel, Sandy, and Nick are investigating socialism. They agree to research certain aspects of socialism and combine their information into a final report. The day before the presentation is due, all the students are ready except Nick. When they ask him to do his part, he says he has a job after school and doesn't have time. The other four students are concerned that their presentation will be incomplete because Nick hasn't done his assignment.

What courses of action are open to the four students? What is the best way to resolve this problem?

*A lucky find:* Freda and Elena were following Mrs. Gomez, a wealthy widow, out of the grocery store one day. As she put her change back in her purse, a ten-dollar bill drifted down. Mrs. Gomez didn't notice she had lost the money, but Freda and Elena saw the bill fall to the sidewalk. They looked at each other; then Freda walked over and picked it up. They had never had so much money at one time before. Freda started to catch up to Mrs. Gomez to return the money to her, but Elena put her hand on Freda's arm and stopped her.

What do they say to each other? What do they finally decide to do?

*Everyone gets punished:* For three days, Mrs. Conner has punished the entire class because Patti, Mike, and Jessie were laughing and cutting up. The students lost five minutes of recess time on Tuesday, and on Wednesday each student had to write "I will not talk" 25 times. Thursday the students had to put their heads down for ten minutes. Carmen, Russ, Ron, and Cindi had behaved themselves, and are now discussing the situation after school.

How do Carmen, Russ, Ron, and Cindi feel? What choices do they have for changing the situation?

## Creative Dramatics

Creative dramatics is similar to simulation and role playing, and you can use it effectively in the classroom for interpreting literature and reenacting episodes from history. Students can become totally involved in creative dramatics through their thinking, speaking, listening, movement, and imaginations. Therefore, they are more likely to understand and remember what they portray than if they were merely to read from a textbook or listen to a lecture.

The procedure for creative dramatics is fairly simple. You do not need props, settings, or scripts, but you do need some space. The students should become totally familiar with a story or historical event, including its sequence of action and the feelings of the characters. Sometimes they do additional research to learn more about the story. Then you choose students to play the parts. If there are not enough parts to go around, some students can be extra villagers or even animals. The students improvise the dialogue as the story unfolds. After the play is over, help them evaluate the performance by asking them what was good about the presentation and what could be done to improve it. Usually, half the class participates while the other half is the audience, and then the play is performed again with students reversing roles.

Almost any historical event can be dramatized. Here are some good scenes to try.

1  The signing of the Magna Carta or the Declaration of Independence
2  Encounters between the Indians and the White Man, including the first Thanksgiving
3  The arrival of the missionaries in Hawaii
4  The Boston Tea Party
5  The assassination of Lincoln or Kennedy

Some stories are better suited to dramatization than others, and in some cases, you will want to dramatize just one or two scenes from a story. Most folktales move quickly, show conflict, and have strong characterizations. Scenes from Shakespeare's plays are also good sources for classroom creative dramatics. These are some other good selections:

*Ask Mr. Bear* by Marjorie Flack (New York: MacMillan, 1932)
*The Three Billy Goats Gruff* by Asbjornsen and Moe (New York: Harcourt Brace Jovanovich, 1957)
*Peddler and His Caps* by Esphyr Slobodkina (New York: William R. Scott, 1947)
*The Pied Piper of Hamelin* by Robert Browning (New York: Scroll, 1970)
*Stone Soup* by Marcia Brown (New York: Scribner, 1947)
*Anne Frank: The Diary of a Young Girl* by Anne Frank (New York: Doubleday, 1967)
*To Kill a Mockingbird* by Harper Lee (Philadelphia: Lippincott, 1960)
*The Pearl* by John Steinbeck (New York: Viking, 1953)
*The Glass Menagerie* by Tennessee Williams (New York: Random House, 1945)
*The Count of Monte Cristo* by Alexandre Dumas (St. Louis: Webster, 1949)

# Discussion Questions

1  Are you motivated to be a good teacher? What motivates you to do your best? Is your motivation primarily intrinsic or extrinsic? Explain your answer.

2 Select a student in your class who appears to be unmotivated. What are some ways you might try to motivate her or him? Looking back through this chapter, can you find some strategies that might work with this student?

3 How would you assign homework so that it relates to what you are studying but doesn't involve the use of texbooks? Can you design it so that it requires problem-solving or creative-thinking skills?

4 Select a goal that you and your students would like to achieve. From Table 6-1, find the purpose that most closely relates to that goal. Can you compose a set of questions appropriate for reaching your goal?

5 What would happen to our society if there were no creativity? Which is more important, knowledge or creativity?

6 What opportunities do the students in your class have for developing creativity? How do you and your cooperating teacher react to creative efforts?

7 What can you do to provide a more creative classroom environment? Would you need to make any changes in the room arrangement, scheduling of class work, types of activities, or assignments?

8 What creative activities are you willing to try in your classroom? What problems can you foresee in doing them?

# Selected References

Bluming, Mildred, and Myron H. Dembo. *Solving Teaching Problems: A Guide for the Elementary School Teacher.* Pacific Palisades, Calif.: Goodyear, 1973.

Brizendine, Nancy Hanks, and James L. Thomas, eds. *Learning Through Dramatics.* Phoenix, Ariz.: Oryx Press, 1982.

Brown, Thomas J. *Student Teaching in a Secondary School.* New York: Harper and Row, 1968.

Callahan, Sterling G. *Successful Teaching in Secondary Schools, A Guide for In-Service Teachers.* Glenview, Ill.: Scott, Foresman, 1971.

Carin, Arthur A., and Robert B. Sund. *Developing Questioning Techniques.* Columbus, Ohio: Charles E. Merrill, 1971.

Crow, Lester D., and Alice Crow. *The Student Teacher in the Secondary School.* New York: David McKay, 1964.

Drayer, Adam M. *Problems in Middle and High School Teaching.* Boston: Allyn and Bacon, 1979.

Ehreich, Harriet W. *Creative Dramatics Handbook.* Urbana, Ill.: National Council of Teachers of English, 1974.

Frymier, Jack. *Motivation and Learning in School.* Bloomington, Ind.: Phi Delta Kappa Educational Foundation, 1974.

Harmer, Earl W., Jr. *Instructional Strategies for Student Teachers.* Belmont, Calif.: Wadsworth, 1969.

Heyman, Mark. *Simulation Games for the Classroom.* Bloomington, Ind.: Phi Delta Kappa Educational Foundation, 1975.

Hoover, Kenneth H. *The Professional Teacher's Handbook,* 2nd ed. Boston: Allyn and Bacon, 1978.

Hoover, Kenneth H., and Paul M. Hollingsworth. *Learning and Teaching in the Elementary School.* Boston: Allyn and Bacon, 1970.

Hunkins, Francis P. *Involving Students in Questioning.* Boston: Allyn and Bacon, 1976.

Inlow, Gail M. *Maturity in High School Teaching.* Englewood Cliffs, N.J.: Prentice-Hall, 1970.

Johnson, James A., and Roger C. Anderson. *Secondary Student Teaching: Readings.* Glenview, Ill.: Scott, Foresman, 1971.

Johnson, James A., and Louis D. Deprin. *Elementary Student Teaching: Readings.* Glenview, Ill.: Scott, Foresman, 1971.

Kim, Eugene C., and Richard D. Kellough. *A Resource Guide for Secondary School Teaching,* 2nd ed. New York: MacMillan, 1978.

McIntyre, Barbara M. *Creative Drama in the Elementary School.* Itasca, Ill.: F. E. Peacock, 1974.

Osborn, Alex F. *Applied Imagination.* New York: Charles Scribner's Sons, 1967.

Torrence, E. Paul. *Encouraging Creativity in the Classroom.* Dubuque, Iowa: W. C. Brown, 1970.

Turner, Thomas N. *Creative Activities Resource Book for Elementary School Teachers.* Reston, Va.: Reston, 1978.

Thompson, John F. *Using Role Playing in the Classroom.* Bloomington, Ind.: Phi Delta Kappa Educational Foundation, 1978.

# 7
# *School Activities*

Ms. Jamison, the student teacher in a fifth grade class, had assigned each class member to write a report on a famous historical figure. As a first step in collecting information, class members were to check encyclopedia accounts and seek additional information. Ricky had been asked to report on James Otis.

Ricky: Ms. Jamison, James Otis isn't in the encyclopedia. I checked all three sets.

Ms. Jamison (puzzled): I'm sure you just overlooked his name, Ricky. I know it is there.

Ricky: No, it's not. I'm sure.

Ms. Jamison (suddenly realizing what she should do): Let's go to the encyclopedia together, and you can show me how you looked for his name.

Ricky (walking toward the reference books): Okay. Oh! I can't show you now. All the "J" encyclopedias are being used.

Ms. Jamison: Why did you look under "J?"

Ricky: His name starts with a "J."

Ms. Jamison: It's his first name that starts with a "J." In the encyclopedia, people's names are alphabetized according to their last names. That's why you couldn't find "James Otis" in the "J" encyclopedia. You should have looked for "Otis" in the "O" encyclopedia. Nobody is using the "O" encyclopedia now. Why don't you try it while I watch?

Ricky (picking up the encyclopedia): Okay. Let's see. Here it is—Otis, James! Thank you, Ms. Jamison.

At this point Ms. Jamison notices that several students seem to be wandering around aimlessly. Several are scanning books in the biography section. The section near the card catalog is strangely empty.

Ms. Jamison: Bryan, what are you doing?

Bryan: Looking for a book on Thomas Jefferson. I've already used the encyclopedia.

Ms. Jamison: Did you try the card catalog?

Bryan: No. Where is it?

Ms. Jamison (pointing): Over by the wall.

Bryan: There aren't books in those drawers, are there?

Ms. Jamison (feeling frustrated): Jana, can you show Bryan how to use the card catalog?

Jana: What is it?

Ms. Jamison (raising her voice): How many of you have checked the card catalog? (three hands) How many of you know how to use the card catalog? (eight hands)

Ms. Jamison (walking toward the card catalog): Please come over here with me for a few minutes, class. . . .

1  What assumption had Ms. Jamison made about the students' research skills when she assigned the lesson? Were they valid? Why do you say so?
2  What might you do before making an assignment like this one to avoid a similar occurrence in your class?
3  Have students always mastered the study skills they have had presented in class?

# Study Skills

Ms. Jamison faced difficulties in teaching a social studies class because the students had not mastered crucial study skills. Students at all levels and in all disciplines need to master a set of basic study skills that will enhance their abilities to learn from content area materials. It is, of course, beyond the scope of this book to teach you *how* to teach study skills; the purpose of this discussion is to make you aware of *what* the important study skills are, so you will not fail to help your students acquire them. Don't assume that students have learned these skills simply because they have been previously exposed to them. Check to see, through pretests, oral questions, and observation of classroom performance, if they have actually acquired them. Many students have been exposed to the skills, but the exposure has not "taken."

Starting with the problem posed by Ms. Jamison's class, the first set of study skills that needs consideration is that of locating information. To carry out many routine assignments in content classes, students need to be able to locate information in trade books (nontextbook reading materials), textbooks, and reference books, as well as be able to locate the books in libraries.

If students are to use trade books and textbooks to best advantage, you must ensure that they understand how to use prefaces and/or introductions, tables of contents, indexes, appendixes, glossaries, footnotes, and bibliographies. Many students do not even know the functions of these book parts, so their chances of using them effectively to locate information are poor. Before some students can use indexes and glossaries to best effect, they may need instruction in the prerequisite skill of alphabetization. For use of the glossary, they may also need instruction in use of guide words and pronunciation keys and in choosing the meaning that fits the context. Some students also need instruction in identifying key words under which to look when using the index. You need to assess the students' knowledge of the skills they need for using trade books and textbooks, and offer information, instruction, and practice as necessary. Informal assessment measures will usually suffice. You can ask students to use each of the book parts and observe their performance, or ask them to explain the function of each part. Primary level students will be concerned only with tables of contents and, by second or third grade, glossaries. Intermediate level students should use all book parts, with the possible exception of the preface and/or introduction, and students in junior and senior high schools should use these parts as well.

Reference books call for a wide variety of skills. Knowledge of alphabetical order and the ability to use guide words are necessary for use of most reference books, especially encyclopedias and dictionaries. Most secondary level students have mastered the use of alphabetical order, which receives initial attention in first grade, but some will have difficulty with alphabetizing beyond the first letter. Many secondary students, however, still have trouble with use of guide words, although most have had repeated exposure to them since at least fourth grade. The ability to use cross references is particularly important for using an encyclopedia. Of course, for use of the dictionary, students need the same skills they need for use of a glossary, including ability to use pronunciation keys and to choose

**Figure 7-1   Graph for Estimating Readability—Extended***

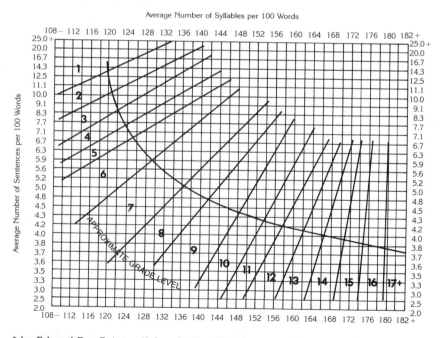

* by Edward Fry, Rutgers University Reading Center, New Brunswick, N.J. 08904; this "extended graph" does not outmode or render the earlier (1968) version inoperative or inaccurate; it is an extension. (Reproduction permitted, no copyright)

the meaning that fits the particular context. To use encyclopedias, students must be able to determine which volume of a set contains the information they seek, which was Ricky's problem at the beginning of this chapter. Encyclopedia users must also be able to determine key words under which they can find related information. To use atlases, students need to know how to interpret a map legend how to interpret map scale, and how to locate directions on a map.

Reference books are often written on relatively high readability levels, considering the populations for which they are intended. Guard against assigning students to look up information in reference books with readability levels far above their reading abilities. They will not learn from such assignments and are likely either to do nothing or merely copy from the reference book without understanding. These responses will not result in the learning outcomes you anticipated. Readability information on some reference books may already be available, but if it is not, you may wish to use a readability formula on selected portions of the books to estimate their levels of difficulty. The Fry Readability Graph (Figure 7-1) is a relatively quick and easy formula to use.

Figure 7-1   Graph for Estimating Readability—Extended* (continued)

1   Randomly select three (3) sample passages and count out exactly 100 words each, beginning with the beginning of a sentence. Do count proper nouns, initializations, and numerals.

2   Count the number of sentences in the hundred words, estimating length of the fraction of the last sentence to the nearest one-tenth.

3   Count the total number of syllables in the 100-word passage. If you don't have a hand counter available, an easy way is to simply put a mark above every syllable over one in each word, then when you get to the end of the passage, count the number of marks and add 100. Small calculators can also be used as counters by pushing numeral 1, then pushing the + sign for each word or syllable when counting.

4   Enter graph with *average* sentence length and *average* number of syllables; plot dot where the two lines intersect. Area where dot is plotted will give you the approximate grade level.

5   If a great deal of variability is found in syllable count or sentence count, putting more samples into the average is desirable.

6   A word is defined as a group of symbols with a space on either side; thus, *Joe, IRA, 1945,* and *&* are each one word.

7   A syllable is defined as a phonetic syllable. Generally, there are as many syllables as vowel sounds. For example, *stopped* is one syllable and *wanted* is two syllables. When counting syllables for numerals and initializations, count one syllable for each symbol. For example, *1945* is four syllables, *IRA* is three syllables, and *&* is one syllable.

Even if students know how to use trade books, textbooks, and reference books effectively, they may not have an opportunity to do so because they do not know how to locate the books in the library. At the beginning of this chapter, Ms. Jamison gave a library assignment before assessing the students' ability to use the library facilities to best advantage. She at last recognized her error and began to try to rectify her mistake, but she had already essentially wasted a period of instruction which was irretrievable. A check-up on library knowledge *before* the class went to the library would have been in order. Areas in which students showed weaknesses—library arrangement (location of books and magazines, reference materials, and card catalog), Dewey Decimal System or Library of Congress System of shelving books, and use of the card catalog—could then have been given attention before the trip to the library or in the inital portion of the trip.

You could plan cooperatively with the librarian to do initial teaching or to review library skills. The librarian may have access to teaching aids of which you are not aware, such as special mini-card catalogs, posters on catalog cards and/or such topics as the Dewey Decimal System, films, or filmstrips. In addition, his or her high degree of familiarity with the library may have made the librarian aware of potential uses you have overlooked. Consider the librarian, as all support personnel in the school, an ally in your teaching endeavor.

Organizational skills are highly important to students working on reports for content area classes. These skills include notetaking,

*Students at all levels must learn to master basic study skills.*

outlining, and summarizing, and are most easily taught in conjunction with an assignment on report writing, since students can best see the need to learn them at such a time. These skills are usually not taught before the intermediate grade levels, but ordinarily receive attention then. Still, many secondary students have not mastered them, perhaps because they were never taught in a functional setting. If you are teaching above the primary level, you need to assess students' mastery of these skills and help them acquire the skills if they have not yet done so. Primary teachers lay the groundwork for these skills, especially outlining, when they help students determine main ideas and supporting details. They lay the groundwork for notetaking and summarizing especially, when they encourage students to paraphrase what they have just read.

A major goal of content area learning is retention of subject matter. Teaching students how to study so they will retain what they read will be an important task for you. Here are some ways you can help students retain content, coded as to the appropriate levels: A = all levels, primary through secondary grades; I = intermediate grades; and S = secondary grades.

1   Have class discussions over all material you assign students to read. (A)
2   Encourage students to evaluate what they read. (A)
3   Give the students an opportunity to apply what they have read. (A)
4   Use audiovisual aids to illuminate concepts presented in the reading. (A)
5   Prepare students before they read by giving them background about the topic. (A)
6   Encourage students to picture in their minds what the author is trying to describe. (A)
7   Have students retell what they have read, in their own words, to you or a classmate soon after they finish reading. (A)
8   Always give students purposes for which to read. Never just say, "Read pages 2–9 for tomorrow." Tell them what to look for as they read. (A)
9   Teach your students a study method such as SQ3R[1], SQRQCQ[2], EVOKER,[3] REAP,[4] or PANORAMA.[5] (I, S)

[1]Francis P. Robinson, *Effective Study*, (New York: Harper & Row, 1961), chapter 2.
[2]Leo Fay, "Reading Study Skills: Math and Science," in *Reading and Inquiry*, J. Allen Figurel, ed. (Newark, Del. International Reading Association, 1965): 93–94.
[3]Walter Pauk, "On Scholarship: Advice to High School Students," *The Reading Teacher*, 17 (November 1963): 73–78.
[4]Marilyn G. Eanet and Anthony V. Manzo, "REAP—A Strategy for Improving Reading/ Writing/Study Skills," *Journal of Reading*, 19 (May 1976): 647–52.
[5]Peter Edwards, "Panorama: A Study Technique," *Journal of Reading*, 17 (November 1973): 132–35.

10   Encourage students to analyze the author's organization. (I, S)

11   Have students take notes on the main points in the material. (I, S)

12   Have students write summaries of the material after they finish reading. (I, S)

13   Hold periodic classroom review sessions on material that has been read.(A)

14   Prepare study guides for students to use as they read the material. (I, S)

15   Have students apply mnemonic devices to aid memory. (I, S)

16   Give students immediate feedback on correctness of oral or written responses to the reading material. (A)

17   Encourage students to classify the ideas in their reading material. (A)

These techniques will bolster the students' retention.

Another useful study skill your students need to acquire is the ability to adjust reading rate to fit the purpose for reading and the material. Many students have never had help in developing flexibility in reading rates. As a result, they frequently read everything at the same rate. Some employ a painstakingly slow rate that is inappropriate for reading light fiction, for locating isolated facts, or for seeking only general themes. Others use a rapid rate that is inappropriate for reading mathematics story problems, science experiments they must perform, or any type of intensive study material.

Make the students aware that good readers use many different reading rates, matching the rate to the purpose for reading and the nature of the material. Offer them opportunities to practice varying reading rates in the classroom; for example, have them scan for isolated details, skim for main ideas, and read slowly and carefully to solve a mathematics problem.

The ability to interpret graphic aids in content materials is another vital area. Students need to be able to interpret maps, graphs, tables, and illustrations in their textbooks, or they will not gain all they should from the content. Students tend to skip graphic aids when they encounter them in textbooks, perhaps because their teachers have never explained the informative nature of these aids, or because they have never been shown *how* to interpret these aids. We have already mentioned the skills necessary for reading maps. When reading graphs, students must be able to decide what is being compared, the units of measure involved, and how to extract specific information from the graph and make overall generalizations based on the graph. When reading tables, students must be able to decide what type of information is included, the meanings of the columns and rows, and how to extract specific facts. Illustrations such as diagrams present problems because of their abstract nature, distortion of reality, and oversimplification. Realistic illustrations may be looked upon as decorative features, when they really convey information.

You should assess the students' ability to deal with graphic aids and help them interpret those that present problems. Students at all levels need appropriate instruction in these important skills.

You may also find that your students have very poor study habits. They must learn that study should take place in an environment that is as distraction-free as possible (many may not have a distraction-free option), that they should gather their study tools (books, pens, pencils, paper) *before* they start to study, that they should budget their study time so that nothing is left out, and that they should set aside a time for study that they will not be constantly relinquishing to other activities. Those who just do not have a good place to study at home should be encouraged to use school study periods as effectively as possible. Students who change classes should learn to gather all necessary study materials before they go to the study hall period, to have all homework assignments written down to take with them, and to concentrate on homework tasks during the study period rather than visit with other students.

## Functional Learning

You will find that some students come to school eager to learn. They look up to their teachers and are willing to try whatever the teachers ask them to do. Other students, however, seem uninterested in participating in classroom activities. One boy surprised his student teacher by refusing to participate in a number of planned activities. When the student teacher asked him to "cooperate please," the boy asked, "What's in it for me?" Like this boy, many children do not see the relevance of the instruction they receive in school to their lives, and therefore they may be difficult or indifferent students. You can make a difference by showing them the need they have for what you are teaching. Remember that not all your students will go to college, and many have no understanding of long-term goals. They will not necessarily see the relevance of something simply because you tell them they will need it in the distant future; instead, show them how your instruction relates to the here and now.

For example, explain that reading allows you to tell what is in foods you buy at the store, so that you get what you really want. It allows you to read advertisements to find out where to shop for things you want; to read danger signs and traffic signs for your protection; to read about current news or results of sports events; to read for entertainment; and to read directions for making things, from model airplanes to cakes.

Mathematics allows you to handle your money wisely (to buy things and make change); to measure things; to divide possessions fairly; to figure interest on loans or savings; to determine the area of a field or room; and to figure cash discounts on purchases.

Science helps you understand how to care for plants, how automobiles and motorcycles run, how to interpret weather signs and read newspaper weather maps, how to read thermometers and other scientific instruments, and how the wiring in your house works.

English helps you communicate with others clearly in oral and written form, and it helps you find enjoyment through literature.

Social studies helps you understand how your government works and what you must do to be a good citizen. It also helps you understand things that constantly affect your life, such as taxes and inflation.

Physical education helps you keep your body fit and teaches you how to participate in a variety of sports.

Business courses give you skills such as typing (for school papers) and bookkeeping (for keeping track of money).

Shop courses help you learn to make useful objects—tables, racks, etc.

Auto mechanics courses help you learn to repair automobiles (yours and others').

Home economics teaches you to sew, prepare food, plan healthy meals, and keep a budget.

Learning can also be made more meaningful to students if it is not merely textbook-centered. Here are some different approaches.

1   Use the newspaper to teach reading, current events, propaganda detection, consumer skills, mathematics (with grocery and other advertisements), home economics (shopping for food and clothing), business (stock market analysis, job market as indicated by classified advertisements), and weather analysis.

2   Use television advertisements and political speeches when studying propaganda.

3   Use restaurant menus when teaching reading, mathematics, and home economics.

4   Use directions for making things to teach reading and vocational/technical subjects.

5   Use medicine labels to teach reading, mathematics, and health.

6   Use catalogs to teach reading, mathematics, and home economics.

If, in the course of their school day, students learn to find and use information in the newspaper, intelligently analyze what they see on television, read restaurant menus effectively, read and follow directions accurately, take medicine safely, and order goods they want, they will be more active participants in the learning process, because learning becomes more important to them personally. It is up to you to see that students make this connection between learning and everyday living.

# Extracurricular Activities

In some elementary schools and most secondary schools, students participate voluntarily in a number of school-sponsored activities. School sponsorship makes faculty involvement in these activities important. As a student teacher, you will probably be involved in the extracurricular activities in which your cooperating teacher is involved. You may, however, be asked to help with other extracurricular activities in which you have special interest and/or expertise. You may be asked to do something as simple as taking tickets or chaperoning a dance or something as difficult as directing a dramatization or coaching defensive ends.

Typical extracurricular activities are membership in clubs (science, photography, mathematics, drama, foreign language, community action, future teachers, future homemakers, etc.); working on school publications (magazines, annuals, newspapers); athletic teams (football, basketball, baseball, track, golf, volleyball, wrestling); musical groups (marching band, jazz band, orchestra, chorus); and scholastic honor societies (Beta Club, Quill and Scroll, National Honor Society). School-sponsored dances, carnivals, and festivals also qualify as extracurricular activities. This variety gives you a wide range from which to choose if you are asked to participate. The list of possibilities for after-hours involvement seems endless. You may help with science fair projects or work at a book fair; you may judge a storytelling contest or a debate; you may coach intramural sports, accompany students on special trips, mend costumes for a play, paint sets, move band equipment, organize the safety patrol—the list goes on and on. Students involved in extracurricular activities are usually highly motivated in the chosen area and therefore make the sessions enjoyable, so go ahead and give a chosen activity a try.

You may think of extracurricular activities as just another intrusion on your already vanishing free time, or you may remember that extracurricular activities were really important to you when you were your students' age. Contribute some time and effort to give your students some valuable experiences.

If your school has a handbook, read the section on extracurricular activities. Find out what roles faculty members play and the rules and restrictions for each activity. Then you will be able to choose activities or assist with assigned activities knowledgeably.

## Student Supervision

Chances are that you will also share your cooperating teacher's assigned supervisory responsibilities, such as cafeteria, hall, or bus duty, or keeping detention hall. Each school has its own policies regarding supervision of students waiting for buses, moving through hallways, eating in the cafeteria, and working in study or detention halls. Observe your cooperating teacher closely, and learn the ground rules for these situations, so you can handle them properly.

Supervision of students in the lunchroom is more likely to be a responsibility of an elementary or middle school teacher than of a secondary school teacher. If you are lucky, even at the lower levels, cafeteria supervision will be handled by staff members or volunteers so you can enjoy a quiet, uninterrupted meal.

A nutritious and relaxing lunch is important for helping students make it through the afternoon. Routine procedures are usually followed, so students know where to sit and what rules are in effect. If you are helping to supervise students in the cafeteria, you need to know what to do if any of these situations arise: the noise level gets too high; a student drops a tray; a child breaks a thermos; a slow eater doesn't finish in time; a student loses a lunch box or bag; a student forgets lunch money; students want to trade food; someone offers you a sandwich. If there is no policy concerning such matters, keep in mind that students need to eat a nourishing lunch in an atmosphere that enables them to digest it!

*By permission of Johnny Hart and Field Enterprises, Inc.

Bus and hall duty may exist in your school. Hall duty simply means that teachers are stationed in school corridors when students change classes to keep an orderly flow of traffic, direct new students, and help with problems. In some schools, bus duty is handled by each student's homeroom teacher; in other schools, students assemble in a central location, where they are supervised by one or more teachers. If you must assist your cooperating teacher in supervising groups of students from different classes, you might suggest ideas for passing the time constructively. Students may be asked to bring a library book to read, or you can read to them, show films, lead singing, or let them play guessing games.

Some secondary teachers may have responsibility for supervising a study hall during a period when they do not have a scheduled class. The study hall provides a place for students to study during free periods, and the study hall supervisor is generally expected to maintain a quiet, orderly study environment. A student will sometimes ask for help with an assignment. If your school has formal study halls, find out what rules the students are expected to obey and the responsibilities of the supervisor. You may be called upon to supervise a study hall with your cooperating teacher or alone.

Some schools still use detention after school hours as punishment for minor infractions of school rules. Generally in the elementary grades, each teacher supervises the students he or she has detained. In secondary schools, there are often detention halls to which all misbehaving students are sent. Responsibility for supervising detention halls usually rotates among the teachers. If your cooperating teacher is assigned to supervise detention hall, you will probably be expected to help check the roll, hand out special assignments to be completed as a condition of the detention, take up any special detention assignments, and monitor the students' behavior. Many schools do not use detention as a means of punishment because of bus schedules, interference with extracurricular activities, and interference with after-school employment.

## Discussion Questions

1  What is the most appropriate time to teach outlining, summarizing, and notetaking skills? Why do you think so?

2  How can you and the librarian cooperate to ensure that students master important library skills?

3  How can inappropriate and inflexible reading rates inhibit students' learning? What can you do to change these habits?

4  What study methods might you use in your grade or discipline? Why would these methods be appropriate?

5  What kinds of graphic aids are most common in your content area or areas?

6  Why should you bother to include functional learning activities in the curriculum? How can such activities fit into your class instruction?

7  What can you do to help with extracurricular activities? What have you done so far? Can you think of a way to help that no one else is doing? What is it?

8   What special talents or interests do you have that could help you with your involvement with extracurricular activities?

9   Why is it important to find out the ground rules related to supervisory tasks *before* you attempt them? What could happen if you fail to do so?

## Selected References

Burns, Paul C., and Betty D. Roe. *Teaching Reading in Today's Elementary Schools.* Boston: Houghton Mifflin, 1980.

Drayer, Adam M. *Problems in Middle and High School Teaching.* Boston: Allyn and Bacon, 1979.

DuBey, Robert E., et al. *A Performance-Based Guide to Student Teaching.* Danville, Ill.: Interstate, 1975.

Edwards, Peter. "Panorama: A Study Technique," *Journal of Reading,* 17 (November 1973), pp. 132–35.

Eanet, Marilyn G., and Anthony V. Manzo. "REAP—A Strategy for Improving Reading/Writing/Study Skills," *Journal of Reading,* 19 (May 1976), pp. 647–52.

Fay, Leo. "Reading Study Skills: Math and Science," in *Reading and Inquiry,* ed. J. Allen Figurel. Newark, Del.: International Reading Association, 1965, pp. 93–94.

Johnson, James A., and Roger C. Anderson. *Secondary Student Teaching: Readings.* Glenview, Ill.: Scott, Foresman, 1971.

Pauk, Walter. "On Scholarship: Advice to High School Students," *The Reading Teacher,* 17 (November 1963), pp. 73–78.

Robinson, Francis P. *Effective Study.* New York: Harper and Row, 1961.

Roe, Betty D., et al. *Secondary School Reading Instruction: The Content Areas.* Boston: Houghton Mifflin, 1983.

# 8
# *The Exceptional Student*

It probably comes as no surprise that you will find all types of students when you enter the classroom. Taking one characteristic as an example, students will range in ability from highly intellectual to slow learning. There may also be learning disabled, culturally different, and physically disabled students. With mainstreaming, many kinds of students will need your consideration. It will take your best efforts to challenge, help, provide for, and understand these youngsters.

---

In January, Carlos, an eight-year-old boy from Cuba, enters a mostly white, middle class school in a suburb of a northern city. Carlos is a shy child who knows only a little English. Mrs. Hearn, the cooperating teacher, and Miss Vaughn, the student teacher, encourage the class to accept Carlos and try to make him feel part of the class. Mr. Ray is a student teacher in the fourth grade.

Mrs. Hearn: Boys and girls, I'd like you to meet Carlos. He has just moved here from Cuba and I want you to make him feel welcome. Carlos, we're glad to have you. Here is your seat, right between Nancy and John.

John (at recess): Come on, Carlos. We're going to play kickball. You can be on my team.

Carlos: No. I no play ball.

Terry: We'll show you how. It's easy.

Carlos: No. (He moves away from the boys and stands off by himself.)

John: Suit yourself. Let's get started.

Hank (at lunch): Did you bring your lunch, Carlos?

Carlos: Sí.

Hank: Here, you can eat at our table.

Carlos: No. I eat over here. Myself.

Hank: O.K. Whatever you say.

Miss Vaughn (one week later): Mrs. Hearn, I'm worried about Carlos. I think the class tried to make him feel welcome at first, but now the children ignore him. He just stays by himself and looks so sad and lonely. We should be able to do something.

Mrs. Hearn: I'm concerned about him too, but I don't know what to do. I've talked to some of the children about him and they say he never wants to do anything with them, so they don't ask him any more.

Miss Vaughn: What's even worse is that some of them are beginning to laugh at him and make fun of him because he brings unusual food to lunch and acts strangely sometimes. I'll try talking to him about it and see how he feels.

Miss Vaughn: Carlos, how are you getting along?

Carlos: Not so good. Boys and girls, they no like me.

Miss Vaughn: Sure, they like you. They want you to be their friend.

Carlos: No. I no like them.

Miss Vaughn (to herself): I didn't get any place with him. I've just got to think of something.

Miss Vaughn (a few days later): Mr. Ray, aren't you teaching a unit on Mexico?

Mr. Ray: I'm right in the middle of it.

Miss Vaughn: How would you like your children to learn some Spanish words?

Mr. Ray: That'd be great. What do you have in mind?

Miss Vaughn: I've got this little guy from Cuba who is having a really hard time in our class. I thought maybe you could ask him to help you with some Spanish words.

Mr. Ray: Sure. Could he come over tomorrow about 10:30?

Miss Vaughn: That'll be fine.

Miss Vaughn (back in her own class): Carlos, the class down the hall is learning about Mexico. The teacher can't speak Spanish. Could you go there and tell them some Spanish words tomorrow?

Carlos: I don't know. They no like me either.

Miss Vaughn: They'll like you. Don't worry about that. Anyway, you know Spanish words and they don't know any.

Carlos: Well, maybe.

Mr. Ray (next day at 10:30): Class, this is Carlos from Mrs. Hearn's room. He knows how to speak Spanish and is going to tell us some words we need to know.

Jean: Terrific! I'm working on a scrapbook. I can put in some Spanish words. Carlos, how do you say *family* in Spanish? How about *dinner*? And *school*?

Barry: Can you teach us how to count in Spanish?

Elaine: Say something to us in Spanish.

Mr. Ray: Whoa. Wait a minute. Give Carlos a chance to answer. Carlos, can you tell Jean the words she wants to know first?

Carlos (beginning very cautiously): Sí. Word for *family* is *familia*. What else you want to know? (Carlos answers more questions, gradually builds confidence, then seems eager to answer questions about Spanish.)

Mr. Ray: That's great, Carlos. You've helped us a lot. Maybe you can come back again.

Carlos (with a big grin): Sí. I come back.

Mr. Ray (that afternoon): Thanks, Miss Vaughn. Having Carlos come was really good for my class.

Miss Vaughn: It seemed to help Carlos, too.

John (three days later): Hey, Carlos. I hear you've been teaching the kids down the hall to speak Spanish. How about teaching us?

Carlos: Sí. I teach you. What you want to know?

Terry: I know. You teach us some Spanish and we'll teach you how to play kickball. Is it a deal?

Carlos: O.K. Now we go play ball. You show me. O.K.? Then I teach you Spanish.

1  Why do you think Carlos had trouble getting along with the boys and girls?
2  What are some indications that he is beginning to feel more comfortable in his new school?
3  Why did Miss Vaughn's idea about having Carlos teach Spanish to a group of children seem to help him when other attempts to help had failed?
4  Can you think of other plans that might have helped Carlos adjust to his new class?

## Challenging the Gifted Student

Gifted students often progress academically one and a fourth (or more) years within one calendar year, compared to the average student who shows one year of academic growth each year. As a student teacher, you should be aware that there are both "normal" achievers and underachievers among the gifted; they do not always live up to their potential. Usually, gifted students possess some of these characteristics:

1  An interest in books and reading
2  Large vocabularies and ability to express themselves verbally in a mature style

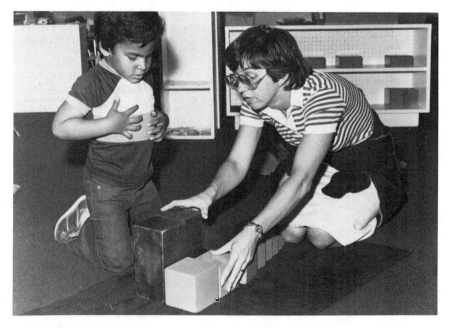

*Even gifted children need to begin by working with concrete objects.*

3　A curiosity to learn, with long attention span
4　A high level of abstract thinking
5　A wide range of interests

Gifted students have the same needs as other students in terms of acceptance, achievement, and interaction with others. They need the same basic academic tools as others, but to a different degree and at different times. While gifted students are able to direct many of their own activities, some teacher direction is needed.

Within the school program, you will find many opportunities to attend to the special needs of gifted students. These are some suggested instructional procedures:

1　Make use of trade (library) books in the program.
2　Develop units of work that provide opportunity for in-depth and long-term activities, as well as library research.
3　Utilize special tables and bulletin boards for interesting and challenging problems, puzzles, worksheets, etc.
4　Use special enrichment materials appropriate to the content areas.
5　Encourage oral and written reports on topics under discussion and related topics.
6　Provide opportunity for participation in special clubs or groups designed to challenge gifted students.

Marty Williams describes her recent experiences in teaching some gifted students.

---

## MATH WIZARD: A Course in Informal Geometry

During the summer, I taught a mini-course in informal geometry geared to gifted children in grades 4–6, as part of the Summer Enrichment Program. Since geometry is an indispensable tool of mankind, used constantly in many professions—by the builder, the engineer, the navigator, the astronomer, the artist, the musician, the inventor—gifted children should learn this material to have a solid foundation on which to build more complex geometric skills as their education progresses.

Some of the concepts taught and investigated in this mini-course were the three basic shapes; the ideas of proximity, separation, order, and enclosure; the relationship of sides and angles; the ideas of congruent, similar, and different; the Platonic Solids and Euler's Formula; and the visualization and creation of two- and three-dimensional objects.

Gifted children need to begin by working with concrete objects, even though they are quick to perceive the abstract. From concrete objects they can move to semiconcrete or pictorial representations and then to abstract thinking.

Integration of mind and body is also essential for the gifted student, and with this in mind, I made it a point to involve the students physically with the concepts we studied. For example, they used their and/or other students' bodies to demonstrate the ideas of proximity, separation, order, and enclosure, and we had a relay race as a follow-up to the section of visualization and creation of two- and three-dimensional objects.

Every few days we had a "Tricky Puzzle"—a mathematical brainteaser—to serve as a follow-up of the lesson. These puzzles also served as a lesson carry-over to get things rolling the next day by having the students present their solutions of the previous day's puzzle. "Tricky Puzzle" time was definitely the highlight of the day!

As the culminating experience for this mini-course, the students created box sculptures from "garbage" they had been collecting since the first day of class. The only criteria were that they have an "idea" from which they were constructing, and be able to name the geometric shapes involved in their sculpture. This served as a good way to wrap up the course and ended things on a pleasant note.

---

As a student teacher, you should begin collecting a file of creative and unusual ideas for use with gifted students. Here's one with which to start your file.

> File Card for Able Students
> ### BOX O' BALLADS
>
> Have a copy available of Carl Sandburg's book, *The American Songbag*. Provide time and materials for students to do one of the following related projects after discussing and enjoying some of the ballads.
>
> (a) Draw a panorama representing one of the cowboy ballads.
> (b) Write some imaginative ballads of your own about the pioneers or the railroad workers.
> (c) Create a shoe-box diorama representing one of the lumberjack ballads.
> (d) Plan and present a short creative drama representing the ballad of your choice.

Although our discussion has centered on intellectually gifted students, do not overlook other types of talented students. These other talented students may be:

Students who engage in divergent thinking, differing from the "normal," "expected," or "standard;"
Students with leadership abilities;
Students with visual and performing arts ability; and
Students with specific ability, such as psychomotor ability.

All such students have special needs and can profit from specially planned activities beyond those normally provided by the standard school program.

Recognition of various types of talents cannot be made only on the basis of intelligence or achievement tests. Additionally, other classroom options should be available, such as special programs outside the classroom, use of resource teachers, mini-courses, summer programs, independent study, advanced placement, community programs, and study groups. For example, your school system may have a special teacher for the gifted and talented, who can give you a great deal of help with materials and program planning. As the student teacher, you will need to enjoy learning from gifted students, to respect their ideas, to encourage a wide range of classroom activities (from independent study to much group interaction) as a way of individualizing instruction—and perhaps, above all, you will need a sense of humor. How helpful it is to admit mistakes and laugh at oneself!

# Helping the Slow Learner

A primary characteristic of slow learners is that they do not learn as readily as do others of the same chronological age. You will have to make some adjustments for instructing students of low-normal ability such as:

1  Paying careful attention to readiness for any task
2  Moving more slowly and gradually than with the normal learning student
3  Taking opportunities to develop ideas with concrete, manipulative, and visual materials
4  Using simplified materials that do not demand too much at one time from the student
5  Varying activities because of short attention span
6  Relating learnings to familiar experiences (school, lunchroom, gymnasium, current events, community projects, holiday celebrations, etc.)
7  Providing for large amounts of practice to fix new learnings
8  Reviewing with closely spaced, cumulative exercises to encourage retention

To develop and maintain positive attitudes toward school subjects, it is necessary to provide slow learners with situations that relate to their experiences and to the real world in which they live. For example, where students have had experience with money, many of the computational operations can be approached in terms of money:

$$
\begin{array}{ccccc}
42 & & 4 \text{ dimes} + 2 \text{ cents} & & 3 \text{ dimes} + 12 \text{ cents} \\
\underline{-18} & \rightarrow & \underline{-1 \text{ dime} \; + 8 \text{ cents}} & \rightarrow & \underline{-1 \text{ dime} \; + \; 8 \text{ cents}} \\
& & & & 2 \text{ dimes} + \; 4 \text{ cents}
\end{array}
$$

Similarly many student teachers have found ways to present subject matter concepts through newspapers and magazines, "how to" books, telephone directories, mail order catalogues, TV guides, scouting manuals, menus, greeting cards, hobby materials, food and medicine containers, road signs, and nature guide materials. If a slow learner is having difficulty with a particular concept or idea, you may need to utilize corrective exercises and materials.

If You're Still Having Trouble With These Words . . .

"That's my son."

"The sun is high in the sky."

sun
A

son
B

1. Do sun and son sound alike?
2. What is different in the spelling of the words?
3. Draw a picture to fit these sentences.
   a. The sun is shining.
   b. Mother is with her son.
4. Write a sentence using the word sun. Then write a sentence using the word son.

Directions: Circle the picture word that fits these sentences.
5. The _____ was behind the clouds.
       (sun, son)
6. Bill is Mr. Brown's _____.
              (sun, son)

# Providing for the Learning Disabled Student

Students with a learning disability usually demonstrate a significant discrepancy between intellectual potential and actual level of performance. They exhibit behaviors that point to an impairment, usually involving perceptual difficulties. In other words, there is difficulty in processing auditory and visual sensations or stimuli, resulting in a faulty interpretive response. On the other hand, these students are not below average in intelligence, visually or hearing impaired, or "educationally deprived."

Students with learning disabilities usually profit most from concrete, manipulative materials and direct, hands-on experiences, depending upon the specific learning disability. These are areas in which learning disabilities can occur:

Memory—failure to remember newly presented information

Visual-auditory discrimination—failure to see or hear likenesses and differences

Visual-auditory association—failure to associate visual and auditory stimuli

Perceptual-motor skills—failure of visual, auditory, tactile, and kinesthetic channels to interact appropriately with motor activity

Spatial orientation—failure to master temporal, spatial, and orientation factors

Verbal expression—failure to express ideas, communicate, or request information

Closure-generalization—failure to extrapolate beyond an established set of data or information

Attending—failure to attend selectively or focus upon tasks

General guidelines for working with learning disabled students usually involve ideas relating to attention span, hyperactivity, and related organizational patterns. These are useful ideas:

1   Increase attention span by removing distractions, including any materials other than those necessary for the assigned task.
2   Teach the student how to organize his or her desk, belongings, and materials.
3   Try to improve one behavior at a time, rewarding appropriate behavior, and involving the student in recording behavioral progress. Discuss appropriate ways to expend extra energy.
4   Carefully structure the learning environment and tasks with specific standards, limits, and rules.
5   Consistency is an important ingredient—in rules, di-

rections, and the like. Make consequences for rule infractions clear.

6   Assign one task at a time, at first using a step-by-step procedure. This means short, sequential assignments, with breaks between tasks.

7   Use a variety of media to present content (films, tapes, printed material, etc.)

8   Utilize active methods (simulation games, experiments, role playing, etc.) in the instructional strategies.

9   Employ materials for differing learning patterns (pictures, tapes, concrete objects).

10  Prepare peers or partners to serve as tutors in certain skills or content areas.

Here are some examples of instructional procedures in mathematics for certain types of learning disabled students.

**Instructional Strategy 10.1.1: Use structured algorithms**   Some of the historical computational procedures help to circumvent errors due to misplacement of digits within an algorithm, reversed sequence of procedure, or messy writing.

**Instructional Strategy 10.1.2: Use hand calculator**   For those students displaying expressive disabilities, such as inability to say or write an answer on demand, use of a hand calculator allows circumvention of the problem. This is also a good drill activity—every time the child punches the keys and thinks "three plus five equals eight," he is practicing this basic fact.

**Instructional Strategy 10.1.3: Restrict number of computations**   Some children with specific learning disabilities tend to expend a great deal of energy when engaged in fine motor activities—for example, writing computations. Such children may produce an excess of saliva and/or show a noticeable degree of fatigue half-way through such activities. Therefore, give them only enough computations to permit them to demonstrate their knowledge. Three to five computations within an operation should be sufficient and should control for guessing or random errors. A page of 20 or more computations is punishing.

**Instructional Strategy 10.1.4: Develop a time schedule for completing a task**   Some children with specific learning disabilities seem to be in a constant battle with time. They often wait until the last minute to study for an exam; they attempt to write a term paper the night before it is due; or they are unable to pace themselves during a task, taking too much time on some items and not enough on others—or else they don't finish at all. The teacher can help such children write a time schedule and can remind them when time sequences are up. A fading-out technique, utilizing the child's own attention to the end of a predetermined sequence for a portion of a task, builds independent pacing by the child. By teaming tasks and tests, a peer can be used to help such a child with his pacing schedule.

**Instructional Strategy 10.1.5: Use tactile experiences**
The child's ability to use symbols—the digits, the operation signs, the equality and inequality signs and the set operations signs, all of which are arbitrary associations—is affected by visual perception disabilities. To compute basic facts, a child must have a working knowledge of these symbols. Some children need practice with tactile experiences (tracing clay or cutout symbols) in order to produce these symbols correctly.

**Instructional Strategy 10.1.6: Use fixed representation of number** Using fixed examples of a number—dominoes, playing cards, or pictures of objects—helps to circumvent visual perception disabilities. The physical appearance or spatial arrangement of objects used can make the number property of equivalent sets hard to detect.[1]

Practices frequently used with learning disabled students at the secondary level include: generalized learning strategies (such as notetaking, test taking, outlining, and study skills); greater emphasis on multimedia presentation of material (films, tapes, transparencies, etc.) than upon lecture/textbook; and provision for alternatives (such as oral instead of written examinations).

Other secondary school programs focus instruction for the learning disabled on practical skill applications: for example, planning a budget; filling out job applications; learning social skills needed in family and job situations; and using independent living skills, such as food preparation, home management, personal hygiene, and safety. Still other functional curriculum programs incorporate career education, prevocational study, specific vocational skills, and/or on-the-job training in certain areas.

# Understanding the Needs of the Culturally Different Student

Many students may be different in terms of cultural background—students who are not native to the United States, or students from the inner city or from rural areas, such as Southern Appalachia. Teachers should be aware of concerns related to culturally different students.

[1]Fredricka K. Reisman and Samuel H. Kauffman, *Teaching Mathematics to Children with Special Needs* (Columbus, Ohio: Charles E. Merrill, 1980), pp. 178, 181–82.

### Ethnicity

Ethnicity refers to groups of people who are unique in ancestry, language, religion, physical characteristics, or customs. Ethnic groups exist within a larger, dominant society. Ethnic groups with which you may deal are the Chicanos, blacks, and Native Americans.

In a pluralistic society, ethnic or minority groups continue to practice aspects of their cultural heritage while also observing the customs of the dominant society. Pluralism is a compromise between segregation and assimilation. Under segregation, there is complete separation between the dominant society and minority groups. Assimilation is the total absorption of a minority group by the dominant society.

Our nation was founded on the principle of assimilation—the melting pot. Ethnic differences were supposedly combined to create a superior, unified nation with common traditions, purposes, values, and responsibilities. Each immigrant group gave up much of its individuality to become part of the great American society. An opposing point of view, the salad bowl or cultural pluralism concept, permits the various ethnic groups to retain different elements of their cultures while living in America.

Students who speak no English are entering the United States from Cuba, Viet Nam, and elsewhere. Some states have laws that require school districts to employ teachers who can speak the student's language. Students who only speak other languages need your help in learning English as quickly as possible in order to benefit from the educational experiences offered in an English-speaking school. As they learn English, they may also help the other students to learn a second language, as Carlos did in his school.

In certain geographic areas, you will need to recognize the importance of the Bilingual Education Act. This act has been interpreted to require that a school district offer a bilingual program (education in two languages, one of which is English) where there are a number of limited English-speaking students. A well-known part of bilingual education is English as a Second Language (ESL). ESL focuses first upon helping students understand and speak oral English, then to read and comprehend written English, and finally to write in English.

Multiethnic or multicultural education is a way of observing the rights of various cultural groups within the schools. It "is concerned with modifying the total educational environment, so that the environment is more reflective of the ethnic diversity of American Society."[2] Supporters of multicultural education believe that material related to ethnic groups should be an integral part of the curriculum, beginning in kindergarten and continuing throughout

[2]James Banks, *Multiethnic Education: Practice and Promises* (Bloomington, Ind.: Phi Delta Kappa Educational Foundation, 1977), p. 21.

the grades. In social studies, you may want to have students study world events from different perspectives. Instead of having them consider only the American point of view, you can lead them to consider also how Mexicans, Asians, or Arabs view international events. In literature, you can have them read stories with varied ethnic and racial content from the preprimer level onward. You can also incorporate multiethnic themes into the art, music, science, mathematics, and physical education portions of the curriculum.

A much less effective approach to multiethnic education that some teachers take is the "heroes and holidays" observance. Two or three times during the year, certain periods are set aside to celebrate a particular event related to an ethnic group. For example, at Thanksgiving children may dress as Indians and construct teepees, or in observance of Martin Luther King's death, students might prepare a "soul food" meal. Such observances do little to promote understanding of racial and ethnic groups, but rather reinforce misconceptions and stereotypes. As a student teacher, you should consider taking a more comprehensive approach to multiethnic education.

Multiethnic content in the curriculum can be more meaningful than material about Anglo-Saxons for students of particular ethnic groups. Your black students will be more interested in reading stories about Harriet Tubman's heroic efforts to free slaves or George Washington Carver's ingenuity in finding ways to use peanuts than about many situations involving no black characters. When students have greater interest in reading material, they are likely to develop more skill in reading. The same principle applies to other subject matter areas where students work with information pertaining to their own ethnic groups.

One aspect of multicultural education does not deal with the curriculum itself, but with attitudes toward ethnic groups. Research has shown that many preschool children are already aware of racial differences. They have acquired negative impressions of various races from their parents, television, and movies. These negative attitudes become more widespread as students progress through school, and are damaging to students of all groups, but particularly to students who belong to those groups that are viewed negatively. These students often find the school environment hostile, unaccepting, and damaging to their self-concepts.

You need to be sensitive to the special needs of the minority students in your classroom. In your student teaching, you need to be aware of ways to work with these students that take into consideration their needs and feelings. You should respect their ethnic and racial backgrounds. While some students have no problems with their ethnicity, others feel insecure and ill at ease in a different culture. You should respond in a helpful and constructive way to students with ethnic identity problems.

You also need to be conscious of ways to use multicultural content in your lessons. Keep in mind that multicultural education is not simply a matter of adding a bit of information about a minority group to your lessons now and then. It is a total commitment to presenting material from a global perspective that values the contributions and lifestyles of each ethnic group.

Although you may not mean to offend minority students, you may unconsciously reveal negative feelings toward them. Here are behaviors to avoid in working with minority students:

1  Assigning them a large number of menial tasks.
2  Using derogatory labels for different racial and ethnic groups.
3  Referring to students according to negative stereotypes.
4  Verbally or nonverbally expressing dislike or disapproval.
5  Becoming impatient when they misinterpret your questions or fail to respond as quickly as other students.
6  Ignoring them when they want your attention.
7  Being condescending toward them (appearing to be nice while actually feeling superior).
8  Avoiding physical closeness or actual contact.
9  Constantly criticizing their use of dialect.
10  Failing to give them opportunities for leadership.
11  Blaming the minority student when it is unclear who is at fault.

In your daily work with these students, you should be able to find many ways to encourage and support them. Expressing interest in what they are doing or granting them a special privilege for work well done are examples of ways to show that you care.

Several strategies can be used to encourage students to accept their peers who come from different racial or ethnic origins. Role playing helps students understand how it feels to be a member of a different ethnic group. Assigning children of different ethnic heritages to work together on a committee helps them realize that each member of the group can make an important contribution. You can create other situations in which problems can be solved only through the cooperation of each member of an ethnically-mixed group.

Culturally different students need to acquire the values and behavior essential for success in the dominant society while retaining important aspects of their own subcultures. While you cannot do much to further this concept in a short period of time, your awareness of cultural differences, your attitudes toward your students, and the focus of your lessons can make a difference.

# Mainstreamed Students

Because students who had previously been enrolled in special education classes are now being integrated into regular classes, you will probably be responsible for other exceptional students. This practice is referred to as "mainstreaming."

You should be familiar with the Education for All Handicapped Children Act of 1975 (Public Law 94–142).[3] These are some of its important points:

Handicapped students should be educated with nonhandicapped students to the extent possible.

Handicapped students, prior to mainstreaming, shall be tested with nondiscriminatory materials. The test should be printed in the student's native language, be valid, and be administered by appropriate personnel. The test must not reflect the student's impairment except where that particular factor is being measured by the test. No single test shall be used as the sole criterion for determining the program for a handicapped student.

On the basis of test materials and appropriate records, an evaluation is made by an "M-Team" (multidisciplinary team). The team is composed of the child's teacher, one or both of the child's parents, and a representative of the local education agency (other than the child's teacher). It may also include the child and additional professional personnel. The M-Team writes the Individual Education Program (IEP). Figure 8-1 is a sample IEP.

Due process must be observed in all evaluation and placement of the student. Parents (or guardians) must consent to formal evaluation, be informed of results, and be involved in developing the IEP. They have the right to examine records and to present complaints with respect to any matter related to evaluation or placement of the student. Additionally, the Buckley Amendment (Family Educational Rights and Privacy Act of 1974) prohibits the release of a student's records without parental consent and provides that all information be kept confidential.

One of the first steps is to become familiar with the IEP for the student. The IEP provides a synthesis of all assessment information, as well as classroom accommodations and instructional plans. The format will probably include items such as these:

1 A statement of the student's present levels of educational performance, including academic achievement, social adaptation, prevocational and vocational skills, psychomotor skills, and self-help skills.

[3]The following information is summarized from *Federal Register*, November 21, 1975, and *Federal Register*, August 23, 1977.

# Figure 8-1  Individual Education Plan*

## Checklist

|  |  |
|---|---|
| 9-1-77 | Referral by Louise Borden |
| 9-3-77 | Parents informed of rights; permission obtained for evaluation |
| 9-15-77 | Evaluation compiled |
| 9-16-77 | Parents contacted |
| 9-18-77 | Total committee meets and subcommittee assigned |
| 9-28-77 | IEP developed by subcommittee |
| 9-30-77 | IEP approved by subcommittee |

## Yearly Class Schedule

| | Time | Subject | Teacher |
|---|---|---|---|
| 1st semester | 8:30–9:20 | math | Franks |
| | 9:30–10:20 | language arts | Bambara (Resource) |
| | 10:30–11:20 | social studies | Bambara |
| | 11:30–12:20 | science | Franks |
| | | lunch | |
| | 1:10–2:00 | art | Shaw |
| | 2:10–3:00 | P.E. | King |
| 2nd semester | 8:30–9:20 | math | Franks |
| | 9:30–10:20 | language arts | Bambara (Resource) |
| | 10:30–11:20 | social studies | Bambara |
| | 11:30–12:20 | science | Franks |
| | | lunch | |
| | 1:10–2:00 | art | Shaw |
| | 2:10–3:00 | P.E. | King |

## Continuum of Services

| | Hours per week |
|---|---|
| Regular class | 20 hours |
| Resource teacher in regular classroom | 6 hours |
| Resource room | 4 hours |
| Reading specialist | |
| Speech/language therapist | |
| Counselor | |
| Special class | |
| Transition class | |
| Others: | |

## Committee Members

Mrs. Louise Borden

Teacher

Mrs. John Thomas (Sp. Ed. Coordinator)

Other LEA representative

Mrs. John Doe

Parents

Mrs. Mary Franks

Mrs. Joan Bambara

Mrs. Alice King

Date IEP initially approved
9-30-77

## Identification Information

Name  John Doe

School  Beecher Sixth Grade Center

Birthdate  5-15-65    Grade 6

Parents:
Name  Mr. and Mrs. John Doe

Address  1300 Johnson Street Raleigh, N.C.

Phone: Home  none    Office  932-8161

## Testing Information

| Test Name | Date Admin. | Interpretation |
|---|---|---|
| PIAT | 9-10-77 | spell—1.7, math—5.7, read recog—1. read comp—N.A., gen. info—6.3 |
| test of initial consonants (CRT) | 9-11-77 | knows eight out of twenty-one initial consonant sounds    total 2.0 |
| CRT Reading Checklist | 9-12-77 | oral comprehension—6th grade reading skills—primary level |
| Carolina Arith. Inventory (Time) | 9-2-77 | Level IV |
| Carolina Arith. Inventory (Number concepts) | 9-2-77 | Level IV |

## Health Information

Vision:  good

Hearing:  excellent

Physical:  good

Other:

Student's Name    John Doe

Subject Area    Reading

Level of Performance    primary reading recognition, 6th grade comprehension of oral material.

Teacher    Mrs. Bambara—resource teacher

ANNUAL GOALS:
1) John will successfully complete the primer level of the Bank Street Reading Series.
2) John will recognize and correctly say 90 new sight words.
3) John will master 14 initial consonants.

| | SEPTEMBER | OCTOBER | NOVEMBER | DECEMBER | JANUARY |
|---|---|---|---|---|---|
| OBJECTIVES | Referred | 1. Recognize and correctly state the sounds of the initial consonants b and f 100% of the time. | 1. Recognize and correctly state the sounds of the initial consonants s and m 100% of the time. | 1. Correctly recognize and state the sound of the initial consonant g 100% of the time. | 1. Review and correctly state the sounds of the initial consonants b, f, m, s, and g 100% of the time. |
| | | 2. Recognize and correctly say ten new sight words 100% of the time. | 2. Recognize and correctly say ten new sight words 100% of the time. | 2. Recognize and correctly say five new sight words 100% of the time. | 2. Recognize and correctly state the sound of the initial consonant h 100% of the time. |
| | | 3. Complete the first three stories of the primer, reading the material with 50% accuracy. | 3. Complete the next three stories in the primer, reading the material with 50% accuracy. | 3. Complete the next story in the primer, reading the material with 50% accuracy. | 3. Review and correctly say 25 previously learned sight words 100% of the time. |
| | | | | | 4. Recognize and correctly say five new sight words 100% of the time. |
| | | | | | 5. Review the previously read stories in the primer, reading the material with 60% accuracy. |

195

## Figure 8-1 (continued)

Student's Name   John Doe        Subject Area   Reading

Level of Performance  reading recognition, (1.2 PIAT) 6th grade comprehension of oral material (CRT).       Teacher   Mrs. Bambara—resource teacher

ANNUAL GOALS: 1) John will successfully complete the primer level of the Bank Street Basal Reading Series.

2) John will recognize and correctly say 90 new sight words.

3) John will master 14 initial consonants.

|  | FEBRUARY | MARCH | APRIL | MAY | JUNE |
|---|---|---|---|---|---|
| **OBJECTIVES** | 1. Recognize and correctly state the sounds of the initial consonants l and d 100% of the time.<br><br>2. Recognize and correctly say 15 new sight words 100% of the time.<br><br>3. Complete the next three stories in the primer, reading the material with 60% accuracy and mastering the skills that accompany the stories. | 1. Recognize and correctly state the sounds of the initial consonants r and w 100% of the time.<br><br>2. Recognize and correctly say 15 new sight words 100% of the time.<br><br>3. Complete the next three stories in the primer, reading the material with 60% accuracy and mastering the skills that accompany the stories. | 1. Recognize and correctly state the sounds of the initial consonants c and t 100% of the time.<br><br>2. Recognize and correctly say 15 new sight words 100% of the time.<br><br>3. Complete the next three stories in the primer, reading the material with 95% accuracy and mastering the skills that accompany the stories. | 1. Recognize and correctly state the sounds of the initial consonants n and y 100% of the time.<br><br>2. Recognize and correctly say 15 new sight words 100% of the time.<br><br>3. Complete the next three stories in the primer, reading the material with 95% accuracy and mastering the skills that accompany the stories. | Evaluation |
| **MATERIALS** | Bank Street Basal Reading Series, Hoffman Phonetic Reading Program, teacher-made materials | Bank Street Basal Reading Series, Hoffman Phonetic Reading Program, teacher-made materials | Bank Street Basal Reading Series, Hoffman Phonetic Reading Program, teacher-made materials | Bank Street Basal Reading Series, Hoffman Phonetic Reading Program, teacher-made materials |  |
| **AGENT** | regular teacher<br>resource teacher | regular teacher<br>resource teacher | regular teacher<br>resource teacher | regular teacher<br>resource teacher |  |
| **EVALUATION** | 1. information assessment<br>2. Criterion Referenced Test (CRT) | 1. informal assessment<br>2. CRT | 1. informal assessment<br>2. CRT | 1. informal assessment<br>2. CRT |  |

*Source: A.P. Turnbull, Bonne Strickland, and John C. Brantley, *Developing and Implementing Individualized Education Programs.* (Columbus, Ohio: Charles E. Merrill, 1978).

2 A specific statement describing the student's learning style.

3 A statement of annual goals describing the educational performance to be achieved by the end of the school year.

4 A statement of short-term instructional objectives, which must be measurable intermediate steps between present level of educational performance and annual goals.

5 A statement of specific educational services needed by the student (determined without regard to the availability of those services), including a description of all special education and related services necessary to meet the unique needs of the student, including the type of physical education program in which the child will participate and any special instructional media and materials needed to implement the individualized education program.

6 The date when those services will begin and length of time the services will be given.

7 A description of the extent to which the student will participate in regular education programs.

8 A justification for the type of educational placement the student will have.

9 A list of the individuals responsible for implementation of the individualized education program.

10 Objective criteria, evaluation procedures, and schedules for determining, on at least an annual basis, if the short-term instructional objectives are being achieved. (Annual and short-term goals must be revised at least annually.)

Figure 8.1 is a sample IEP.

The following ideas may be useful in teaching the mainstreamed student.

1 Build rapport with the handicapped student. Let the student know you are genuinely interested in seeing that he or she overcomes his or her difficulties. A comfortable, relaxed atmosphere also enhances rapport.

2 Formulate a plan for alleviating the difficulty as much as possible. Instruction must be tailored to meet the needs of the individual student. Skills to be taught must relate to the student's learning characteristics and potential. Different approaches will succeed with different students, so you must be flexible in your approaches and familiar with many different approaches.

3 Adjust the length of the instructional session to fit the

student's attention span. In fairly long sessions, you will need frequent changes of activities. Repeated drill may be necessary because of poor retention.

4   Identify the basic life skills and relate them to subject content. For example, in mathematics, note skills related to such everyday areas as these: newspaper advertisements; price tags; money values; calendar; road signs; road maps; recipes; timetables; measurement units; thermometers; clocks; sales slips; making change; budgeting money; planning meals; and personal checks.

5   The mainstreamed students' interests need to be utilized. Where a student is interested in a particular topic (hobby, game, sport, or the like), he will tend to put forth a great deal of effort to master a particular concept or skill that relates to the interest.

Help is available for classroom teachers who work with mainstreamed students. Work closely with the special education teacher and other personnel to maximize the student's potential without duplication of efforts. A paraprofessional (such as a teacher aide) may be available. Peers may act as tutors—either student tutors from the same classroom or students from more advanced grade levels. Finally, be sure to take a course in the Education of Exceptional Children, and consider courses dealing with diagnosis and correction of classroom problems in reading, mathematics, or language arts.

## Case Study: Planning for Differences

Mr. Hernandez, a student teacher, is planning a study of the Civil War for his American History class. He is aware of the need to adjust instruction for the students' varying achievement levels, as well as for some of their personal characteristics. For example, he plans to encourage several advanced students to read widely from a prepared bibliography and plan to present to the class some of the information they glean from their reading—through formal reports, panel discussions, dramatizations, and the like. Some students will be assigned chapters from the textbook in their search for answers to a list of questions prepared cooperatively by the students and teacher. The teacher will prepare reading aids, such as study guides, to help the students focus on particular information.

Several slower-learning students will use some easy-to-read books and other supplementary materials to prepare for group discussion about the Civil War. They will also view several filmstrips as part of their study. A few of the slower learners will be assigned a student "tutor" to help when difficulties arise.

An assignment for one set of students will include reading about Harriet Tubman's efforts in freeing the slaves and preparing a role-playing report. One learning disabled student who has difficulty paying attention will be given an individual set of short, sequential assignments, with a specific "date due" schedule. A visually limited student will listen to several tape recordings prepared by the teacher. Also, Mr. Hernandez is planning to read key information aloud while the study is in progress. Through these and other ways, Mr. Hernandez hopes he has made appropriate adjustments for the needs of the students in the classroom.

1 What is your opinion of the way Mr. Hernandez adjusted assignments to meet differing needs?
2 What additional ideas can you suggest for adjusting to individual differences?

## Discussion Questions

1 How would you identify the following types of students: (a) gifted; (b) slow learner; (c) learning disabled; (d) culturally different; (e) mainstreamed?
2 Consider one content or subject area. How would you challenge the gifted student?
3 Again, consider one content area. How would you help the slow learner in this area?
4 How would you help the learning disabled? Relate your answer to a specific content area.
5 How can the needs of the culturally different be considered in the instructional program?
6 What are the teacher's responsibilities toward the mainstreamed student?
7 How can you and special resource personnel cooperate to ensure the best program for the exceptional student?

## Selected References

Affleck, J. S. et al. *Teaching the Mildly Handicapped in the Regular Classroom*, 2nd ed. Columbus, Ohio: Charles E. Merrill, 1980.

Banks, James. *Multiethnic Education: Practice and Promises.* Bloomington, Ind.: Phi Delta Kappa Educational Foundation, 1977.

Barbe, Walter B., and Joseph S. Renzulli, eds. *Psychology and Education of the Gifted*, 3rd ed. New York: Irvington, 1980.

Hasazi, Susan E., et al. *Mainstreaming: Merging Regular and Special Education.* Bloomington, Ind.: Phi Delta Kappa Educational Foundation, 1979.

Herlihy, John G., and Myra T. Herlihy, eds. *Mainstreaming in the Social Studies.* Washington, D.C.: National Council for the Social Studies, 1980.

Herman, Barry E. *Winchester: A Community School for the Urbanvantaged.* Bloomington, Ind.: Phi Delta Kappa Educational Foundation, 1977.

Johnson, Stanley. *Arithmetic and Learning Disabilities.* Boston: Allyn and Bacon, 1979.

Khatena, Joe. *The Creatively Gifted Child: Suggestions for Parents and Teachers.* New York: Vantage Press, 1978.

Lerner, Janet W. *Children with Learning Disabilities,* 2nd ed. Boston: Houghton Mifflin, 1976.

Mallis, Jackie, ed. *Ideas for Teaching Gifted Students.* Blauvelt, N.Y.: Multimedia, 1979.

Markoff, Annabelle M. *Teaching Low Achieving Children Reading, Spelling, and Handwriting.* Springfield, Ill.: Charles C. Thomas, 1976.

Smith, Deborah. *Teaching the Learning Disabled.* Englewood Cliffs, N.J.: Prentice-Hall, 1981.

Warger, Cynthia L. et al. *Mainstreaming in the Secondary School: Role of the Regular Teacher.* Bloomington, Ind.: Phi Delta Kappa Educational Foundation, 1983.

Washburn, Winifred Y. *Vocational Mainstreaming.* Novato, Calif.: Academic Therapy Publications, 1979.

Wilkins, Gloria, and Suzanne Miller. *Strategies for Success: An Effective Guide for Teachers of Secondary-Level Slow Learners.* New York: Teachers College Press, 1983.

Woodward, Dolores M. *Mainstreaming the Learning Disabled Adolescent.* Rockville, Md.: Aspen Systems, 1980.

# 9

## *Evaluation*

In terms of evaluation, as a student teacher you will wear two hats. You will wish to check student progress through various means— observation, informal techniques, and formal tests. At the same time, you will be monitoring your own performance through a variety of methods.

Mike, a student teacher in a sixth grade, thought he would gather some data about several students to learn their present status and how to better evaluate their progress under his instruction. He thought the most important information would include students' academic aptitude test data (often called "intelligence scores"), their achievement test data, their interests and hobbies, and comments by the classroom teacher about the students.

Here are data about twelve students. Study the data and try to answer the questions Mike asked himself.

**TABLE 9-1**   Data about Twelve Sixth-Grade Students

| Name | Academic Aptitude Test Data | Overall Achievement Test Data | Interests/Hobbies | Comments |
|------|------|------|------|------|
| Mary | 100 | 6.8 | tennis/stamp collecting | Mary is very cheerful and enthusiastic about her school work. |
| Diane | 86 | 5.2 | crafts/sewing | Diane appears to have potential, but does little more than required. |
| Sara | 94 | 6.0 | babysitting/reading | Sara is a conscientious student. |
| Mark | 110 | 7.3 | science projects/ jumping rope | Mark reads well and enjoys it. |
| Joe | 95 | 7.0 | comic books/ skateboards | Joe spends a lot of his time doodling. |
| John | 102 | 6.9 | collecting baseball cards/bicycles | John usually does his school work, but has been called a "troublemaker" by some teachers. |
| Lisa | 96 | 6.5 | piano/modeling | Lisa reads well; she reads for information as well as enjoyment. |

| Bill | 75 | 4.0 | T.V./remote control airplanes | Bill is a slow learner, but he tries hard. |
|------|-----|-----|------|------|
| Wendy | 90 | 5.8 | ballet/cooking | Wendy is a very good reader; however, she daydreams much of the time. |
| James | 98 | 6.3 | all sports/building go-carts | James enjoys reading about sports. |
| Pam | 118 | 7.7 | creative writing/ reading | Pam has developed very good composing skills and seems to enjoy writing for pleasure. |
| Ben | 89 | 5.5 | skateboards/T.V. | Ben has difficulty reading; he attends the remedial reading class. |

1 What factors should I consider in evaluating students?
2 Which of these students are capable of doing better work? How could I encourage them to do so?
3 In my evaluation of them, how can I give credit to students with lower academic ability who do their best work?
4 From the data, which students appear to be working up to their potential?
5 In terms of test interpretation, what assistance can the school guidance counselor provide?

# Student Progress

Student progress may be determined by observation, informal techniques, and formal tests.

## Observation

Observing a student at work is a good way to find out how well the student is doing. Numerous situations are available to you as an observant student teacher.

1 Responding to questions. (Does the student grasp the main ideas or important ideas?)

2 Following directions or instructions. (Does the student carry out oral/written directions?)

3 Using resource materials. (Is the student able to use reference sources as revealed by an oral report?)

4 Reacting to the subject. (Does the student appear eager to participate?)

You may find it helpful to develop lists of behaviors for recording results of student observations. Table 9-2 shows one type of form you can use for observation.

## Informal Techniques

**Work Products**   To file the information you gather, you may keep a folder for each student. You may keep samples of the student's work, such as workbook pages, written class work, and quizzes given during a particular report period. Such materials can show patterns of strengths and weaknesses. Teacher's manuals for particular textbook series frequently provide testing materials for the content, which can help determine whether students have learned the content of a specific topic or unit. Where workbooks accompany a particular textbook, the tests built into them can show the types of difficulties students are having with the material. You also have other student work to consider, such as the notebook for the subject, or perhaps a special project done for the course. A student-teacher conference to explore a student's understanding of the subject will provide additional information.

**Teacher-made Quizzes**   If you have not had a course in constructing classroom tests, these ideas will help you prepare teacher-made tests.

**TABLE 9-2**   Observation Guide

| | | |
|---|---|---|
| _____1 | Volunteers to answer question posed to class | Key: |
| _____2 | Listens carefully during class time; follows directions | A—always occurs |
| _____3 | Asks questions about what is not understood | B—often occurs |
| _____4 | Completes homework assignments | C—occasionally occurs |
| _____5 | Participates in voluntary projects | D—seldom occurs |
| _____6 | Likes to help others and share activities with them | E—never occurs |
| _____7 | Projects a good self-image | |
| _____8 | Attends regularly | |
| _____9 | Performs well on quizzes | |

A review quiz can be part of a lesson plan. The quiz may be oral, or it may be a short paper-and-pencil one of usually three to five questions, limited to the material taught in the immediate lesson. It should be varied, with true-false, short-answer, and multiple-choice items. The main purpose of such a quiz is to see what concepts the student has not grasped or perhaps has misunderstood. It may be marked by the students and then checked by you.

A longer test may be appropriate about once every ten days. It may have 20 to 25 true-false, multiple-choice, and short-answer questions. Such a test should be duplicated, rather than written on the board or dictated.

A unit test covers a larger block of teaching and may require most of a class period to complete. You will want to have several parts, including short essay items. Prepare a standard answer sheet before marking the test.

Some teachers give midterms and final examinations to cover a half or whole semester of instruction. You may want to assign points to each part of the examination in terms of its percentage of the whole test. Construct an answer sheet to go with the test.

You need to consider certain factors when planning your testing program. After identifying the objectives and content to be covered in a test, make sure your test appropriately distributes the emphasis upon the objectives and content. For example, if most instructional time has been spent on identifying main ideas in novels, be sure the greater part of the test asks questions about main ideas in novels, not about interpreting the mood projected by the authors. After assigning relative importance to the objectives and topics to be tested, you must decide what type of test items to use—for example, completion, short answer, essay, true-false, matching, or multiple choice. Completion, true-false, multiple choice, and short-answer items are often used for frequent and short assessment. Essay test items are best for major examinations that require students to organize and present careful discussion.

Completion test items are often used to measure knowledge of names, dates, terms, and other simple associations. Choose only important concepts and make sure only one response correctly completes the statement.

Short-answer test items are similar in format to completion test items.

Essay test items should be phrased carefully to limit the question, specifically defining the expectations for each answer. In other words, directions must be thorough and specific as to the relative time to be spent on each question, the relative score to be assigned to each question, and the like. The answer key should contain the essential components of the answer and papers should be scored against these factors.

True-false test items should test only important objectives and content, not trivial items. Avoid use of words such as "all," "never," and others that may give clues to correct answers. Avoid use of negative statements, since students often miss the item through misreading it, rather than because they don't know the answer. To discourage guessing, a true-false test may call for inclusion of the correct answer to any item marked "false." A "correction for guessing" formula involves subtracting the number of items answered incorrectly from the number of items answered correctly.

Matching test items are often used to test student knowledge of definitions or identification of objects presented graphically or pictorially. To help eliminate guessing, present more response items than are to be used, or include responses that may be used more than once.

*Observing a student while he works is a good way to determine how he is doing.*

Multiple-choice test items should be in the form of a question, involving a complete idea. The four or five possible responses should be grammatically and logically consistent and similar in length, and correct responses should appear in all positions.

Part of testing includes teaching students to follow instructions and how to study for tests. (See the discussion of study skills in chapter 7.) Students must know what materials they will need for the test. Most importantly, make clear to students why they are taking the test. Learn to recognize the overanxious student or the one who may be inclined to cheat, and consider potential problems before the test administration. Part of the test arrangement may require moving desks or students apart. Walk quietly about the room while the test is being taken, and check to see if students are following instructions. Mark the papers as soon as possible and return them, since students have the right to know their results.

After marking the tests, calculate the mean or median, determine the range of scores, and construct a frequency distribution of the scores. A student who has this information as a point of reference can understand the meaning of his or her score.

The mean is found by dividing the sum of the scores by the number of scores. The median is the score midway between the highest and lowest scores. The range of scores simply indicates the difference between the highest and lowest scores.

When applicable, the teacher should make an item analysis of a classroom test. This involves finding the difficulty index and the discriminating power of each item. The difficulty index shows the relative difficulty of a test item; the discriminating power compares the response of "high" students with "low" students to a test item. These data will help you construct a valid and reliable test on which to make educational decisions.

This is how to find the difficulty index for a test item. Compute the sum of the number of correct responses for a test item from 25 percent of the highest test scores and the number of correct responses for the same test item from 25 percent of the lowest test scores. Then divide the obtained answer by the sum of the number of students in the highest 25 percent and the lowest 25 percent of the test scores.

$P$ = Difficulty index  
$R_H$ = Right responses of highest test scores  
$R_L$ = Right responses of lowest test scores  
$N_H$ = Number of highest test scores  
$N_L$ = Number of lowest test scores

$P$ = Difficulty Index

$$P = \frac{(R_H + R_L)}{(N_H + N_L)}$$

A guide for level of difficulty[1] is:

[1]Robert L. Ebel, ESSENTIALS OF EDUCATIONAL MEASUREMENT, 3rd ed. © 1979, pp. 264–267. Adapted by permission of Prentice-Hall, Inc., Englewood Cliffs, N.J.

| Level | P | Desired Percentage of Test Items |
|---|---|---|
| Very easy | .85–1.00 | As many items as |
| Fairly easy | .50–.84 | possible should be |
| Fairly difficult | .16–.49 | around .70. |
| Very difficult | .00–.15 | |

This is how to find the discriminating power for test item analysis. Subtract the number of correct responses for a test item for 25 percent of the lowest test scores from the number of correct responses for the same test item for 25 percent of the highest test scores. Then divide the answer by the number of students in the highest 25 percent of the test scores.

D  = Discriminating Power

$R_H$ = Right responses of highest test scores

$R_L$ = Right responses of lowest test scores

$N_H$ = Number of highest test scores

D  = Discriminating Power

$$D = \frac{(R_H - R_L)}{N_H}$$

Here is a guide that provides level of discriminating power indices for test items.[2]

| Level of Discrimination | Disc. Power Index | Desired Percentage of Test Items |
|---|---|---|
| Good | .40 or better | As many items as |
| Reasonably good | .30–.39 | possible should be |
| Marginal | .20–.29 | .40 or better. |
| Poor | .00–.19 | |

## Formal Tests

Norms are ordinarily applied to formal or standardized tests. There are different kinds of standardized tests: academic aptitude tests to measure potential achievement in school subjects and achievement tests to measure what a person has learned in a particular area or areas.

Many general academic aptitude tests (often called intelligence tests) may be group administered. (Most individual tests must be administered by trained personnel.) You should be cautious in interpreting the scores from group intelligence tests because:

1  Many are language-based tests, causing language disabled students to have low scores.
2  Scores may be influenced by a student's general health, emotional outlook, fear of the testing situation, and other personal factors.
3  Scores may be depressed as a result of cultural bias.

[2]Robert L. Ebel, ESSENTIALS OF EDUCATIONAL MEASUREMENT, 3rd ed. © 1979, pp. 264–267. Adapted by permission of Prentice-Hall, Inc., Englewood Cliffs, N.J.

Do not accept test scores alone as the measure of academic potential. Scores or expectations based on the scores must not be considered static.

Group achievement tests (administered to a number of persons at the same time) serve the purpose of telling the teacher how the *class*, not individual class members, is performing in comparison with other groups of students. The most important score is the class average, which helps you determine whether the class is average, below average, or above average. The teacher can use this information to make instructional decisions.

Some standardized survey tests provide descriptions of what skills the tests measure. Schools often receive an item-analysis report on how groups perform on each item, as well as the percentage of the national sample of students who answered each item correctly.

Standardized tests report norms in several ways:

1   Grade equivalents—the grade level for which a given score is a real or estimated average. Scores are expressed in terms of grade and month of grade, such as 4.8 for fourth grade, eighth month.
2   Percentile rank—expression of test score in terms of its position within a group of 100 scores. The percentile rank of a score is the percent of scores equal to or lower than the given score in its own or in some reference group.
3   Stanine—one of the steps in a nine-point scale of standard scores. The stanine scale has values from 1 to 9, with a mean of 5 and a standard deviation (S.D.) of 2. Each stanine (except 1 and 9) is ½ S.D. in width.

# Self-Analysis

We will discuss four of the ways you can monitor your teaching performance: (a) microteaching; (b) use of a formal analysis instrument, such as Flanders Interaction Analysis; (c) analysis of nonverbal behaviors; and (d) informal critical analysis of lesson success. We have discussed in earlier chapters other items for self-evaluation such as personal characteristics, classroom management, and methods of instruction.

## Microteaching/Videotaping/Audiotaping

The idea of microteaching is to teach a brief lesson, from five minutes up to 15 or 20 minutes, to three to six students. A microteaching lesson concentrates on only one or two specific skills, such as higher-order questions and planned repetition. After the teaching, a supervisor, teacher, or other student gives a critique of the performance. Some evaluative summary may be provided by the students taught. If the lesson is videotaped, there will be opportunity for pre- and post-comments when the lesson is replanned for teaching to a new group of students. In brief, microteaching follows these steps:

1 The prospective teacher receives exposure to a specific teaching skill.
2 He or she practices the technique in a short lesson with four or five school students.
3 The lesson is recorded or videotaped for review by the prospective teacher.
4 A supervisor critiques the lesson.
5 The prospective teacher has an opportunity to replan and reteach the lesson to another small group of students. This session may also be recorded and critiqued.

Instead of having only one person critique the lesson, small groups of students can rotate their roles as teachers and observers—and learn much; or, the teacher of the lesson may want to evaluate his or her own performance. Where videotaping is not possible, audiotape is satisfactory for some of the same purposes. Just turn on a tape cassette for a lesson presentation, and take it home and listen. This is an excellent way to note mistakes and plan for improvement.

Videotaping or audiotaping gives the student teacher a great deal of information about his or her voice, speech patterns, class participation, use of praise or encouragement, variety of questions asked, clarity of directions, classroom climate, and many other factors.

## Flanders Interaction Analysis

At times you may wish to be evaluated on the basis of the quality of your interaction within the classroom. A basic vehicle that treats this idea is *Interaction Analysis* (IA). This idea can be traced to Ned Flanders, who developed the well-known Flanders Interaction Analysis system to measure the extent to which a teacher is direct or indirect in the classroom.

The Flanders system is not suitable for classroom situations in which students are engaged actively in problem solving in small groups. Moreover, the person responsible for evaluating the teacher should be qualified by preparation, experience, and professionalism to do the evaluation. A cooperating teacher or college supervisor, who has had several years of teaching experience with a wide range of students and has used a diversity of teaching styles, is often the evaluator. Interaction analysis can be used in conjunction with microteaching.

The Flanders Interaction Analysis uses these features and arrangements.

1 It has ten categories of verbal behavior: seven of teacher talk, two of student talk, one for silence or confusion. Each is assigned a number.

2 There is a system of encoding the observed behaviors. One may jot down the observed behaviors as they occur or tally the behaviors into the appropriate cells of a prepared matrix.

3 The observer records, on the average, one bit of behavior each three seconds. For example, he or she may jot down

**TABLE 9-3**  Summary of Categories for Interaction Analysis

| | | | |
|---|---|---|---|
| TEACHER TALK | INDIRECT INFLUENCE | 1 | *Accepts feeling: accepts and clarifies the feeling tone of the students in a nonthreatening manner. Feelings may be positive or negative. Predicting or recalling feelings is included. |
| | | 2 | *Praises or encourages: praises or encourages student action or behavior. Jokes that release tension, but not at the expense of another individual; nodding head; or saying "uh hm?" or "go on" are included. |
| | | 3 | *Accepts or uses ideas of students: clarifying, building, or developing ideas suggested by a student. As teacher brings more of his own ideas into play, shift to Category 5. |
| | | 4 | *Asks questions: asking a question about content or procedure with the intent that a student answer. |
| TEACHER TALK | DIRECT INFLUENCE | 5 | *Lecturing: giving facts or opinions about content or procedures; expressing his own ideas, asking rhetorical questions. |
| | | 6 | *Giving directions: directions, commands, or orders with which a student is expected to comply. |
| | | 7 | *Criticing or justifing authority: statements intended to change student behavior from nonacceptable to acceptable pattern; bawling someone out; stating why the teacher is doing what he is doing; extreme self-reference. |
| STUDENT TALK | | 8 | *Student talk–Response: talk by students in response to teacher. Teacher initiates the contact or solicits student statement. |
| | | 9 | *Student talk–Initiation: talk by students, which they initiate. If "calling on" student is only to indicate who may talk next, observer must decide whether student wanted to talk. If he did, use this category. |
| | | 10 | *Silence or confusion: pauses, short periods of silence, and periods of confusion in which communication cannot be understood by the observer. |

*There is no scale implied by these numbers. Each number is classificatory; it designates a particular kind of communication event. To write these numbers down during observation is to enumerate—not to judge a position on a scale.

Source: Flanders, Ned A. ANALYZING TEACHER BEHAVIOR, 1970, Addison-Wesley Publishing Company, Inc., Chapter 2, page 34, table 2–1, "Flanders Interaction Analysis Categories (FAIC)," Reprinted with permission.

4–8 (or place a tally in the 4–8 cell) if the teacher asks a question and a student answers it.

4   The record is then decoded and interpreted.

The trained observer must have the categories well in mind, perhaps through practicing first from tapes and later in actual classrooms. In initial situations, a better-trained observer should check the observer. At least 12 or more hours of practice and training are usually necessary to use the Flanders analysis in a classroom setting. The teacher should also be thoroughly familiar with the instrument before being monitored with it. Again, groups may work together in monitoring, or individuals can monitor their own performances if they are videotaped.[3]

Table 9-3 summarizes the categories for interaction analysis, and Figure 9-1 presents a typical illustration, using the matrix.

The computation at the bottom of Figure 9–1 indicates that 70 percent of the talk in the classroom was by the teacher and 28 percent by the students. The ratio of the indirect to the direct was .38, suggesting that less than half the teacher talk was indirect (for every indirect statement there were two direct statements). The revised I/D ratio gives insight about whether the teacher's approach to motivation and control is direct or indirect. In this case, the teacher was more indirect than direct. (For every two indirect teacher statements, there was only one direct statement.)

Here are questions you may ask in interpreting the matrix:

1   How much time do I spend talking in the classroom? How much time do the students spend talking? Is there adequate student participation in the classroom? (Compare columns 1–7 with columns 8 and 9.)

2   Am I typically a direct or indirect teacher? (Compare columns 1–4 with columns 5–7.)

3   How much time do I spend lecturing? (Column 5)

4   Do I spend enough time in the extension of student ideas? (Cell 3-3)

5   Do students tend to resist my influence? (Cells 6-7 and 7-6)

6   Do I accept, clarify and use student emotions? (Category 1)

Additional data may be utilized with the instrument; for example, questions asked by the teacher (category 4) may be classified as to type of questions. (See chapter 6 for one classification of questions.)

[3]For a full discussion of the Flanders instrument, see Edmund J. Amidon and Ned A. Flanders, *The Role of the Teacher in the Classroom: A Manual for Understanding and Improving Teacher Classroom Behavior*, Rev. ed. (Minneapolis, Minn.: Association for Productive Teaching, 1967).

**Figure 9-1 Illustration of Flanders Interaction Analysis***

Second

First

| | 1 | 2 | 3 | 4 | 5 | 6 | 7 | 8 | 9 | 10 | |
|---|---|---|---|---|---|---|---|---|---|---|---|
| 1 | 1 | | | | 1 | | | | 1 | | |
| 2 | | 4 | 1 | | | | | 2 | | | |
| 3 | | 1 | 6 | 1 | | | | 2 | | | |
| 4 | | | 1 | 14 | | | | 5 | | | |
| 5 | 1 | | | | 48 | | | 6 | | | |
| 6 | | | | | | 1 | | 4 | | | |
| 7 | | | | | | | 4 | | 1 | | |
| 8 | | 2 | 2 | 5 | 6 | 4 | | 11 | | | |
| 9 | 1 | | | | | | 1 | | 9 | 1 | |
| 10 | | | | | | | | | 1 | 2 | Matrix Total |
| TOTAL | 3 | 7 | 10 | 20 | 55 | 5 | 5 | 30 | 12 | 3 | 150 |
| % | 2 | 4½ | 6½ | 13½ | 36½ | 3½ | 3½ | 20 | 8 | 2 | |

| Teacher Talk | Student Talk |
|---|---|
| Columns 1–7 = 105 | Columns 8–9 = 42 |
| 105 ÷ 150 = 70% | 42 ÷ 150 = 28% |

Indirect (1 ÷ 4) – Direct (1–4) plus (5–7) = I/D Ratio

$$\underline{40} \div 40 \text{ plus } 65 = \frac{40}{105} = .38$$

Indirect (1–3) ÷ Direct (1–3) plus (6–7) = Revised I/D Ratio

$$\underline{20} \div 20 \text{ plus } 10 = \frac{20}{30} = .67$$

*Source: Edmund J. Amidon and Ned A. Flanders, *The Role of the Teacher in the Classroom: A Manual for Understanding and Improving Teacher Classroom Behavior*, rev. ed. (Minneapolis, Minn.: Association for Productive Teaching, 1967), p. 36.

## Nonverbal Behavior

It is important to be aware of nonverbal communication in the classroom. Awareness of the possible ways you use nonverbal communication will make you more conscious of what students' silent messages mean, and help you learn to anticipate them. Students often seem extremely adept at "reading" your nonverbal behavior.

TABLE 9-4   Nonverbal Categories and Sample Teacher Behaviors

For observational purposes, underline the appropriate words in the right column which describe the student teacher's nonverbal behavior in the classroom during a five- or ten-minute period.

| | | |
|---|---|---|
| 1.* | Accepts student behavior | Smiles, affirmatively shakes head, pats on the back, places hand on shoulder or head |
| 2.* | Praises student behavior | Places index finger and thumb together, claps, raises eyebrows and smiles, nods head affirmatively and smiles |
| 3. | Displays student ideas | Writes comments on board, puts students' work on bulletin board, holds up papers, secures nonverbal student demonstration |
| 4. | Shows interest in student behavior | Establishes/maintains eye contact |
| 5. | Moves to facilitate student-to-student interaction | Physically moves into position of group member, physically moves away from the group |
| 6.* | Gives directions to students | Points with hand, raises hands, reinforces numerical aspects by showing the number of fingers, extends arms forward and beckons with hand, points to students for answers |
| 7. | Shows authority toward students | Frowns, stares, raises eyebrows, taps foot, throws book on desk, shakes head, walks or looks toward deviant, walks or looks away from deviant |
| 8. | Focuses students' attention on important points | Uses pointer, walks toward person or object, taps on something, thrusts head forward, employs nonverbal movement to give emphasis to a verbal statement |
| 9. | Demonstrates/illustrates | Performs a physical skill, manipulates materials/media, illustrates verbal statement with nonverbal action |
| 10. | Ignores or rejects a student's behavior | Lacks nonverbal response when one is ordinarily expected |

*The names of these categories are the same as those in the Flanders matrix.

Source: Alice M. Love and Jessie A. Roderick, "Teacher Nonverbal Communication: The Development of Field Testing of An Awareness Unit," *Theory Into Practice*, October 1971, pp. 295–96. Copyright © College of Education, The Ohio State University.

Various categories have been established for some of a teacher's nonverbal behavior. Galloway developed one such category dealing with facial expressions, actions, and vocal intonations as ways of encouraging communication or inhibiting communicative behavior.[4] Lail has developed a checklist for observations of teachers' nonverbal communication behavior.[5] Another instrument helpful in recording the teacher's nonverbal behavior is the Love-Roderick Scale, presented in Table 9–4. Notice that the names of some of the categories are the same as those in the Flanders matrix.

As a student teacher, you can use the Love-Roderick Scale to:

1 Observe the teacher.
2 Ask the cooperating teacher or other student teachers to observe you.
3 Note the items on which you need to improve.
4 Develop strategies where there is need for improvement.[6]

## Critical Analysis of Lesson Success

An alternative to the preceding format of microteaching and analysis should be provided for you in the teaching role. Key aspects of instruction should be developed collaboratively by the classroom teacher and the prospective teacher. Figure 9–2 is a sample format that can serve as a model. After completion of a lesson or series of lessons, the two persons should separately rate the lesson. Then in a meeting, notes may be compared and different perceptions clarified and perhaps reconciled. It is hoped that items that need improvement will be improved over a period of time.

The observed lesson will be rated using the following symbols:
(+) for "good" to "excellent"
(o) for "no evidence of this component in the lesson"
(–) for "needs improvement"
Class members may be involved in the analysis of the lesson or unit of work. For younger students, a format like that in Figure 9-3 can be used.

For older students, a format such as that in Figure 9-4 may be appropriate.

You should also arrange for periodic discussion with your cooperating teacher and supervisor for evaluation. Analysis of your

[4]Charles Galloway, *Silent Language in the Classroom.* Bloomington, Ind.: Phi Delta Kappa Educational Foundation, 1976.
[5]Sue S. Lail, "The Model In Use," *Theory Into Practice,* 7 (Dec. 1968): 176–80.
[6]For other information, see "Effective Nonverbal Communication" in chapter 6 of this text; read also Gerard I. Nierenberg and Henry Calero, *How To Read A Person Like a Book* (New York: Simon and Schuster, 1972) or a similar book.

daily lesson plans and informal questioning of students (What did you learn in the lesson? What were the most important points in today's lesson?) will help them judge the degree of instructional success.

**Figure 9-2   Rating Key Aspects of Instruction**

| Component | Rating | Comments |
|---|---|---|
| 1. Gaining and holding student attention | | |
| 2. Telling students what they're expected to learn | | |
| 3. Reminding students of related knowledge or skills | | |
| 4. Presenting new stimuli for learning | | |
| 5. Guiding student thinking and learning | | |
| 6. Providing feedback about correctness | | |
| 7. Judging or appraising the performance | | |
| 8. Helping to generalize what is learned | | |
| 9. Providing practice for retention | | |
| 10. Other | | |

Figure 9-3   Rating Instruction by Younger Students

A.   Marking Responses:

1.   My teacher usually looks like this:

2.   When I ask the teacher for help, he or she looks like this:

3.   After I finish the lesson, I feel like this:

B.   Oral Interview:

1.   If I were the teacher, I would:

2.   When I go to the teacher for help, he or she . . .

3.   I would understand my lessons better, if:

Figure 9-4   Rating Instruction by Older Students

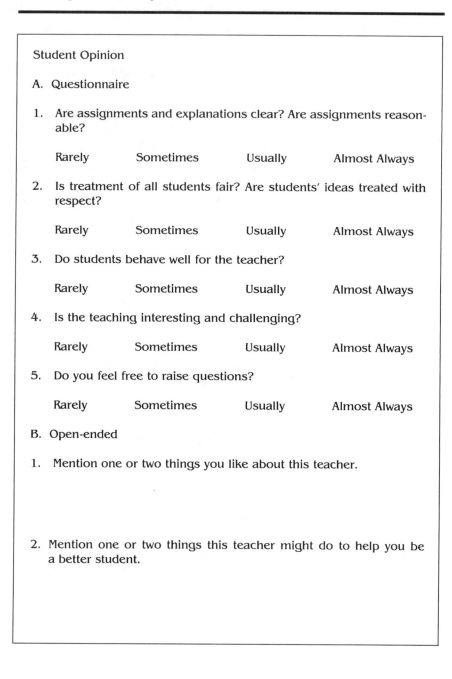

Student Opinion

A. Questionnaire

1.  Are assignments and explanations clear? Are assignments reasonable?

    Rarely          Sometimes          Usually          Almost Always

2.  Is treatment of all students fair? Are students' ideas treated with respect?

    Rarely          Sometimes          Usually          Almost Always

3.  Do students behave well for the teacher?

    Rarely          Sometimes          Usually          Almost Always

4.  Is the teaching interesting and challenging?

    Rarely          Sometimes          Usually          Almost Always

5.  Do you feel free to raise questions?

    Rarely          Sometimes          Usually          Almost Always

B. Open-ended

1.  Mention one or two things you like about this teacher.


2.  Mention one or two things this teacher might do to help you be a better student.

### Case Study: A Challenge to a Student Teacher's Evaluation

A student teacher, Ms. Downey, was teaching a chemistry class. She was trying to keep a close record of student performance in her class. Through observation and analysis of student responses, she quickly noted that three students appeared to have little interest in the subject. Also, their early work products were of rather poor quality. After checking the results of a couple of tests (each covering two weeks of instruction), it seemed clear that the students had not grasped the content presented during that period of time. Ms. Downey thought student-teacher conferences might be helpful. She brought the evidence of her concern to the conferences. During the three conferences, the students responded with comments such as these:

1  "The tests were too hard, so I just guessed."
2  "Most of the students missed the same questions I missed."
3  "Chemistry is mostly for brainy students."
4  "You don't make it clear what I'm supposed to learn."
5  "You talk all the time."
6  "You don't show much interest in the students."

What objective data could Ms. Downey present to respond to each of these comments?

## Discussion Questions

1  How would you modify the student observation guide to fit your particular situation?
2  Using a teacher-constructed test that has been administered to a group of students, perform an item analysis and critique the test. What did you find?
3  Use the suggestions for presenting a microteaching lesson, then critique it. What were the results?
4  What are some strengths and weaknesses of the Flanders Interaction Analysis?
5  Ask someone to observe your nonverbal behaviors while you present a short lesson. What can you do to improve?
6  Present a lesson, having someone rate the presentation according to Figure 9–2. What can you do to improve?
7  What type of student reaction format would be most appropriate in your situation?

# Selected References

Bauernfeidn, R.H. *Building a School Testing Program: Uses and Misuses of Standard Tests.* Bensonville, Ill.: Scholastic Testing Service, 1978.

Beegle, Charles W., and Richard M. Brandt, eds. *Observational Methods in the Classroom.* Alexandria, Va.: Association for Supervision and Curriculum Development, 1973.

Brown, George. *Microteaching.* New York: Methuen, 1979.

Harrington, William. *Measurement in Education,* 4th ed. Dubuque, Iowa: Kendall/Hunt, 1974.

Jensen, Richard N. *Microteaching: Planning and Implementing a Competency-Based Training Program.* Springfield, Ill.: Charles C. Thomas, 1974.

Kirby, Jonell H., et al. *Manual for Users of Standardized Tests.* Bensonville, Ill.: Scholastic Testing Service, 1973.

Scannell, Dale P., and D.B. Tracy. *Testing and Measurement in the Classroom.* Boston: Houghton Mifflin, 1975.

Stallings, Jane. *Learning to Look: A Handbook on Classroom Observation.* Belmont, Calif.: Wadsworth, 1977.

Stodla, Quentin, and Kalmer Stordahl. *Basic Educational Tests and Measurement.* Chicago: Science Research Associates, 1967.

Stubbs, Michael, and Sara Delamont, eds. *Explorations in Classroom Observation.* New York: John Wiley, 1975.

# 10
# Employment and Continued Professional Growth

Mrs. Carruthers and Mr. Martinez are both student teachers. Miss Page and Mrs. Lansing are regular teachers in the school to which the student teachers are assigned.

Mr. Martinez: Have you done any observation in other classrooms yet?

Mrs. Carruthers: Yes, I have. I observed Miss Page and Mrs. Lansing. I guess I chose them because they were both my teachers when I attended Jefferson.

Mr. Martinez: I've observed both of them, too. Mrs. Lansing seems to be using all the latest ideas we studied at school, but Miss Page's class seemed to be strictly traditional. Mrs. Lansing's students were playing a simulation game when I was in there. Miss Page's students were looking up the definitions of five vocabulary words and copying them directly from the dictionary.

Mrs. Carruthers: I noticed the same thing. Miss Page taught her class exactly the way she did when she was my teacher years ago, but I hardly recognized Mrs. Lansing's class. Everything she did had been revised and updated. There was even a boy in the back working on a computer lesson. I mentioned to her something about how things had changed, and she said, "You never stop learning how to be a better teacher." She has gone back to the university and gotten a Master's degree since I was her student, and she still takes occasional classes. She also showed me several professional journals she subscribes to. She said they have wonderful teaching ideas in them.

Mr. Martinez: Miss Page made a disparaging comment about college courses when I had my brief conference with her. I don't think she's done any advanced work at the university.

Mrs. Carruthers: I don't either. I also doubt that she gets many professional publications, because you have to join professional organizations to get many of them, and I heard her mention to another teacher that she wasn't going to waste her money on those useless organizations.

Mr. Martinez: My university supervisor said it's possible to get twenty years of experience in twenty years or to get one year of experience twenty times. It looks like he was right.

Mrs. Carruthers: It surely does. I want to make sure I get a new year's experience for every year I teach. I guess that will mean more school and participation in professional organizations.

1  Did Mr. Martinez and Mrs. Carruthers learn something from their observations besides teaching techniques? If so, what was it?
2  Do you agree with Mrs. Carruthers' summation of the situation? Why or why not?

## Beyond Student Teaching

After you complete your student teaching experience, you will need to search for employment and consider your continued professional growth. You would do well to consider both processes now, well ahead of time, so you will know how to proceed efficiently and effectively after you graduate.

## Employment

In this section, we will talk about searching for employment—where to find a position, how to develop a resumé and inquiry letter, how to get letters of reference, and how to handle interviews. We will also mention some general tips for assuring your best chances for employment.

### Case Study: A Fruitless Interview

John has just graduated from college. He spent four hard years in the study of elementary education, and now he has a Bachelor's degree in education. The next step for John is to find a teaching position. He wants to teach at an elementary school close to his home and to work with fifth grade students.

John was busy during his last quarter of school, so he did not get to visit any schools or superintendents. He looked in the "Jobs Wanted" section of the newspaper, but didn't find a job opening having to do with the fifth grade. He did telephone some teachers at the school where he wants to teach and asked if they knew of any openings for the coming year.

One day at a party, John overheard someone discussing the possibility of a job opening in the fourth grade in a different elementary school in the school system. He wasn't really interested in that teaching position, but he decided to go to see the superintendent.

Before going for the interview, John decided he would compile some kind of resumé. He decided he did not need to make a detailed resumé, since he wasn't very interested in the job. He thought he would take the job if it were offered to him, but he would not try too hard. John thought, "I'll go to the interview, but I won't take it too seriously. I would like to have a job but not in that school. Perhaps if I go, I can talk with the superintendent and he might offer a job in the fifth grade at the school I want."

John took a few minutes to write his resumé. The resumé looked like this:

My name is John Johnson
Age: 24          Sex: Male
College: City University
Degree: B.S. in Education
Experience: I student taught in the third grade at Cordell
            Elementary school. They were nice kids, but I
            like the higher grades, like the fifth, better.

After developing his resumé, John went to the superintendent's office. John walked into the office and asked to see the superintendent. The secretary told John he would need to make an appointment because the superintendent would be busy with meetings all day. John argued with the secretary, trying to get to see the superintendent, but finally agreed to set an appointment for the next day.

John had all kinds of trouble on his way to the office the next day. His car stalled several times, so he was fifteen minutes late. He had dressed in a suit, but it was dirty from working on his car.

When he arrived, John did not apologize for being late. The superintendent looked somewhat shocked at John's appearance, but proceeded to ask him questions about his school experience and his interest in the job. John nervously twitched in his chair and often had trouble getting his thoughts together.

After discussing some questions with the superintendent, John said he really was not very interested in the open position, but would like to teach fifth grade in another school. The superintendent told John he could not guarantee that John would get to teach fifth grade in the school he wanted. John said he was not sure he wanted a job if he could not teach at the fifth grade level in the school of his choice. The superintendent said he would do his best and would let John know if any openings became available.

Before John left, the superintendent asked him for references. John said he did not have a reference list, but would give the superintendent the names of teachers he had worked with in school who might give him a good recommendation.

John walked out of the office and gave a shrug. "I don't need *that* job. I can find the one I'm looking for if I get in touch with the right people."

What suggestions would you make to John about:

1  How to go about finding a job
2  Developing a letter of inquiry and resumé
3  Procedures for applying to a school system
4  Getting letters of reference
5  Interviewing skills

## Where to Find a Position

You need to be aware of employment opportunities for graduates. The data change over a period of time. Mobility and double certification are positive factors in demand and ultimate placement. (You should check trends in your own area and in the latest issue of ASCUS ANNUAL, "A Job Search Handbook for Educators," published by the Association for School, College and University Staffing, Box 4411, Madison, Wisconsin 53711.)

Some special job options that are frequently overlooked are the following:

State government—Educators are employed in state correctional institutions and the state department of education. (Visit the state employment office in your city, and discuss possibilities with your advisor or counselor.)

Federal government—Educators are employed in several federal agencies, such as the Bureau of Indian Affairs (teaching on reservations, etc.), the Bureau of Prisons, the Department of Education, and the National Institute of Education. (Consult directories of government agencies in a library, and discuss possibilities with your advisor or counselor.)

Overseas—Educators, usually with at least two years of full-time experience, are selected for overseas positions. (Consult your library and discuss possibilities with your advisor or counselor.) Several sources of employment for overseas jobs are:

Department of Defense Overseas Dependent Schools (DOD), Office of Overseas Dependent Schools, Department of Defense, 2461 Eisenhower Ave., Alexandria, VA 22331

Office of Overseas Schools of the U.S. Department of State, Office of Overseas Schools, Room 234, SA-6 (A. OS), U.S. Department of State, Washington, DC 20502

The Teacher Exchange Program (known as the Fulbright-Hays Act), Teacher Exchange Section, Division of International Education, U.S. Department of Education, Washington, DC 20202

Schools operated by American firms conducting business overseas. See: Directory of American Firms Operating in Foreign Countries, Juvenal Angel, 9th ed. New York: Uniworld Business Publications, 1979.

Textbook publishers: Educators are employed in several capacities. Specific opportunities include sales representative, demonstrator of materials, leader of inservice sessions when new textbooks are adopted, writer for manuals and workbooks, and the like.*

Through your library, you will find a number of references dealing with employment for teachers, such as directories of public school systems, boarding schools, and private schools, and journals such as *Academic Journal: "The Educators" Employment Magazine* (published biweekly) and *Affirmative Action Register* (published monthly).

Some private employment agencies specialize in teacher placement, but they vary widely in quality and types of services they provide. City newspapers also run classified ads for teaching positions in the employment section. The cooperating teacher or principal where you did student teaching may know of openings outside or within their school systems, and job vacancies are often advertised at professional meetings. One of the best sources of help is the college or university career planning and placement office; it should have a complete and current placement file.

If you are considering alternate and/or satellite careers for teachers, the career/placement office can probably give you a list of possibilities. Career counseling will be provided and credentials (or placement papers) are filed in this office to support your applications to prospective employers. You will also find a career library in the placement office, including: brochures and applications; directories of community service organizations; encyclopedias of associations; audiovisual tapes on interviewing; information on writing resumés; overseas teaching literature; and the ASCUS ANNUAL.

## Developing a Resumé and Inquiry Letter

A resumé is a brief statement about your abilities and experiences to help a prospective employer assess your potential for future success with his or her school system. The resumé can serve as a general introduction to accompany your letter of inquiry or application.

**Preparing a Letter of Inquiry**   Here is a general outline for the cover letter:

Paragraph 1:   Give reasons for writing, indicating the position for which you are applying.

Paragraph 2:   State concrete reasons for wanting to work for the particular employer. Give evidence that you understand the requirements of the position and that you possess the necessary qualifications for success in the position.

---

*For a comprehensive book that deals with alternatives for education graduates, see Bill McKee, *New Careers for Teachers* (Chicago: Henry Regnery, 1972).

Paragraph 3:  Refer the reader to the enclosed resumé and emphasize relevant personal qualities not cited elsewhere.

Paragraph 4:  Provide at least three references with complete addresses.

Paragraph 5:  Request a response and ask for an interview (Figure 10-1 provides a sample letter of inquiry.)

**Resumé**    The resumé should be confined to one page, if at all possible. A reference on details of resumé writing is Burdette Bostwick's *Resume Writing: A Comprehensive How-To-Do-Guide* (New York: John Wiley, 1976). Figure 10-2 is a sample resumé showing an acceptable format and what data to provide; it can be modified according to your specific experiences and qualifications.

## Getting Letters of Reference

Letters of reference increase the employer's confidence in the applicant's ability. Avoid including references who might be considered biased, such as relatives. Letters from appropriate persons (your adviser, student teaching supervisor, cooperating teacher, professors of courses you have taken, and the like) should reflect the writer's knowledge of your academic preparation and career objectives and should be positive statements of support for the position you seek. With an "open file" (nonconfidential), you can read the letters; with a "closed file" (confidential) you are unable to read your letters of recommendation.

## Interviewing Skills

The best advice for an interview is to "be prepared." One way to prepare is to anticipate questions you may be asked.

Research the school system as much as possible. Find out about its reputation, school/community relationships, organizational structure, teacher-pupil ratio, benefits and services provided to teachers, and other considerations.

Think through some responses for the questions likely to be asked, such as: Why did you select teaching as a career? How would you handle certain problems—such as motivation, discipline, parental concerns? Why do you want to teach in this particular system? How would you like to organize your class? How would you take care of individual differences? What instructional materials have you found helpful? How would you evaluate students? How would you diagnose difficulties of students? What magazines, periodicals, or books relative to your field do you subscribe to or read regularly? What are your long-range goals in the teaching field? What are your strengths and weaknesses in teaching? How are your human rela-

Figure 10-1   Sample Letter of Inquiry

---

Box 145
University of Parkersburg
Parkersburg, Tennessee 55519
May 2, 1984

Dr. John Doe
Superintendent of Schools
Cumberland County Schools
Hillside, Delaware 24970

Dear Dr. Doe:

It has come to my attention that a teaching position in mathematics will be open next year at the Parkview School. I plan to graduate in June from the University of Parkersburg with a M.S. Degree in Mathematics Education and would like to apply for this position.

Your school system is often cited as outstanding because of its strong instructional program. The extensive use of media in your school system and the availability of facilities and equipment are impressive. My program of study included media courses that provided practical information for using audiovisual aids in the classroom. I am eager to put my educational experiences into practice in a full-time teaching position.

Enclosed is a copy of my resumé which will give you some insight into my background, education, and experience. A videotape of my teaching performance is also available upon request, and a copy of my placement file can be obtained from our Career Planning and Placement Service.

Below you will find three references you may contact about my qualifications for the position. I have received permission from all three people to use them as references.

Dr. Buford Jenkins        Mr. A. J. Metcalf
1245 Park City Hill        Jenkins Square
Park City, TN 55516        Barkley, TN 55542

Mr. Jack Harris
1111 Memphis Avenue
Jacksonville, TN 55503

I will be available at your convenience for an interview and will look forward to hearing from you. Thank you for your consideration.

Sincerely,

*Bob Alfred*

Bob Alfred

**Figure 10-2 Sample Resumé**

---

Bob Alfred                                    Date Available: June 14, 1984
Johnson Avenue
Corbin, Maine 44407

Professional Objective:
  To secure a mathematics teaching position in a secondary school
  that encourages innovation and creativity.

Education:
  June 2, 1984—M.S. in Mathematics Education from the University
  of Highpoint, Greenville, N.D.
  Major: Mathematics Education        Certification: Grades 8–12
  GPA: 3.8                            Minor: Physical Science

Honors and Awards:
  Received Maxwell Student Teacher of the Year Award (1982)
  Was in top ten of secondary education graduating seniors
  (GPA) (1982)

Experience:
  Teaching Assistant, Greenville Secondary School, Greenville,
  N.D., 1983
  Assisted tenth grade teacher for the school year as a paid
  assistant. I worked thirty hours a week.
  Student Teacher, Marks Secondary School, Greenville, N.D., 1982
  Math tutor for gifted children during the summer, 1982

Activities:
  Debate Captain
  Active member in Student Teacher Association
  Volunteer worker at Student Handicap Center

Interests:
  Sports
  Church Activities

References:
  Available upon request from:
  Career Planning and Placement Service

---

tions with principals, supervisors, and students in such extracurricular activities as athletics, dramatics, publications, etc.?

Think through some questions you may wish to ask an interviewer, such as: What are your homework and discipline policies? What incentive is there for advanced study? What kinds of inservice programs will be offered to help me during my first year? What supervisory assistance will I be provided? What is the school's evaluation system for teachers? What types of schools/situations are new teachers placed in? What is the beginning salary, and what are other monetary benefits? May I read the system's contract?

Figure 10-3 is an illustrated sample contract from one school district. For some school systems, memoranda of understanding between the board of education of the system and the local education association will be available for study. These memoranda contain information about agreements reached relative to association rights, management rights, work stoppage, dues deductions, student discipline procedures, personnel files, evaluation, right to representation, grievances, transfer policy, leaves of absence, sick

**Figure 10-3  Sample Contract**

---

### COUNTY OF KNOX, STATE OF TENNESSEE
### CONTRACT BETWEEN THE COUNTY BOARD OF EDUCATION

and _____ as _____
in the Knox County School System.

This contract, entered into this _____ day of _____, 19___, between the aforesaid Board of Education and _____

Witnesseth: That the said Board of Education has engaged the said _____ as _____ in the Knox County School System from the _____ day of _____, 19___, for a term of _____ and agrees to pay him/her the sum determined by the appropriate salary schedule adopted by the Knox County Board of Education for this contract period but not less than ($_____) _____ Dollars, for his/her services. This sum to be paid in 12 monthly installments.

The said _____ agrees to observe all laws, all valid rules and regulations of the Knox County Board of Education and all valid rules and regulations of the State Board of Education.

It is agreed between the parties that the said _____ shall not be entitled to demand a warrant for the payment of his/her salary for any month until he/she has delivered to the Superintendent the correct reports which may be at that time due.

It is further agreed that, should school attendance decrease to the extent that a teaching position is terminated because it cannot be justified under the Rules and Regulations of the State Board of Education, this contract may be cancelled at the discretion of the Knox County Board of Education.

It is understood that this contract is subject to the provisions of all applicable legislative enactments of the General Assembly of the State of Tennessee.

_____

_____

_____

ACCEPTED:

_____                    _____
Employee                                          Chairman, Board of Education

_____                    _____
Date                                                    Superintendent

Source: Reprinted by permission of Knox County, Tennessee, Board of Education.

leave, physical examinations, insurance, salary schedule, and other such matters. Study of the memoranda of understanding will provide further information about the particular school systems you are investigating.

You may wish to take several items with you for the interview session—resumé, transcript, student records, representative lesson/unit plans, audio/videotape of a teaching situation, and student evaluations. Consult with your placement office for videotapes or films on interviewing and books about interviewing skills. Use a mirror, or ask a friend to look for characteristics that could detract from an interview session.

### General Tips for Employment Search

Letters should be:

1　Typewritten on good quality bond paper;
2　Immaculately clean (no smudges or fingerprints);
3　Attractively arranged; and
4　Grammatically perfect and properly punctuated, with spelling carefully checked.

For interviews, you should:

1　Know the name and position of the interviewing official;
2　Arrive promptly for your appointment;
3　Write a letter of appreciation following the interview;
4　Dress formally and moderately;
5　Look the interviewer in the eye when answering questions, look alert and interested, and be a good listener; and
6　Use language well.

Where interest is evident on the part of the student and the prospective employer, there will probably be follow-up telephone calls and letters, and specific materials may be called for, such as an application form, a picture, and transcripts. If you observe the commonsense guidelines in this chapter, the chances are good that you will be successful in your search for a job.

## Continued Professional Growth

After you actually have a job as a teacher, you may be tempted to settle into a routine much like Miss Page at the beginning of this chapter. It is, after all, easier to use the same lesson plans year after year without bothering to revise and update them. If it worked the first time, it ought to be good enough now, right?

Wrong! Every year, you will have students with different abilities and needs, and you must adjust instruction if they are to benefit maximally. There will always be changes going on within your discipline that could render your lessons inadequate and, in some cases, actually incorrect. A teacher like Miss Page will never know.

How, then, can you be sure to stay "on top" of your teaching assignment? Actually, there are many ways. Membership and participation in professional organizations is one excellent way. Reading the publications of the professional organizations to which you belong and of others you will find in your school library or that of a nearby college or university is another. Attending workshops sponsored by your school and outside agencies (professional groups, industries, federal and state agencies) can add much to your professional growth, if you approach these workshops with a desire to learn and not a resentment at being asked or required to attend. Courses at a nearby college or university, if carefully chosen to meet your needs, can be extremely beneficial. In addition, there are growth opportunities within your own school. Serving on textbook selection and curriculum revision committees will expose you to new ideas and materials.

## Professional Organizations and Publications

Professional organizations for teachers abound today—general organizations, encompassing all grade levels and disciplines, and specific organizations, focusing on particular grade or subject areas. These organizations frequently have local, state, regional, and national level activities, and your involvement can vary as you desire. Activities usually include regular meetings (discussion, speakers, panels), conferences and conventions, and service projects. Members often receive benefits such as reduced rates for conferences and conventions, journals and/or newsletters, and group study opportunities. Attending the regular meetings and conferences and conventions and reading the journals and newsletters will keep you up-to-date. By helping with service projects, you can learn more about the discipline and the community. In addition, group study opportunities offer motivation to analyze content, methods, and materials.

Two large general professional organizations are the National Education Association (NEA) and the American Federation of Teachers (AFT). The NEA was formed to promote professional development of educators and improvement of educational practices. It has become politically active in recent years, and has participated in teachers' collective bargaining efforts. The AFT was created as an affiliate of the American Federation of Labor, and functions primarily as a teacher's union by promoting better working conditions and higher salaries. It participates in collective bargaining activities as a main function. You need to analyze the goals and functions of these

*Even after you have become a teacher, you will find it beneficial to continue taking college courses.*

organizations and decide which, if either, is more closely oriented toward your personal philosophy.

Many professional publications can benefit the individual teacher, and many of them are connected with professional organizations. Although there is a limit to the number of professional organizations you can realistically join, there is no reason to limit the journals you consult to help improve your teaching. To round out your professional reading, you should obtain journals to which you do not subscribe from other sources. Other sources include fellow teachers, the school library's professional collection, the public library, the teacher center, and college or university libraries. Articles in these journals cover a wide range of topics, including classroom management, methods, materials, teacher liability, accountability, curriculum revision, new developments in different disciplines, and many others. Search out articles related to your situation and needs, read them, and *grow*.

## Inservice Opportunities and Graduate Work

To keep their teachers up-to-date, school systems budget a certain amount of money each year for inservice education. Inservice programs can be as effective as you and your fellow educators determine. Most systems allow teachers some voice in choosing inservice programs *if* the teachers express a desire to have such a voice. In many cases, programs are chosen without teacher input because teachers have said nothing and administrators assume teachers don't want to be involved. This may be an inaccurate assumption which administrators should investigate, but often such an assumption *is made* and *no* attempt is made to test its accuracy. When teachers do not have input about inservice programs, the programs may not meet their needs, and some teachers will write off inservice education programs as irrelevant. Don't make this mistake. Tell your inservice planners what your needs are, and they are more likely to be met.

Some systems ask teachers to attend a variety of professional functions to earn inservice "points," of which a specific number must be earned during each school year. Such a plan can work to your benefit. You may be able to earn points by attending the meetings and conferences of the professional organizations of your choice, by participating in specially planned activities at your school, or by participating in professional activities such as curriculum development workshops. You may also be able to earn points by taking related graduate courses at a nearby college or university.

Graduate courses can help you improve your teaching if you choose them wisely. Many states require a certain amount of graduate work for renewing teaching certificates. Some teachers take any convenient or reportedly easy course for this purpose. Don't fall into this trap. You are paying for this graduate work; make it pay you back with ideas for better instruction. Choose courses that will increase your skills in the areas you have felt some weakness, alert you to new methods and materials, or give you more insight into your students. If you actually enroll in a degree program and steadily take relevant courses, your activity will also lead in time to a salary increase on the basis of your new degree.

## Personal Contributions

You can also grow while helping others. Speaking at professional meetings or writing for professional journals will help you clarify your thinking and stimulate your mental processes. Your help for others turns into helping yourself. Serving on curriculum revision or textbook selection committees adds extra hours to your workday, but you will find that you also gain new ideas and familiarity with new materials that can improve your teaching. Everybody gains.

# Community Involvement

As a teacher, you are an important member of the community in which you teach. You have the right to voice your concerns about community conditions that may adversely affect the learning climate, such as censorship of books. You also have the responsibility to work toward solutions of community problems. You should be willing to do committee work, fact-finding searches, and other things to help your community find answers to its problems.

You should work as an ambassador for education, helping laypersons see the functions the school fills and the contributions of an educated populace to proper community functioning. Let people hear the good about education instead of only sensationalized bad news. The attitudes of community members toward the schools affect how well they support them. You can help shape positive, rather than negative, attitudes.

You can help keep the community informed about good things in the schools by having the news media cover special projects and programs. Science fairs, book festivals, computer-assisted instructional programs, and programs for the gifted and talented are only a few of the activities you may wish to publicize.

Your participation in parent-teacher organizations is also a positive way to reach the community. Special programs can be planned for disseminating information to parents. A new computer-assisted instructional program, for example, can be explained by allowing parents to play the roles of their children and have hands-on interaction with the computers and programs the students are using in class. A videotape can show students participating in a science laboratory or a physical education class using a new fitness program, and almost any school program can be written up in an attractive brochure to distribute to parents during meetings in which the program is discussed.

If you are employed in a system that engages in collective bargaining with the school board on items such as salary, hours, and working conditions, acting as a goodwill ambassador for educators can be helpful in negotiating a contract. School board members, as well as the public in general, may have the incorrect impression that teaching is an easy job, with many days of vacation. This impression tends to make board members and the public react negatively to requests for salary increases and lower pupil-teacher ratios. You can help by letting people know about the long after-school hours teachers spend in class preparation and grading papers, the stress of being responsible for so many people throughout the school day, and the demands of self-renewal and continuing education that are usually a condition of continued employment. Those long summer vacations are often filled with arduous, albeit satisfying, study. Speak out for the hard work and dedication of teachers, and you will be helping yourself and others in the profession.

## Discussion Questions

1   What options and resources should you consider when looking for a position?
2   What factors should you consider in developing a resumé and a letter of inquiry?

3  From whom and how should you secure letters of reference?
4  What are some necessary interviewing skills?
5  What opportunities for employment are available in your field? Do all of them involve teaching?
6  Where might you relocate to find the right position?
7  Do you have a responsibility to continue your education after you graduate from college and are certified as a teacher? Why or why not?
8  How can you keep up-to-date in your field after you leave the college classroom?
9  What contributions can professional organizations make to your growth as a teacher?
10  How can you obtain professional journals to read for new ideas? What journals are designed for your particular field?
11  Do inservice programs serve a useful function? Why or why not?
12  Are there any advantages to doing graduate study when you are employed as a teacher? If so, what are they?
13  Find a current directory of job opportunities or check with your placement office about the availability of positions. What good prospects are available?
14  Role play an interview with a peer. How could you improve your performance?
15  Develop a sample resumé and letter you might use. Have you presented yourself effectively?

# Selected References

Bolles, Richard Nelson. *What Color Is Your Parachute?* New York: Ten Speed Press, 1981.

Callahan, Sterling G. *Successful Teaching in Secondary Schools.* Glenview, Ill.: Scott, Foresman, 1971.

Crystal, John C., and Richard N. Bolles. *Where Do I Go From Here With My Life?* New York: Ten Speed Press, 1979.

Dubey, Robert E., et al. *A Performance-based Guide to Student Teaching.* Danville, Ill.: Interstate, 1975.

Figler, Howard. *The Complete Job-Search Handbook.* New York: Holt, Rinehart and Winston, 1979.

Flygare, Thomas J. *Collective Bargaining in The Public Schools.* Bloomington, Ind.: Phi Delta Kappa Educational Foundation, 1977.

Inlow, Gail M. *Maturity in High School Teaching.* Englewood Cliffs, N.J.: Prentice-Hall, 1970.

Itish, Richard K. *Go Hire Yourself an Employer.* New York: Doubleday, 1978.

Johnson, James A., and Louis D. Deprin. *Elementary Student Teaching: Readings.* Glenview, Ill.: Scott, Foresman, 1971.

Keach, Everett J. *Elementary School Student Teaching: A Casebook.* New York: John Wiley, 1966.

Lathrop, Richard. *Who's Hiring Who.* New York: Ten Speed Press, 1980.

Medley, Anthony. *Sweaty Palms: The Neglected Art of Being Interviewed.* New York: Lifetime Learning Publications, 1978.

Scheele, Adele. *Skills for Success.* New York: Ballantine Books, 1981.

Schmidt, Peggy J. *Making It on Your First Job: When You're Young, Inexperienced, and Ambitious.* New York: Avon Books, 1981.

Sund, Robert B., and Leslie W. Trowbridge. *Student-Centered Teaching in the Secondary School.* Columbus, Ohio: Charles E. Merrill, 1974.

U.S. Government Printing Office. *Dictionary of Occupational Titles.* Washington, D.C.: U.S. Government Printing Office, 1977.

U.S. Government Printing Office. *The Occupational Outlook Handbook, 1980–81.* Washington, D.C.: U.S. Government Printing Office, 1981.

# Appendix A

## Bibliography of Field Experience Textbooks

Beegle, Charles W., and Richard M. Brandt, eds. *Observational Methods in the Classroom.* Washington, D.C.: Association for Supervision and Curriculum Development, 1973.

Bennie, William A. *Supervising Clinical Experience in the Classroom.* New York: Harper and Row, 1972.

Borich, Gary, and Kathleen S. Fenton. *The Appraisal of Teaching: Concepts and Process.* Reading, Mass.: Addison-Wesley, 1977.

Cartwright, Carol, and Sarah Forsber. *Exceptional Previews: A Self-Evaluation Handbook for Special Education Students.* Belmont, Calif.: Wadsworth, 1979.

Cooper, James. *Classroom Teaching Skills: A Handbook.* Boston: Heath, 1977.

Drayer, Adam M. *Problems in Middle and High School Teaching.* Boston: Allyn and Bacon, 1979.

Elliot, P.G. *Field Experiences in Preservice Teacher Education.* Washington, D.C.: Eric Clearinghouse in Teacher Education, 1978.

Hanson, Derek, and Margaret Herrington. *From College to Classroom: The Probationary Year.* London: Routledge and Kegan Paul, 1976.

Heitzmann, William Ray. *The Classroom Teacher and the Student Teacher.* Washington, D.C.: National Education Association, 1977.

Henry, Marvin A., and W. Wayne Beasley. *Supervising Student Teachers: The Professional Way,* 2nd ed. Terre Haute, Ind.: Sycamore Press, 1976.

Hoover, Kenneth H. *The Professional Teacher's Handbook.* Boston: Allyn and Bacon, 1976.

Hoover, Kenneth, and Paul Hollingsworth. *Handbook for Elementary School Teachers*. Boston: Allyn & Bacon, 1978.

Jarolimek, John. *Social Studies Competencies and Skills*. New York: Macmillan, 1977.

Johnson, Jim, and Floyd Perry. *Readings in Student Teaching*. Dubuque, Iowa: William C. Brown, 1973.

Keach, Everett T., Jr. *Elementary School Student Teaching: A Casebook*. New York: John Wiley, 1966.

Lang, Duaine C., et al. *A Partnership for the Supervision of Student Teachers*. Mt. Pleasant, Mich.: Great Lakes, 1975.

Merrill, Edward C., Jr., and Betty J. Schuchman. *Professional Student Teaching Program*. Danville, Ill.: Interstate, 1973.

Neal, Charles D. *The Student Teacher at Work*. Minneapolis, Minn.: Burgess, 1971.

Putt, Robert C. *Working with the Student Teacher*. Dansville, N.Y.: Instructor Publications, 1971.

Schimmel, David, and Lois Fisher. *The Civil Rights of Students*. New York: Harper and Row, 1975.

Schwebel, Andrew. *Student Teacher's Handbook: A Step-By Step Guide*. New York: Harper and Row, 1979.

Sorenson, Virginia M., and Mary L. Veele. *Student Teacher's Handbook*. Holmes Beach, Fla.: Learning Publications, 1978.

Tanruther, Edgar M. *Clinical Experiences in Teaching for the Student Teacher or Intern*. New York: Dodd, Mead, 1973.

Tisdale, Pamela, and Frances Clayton Welch. *Teaching in the Elementary School: A Guide for Student Teachers*. Springfield, Ill.: Charles C. Thomas, 1983.

Tittle, Carol K. *Student Teaching: Attitude and Research Bases for Change in School and University*. Metuchen, N.J.: Scarecrow Press, 1974.

Wilkens, William H. R. *Today's Student—Tomorrow's Teacher*. Dubuque, Iowa: Kendall/Hunt, 1979.

Woods, John B., Tomas J. Mauries, and Bruce V. Dick. *Student Teacher: The Entrance to Professional Physical Education*. New York: Academic Press, 1973.

# Other Books of Interest

Boehm, Ann E., and Richard A. Weinberg. *The Classroom Observer*. New York: Teachers College, Columbia University, 1977.

Callahan, Joseph F., and Leonard H. Clark. *Teaching in the Middle and Secondary School*, 2nd ed. New York: Macmillan, 1982.

Clark, Leonard H., and Irving S. Star. *Secondary School Teaching Methods*, 4th ed. New York: Macmillan, 1981.

Good, Thomas L., and Jere E. Brophy. *Looking in Classrooms*, 2nd. ed. New York: Harper and Row, 1978.

Dreikurs, Rundall, et al. *Maintaining Sanity in the Classroom: Classroom Management Techniques*, 2nd ed. New York: Harper and Row, 1981.

Hyman, Ronald T. *Ways of Teaching*, 2nd ed. New York: Harper and Row, 1974.

House, Ernest R., and Stephen D Lapan. *Survival in the Classroom: Negotiating with Kids, Colleagues and Bosses*. Boston: Allyn and Bacon, 1978.

Kim, E.C., and R.D. Kellough. *Resource Guide for Secondary School Teaching: Planning for Competence*. New York: Macmillan, 1978.

Klingele, William E. *Teaching in Middle Schools*. Boston: Allyn and Bacon, 1979.

Jarolimek, John, and Clifford D. Foster. *Teaching and Learning in the Elementary School*, 2nd ed. New York: Macmillan, 1981.

Lemlech, Johanna. *Handbook for Successful Urban Teaching*. New York: Harper and Row, 1977.

Lemlech, Johanna. *Classroom Management*. New York: Harper and Row, 1979.

Orlich, Donald. *Teaching Strategies: A Guide to Better Instruction*. Indianapolis, Ind.: D.C. Heath, 1980.

Ryan, Kevin, et al. *Biting The Apple*. New York: Longman, 1980.

Ryan, Kevin, and James Cooper. *Those Who Can, Teach*, 3rd ed. Boston: Houghton-Mifflin, 1980.

Sadker, Myra P., and David M. Sadker. *Teachers Make the Difference: An Introduction to Education*. New York: Harper and Row, 1980.

# *Appendix B*

## Code of Ethics of the Education Profession, Adopted by 1975 Representative Assembly, National Education Association

### Preamble

The educator, believing in the worth and dignity of each human being, recognizes the supreme importance of the pursuit of truth, devotion to excellence, and the nurture of democratic principles. Essential to these goals is the protection of freedom to learn and to teach and the guarantee of equal educational opportunity for all. The educator accepts the responsibility to adhere to the highest ethical standards.

The educator recognizes the magnitude of the responsibility inherent in the teaching process. The desire for the respect and confidence of one's colleagues, of students, of parents, and of the members of the community provides the incentive to attain and maintain the highest possible degree of ethical conduct. The *Code of Ethics of the Education Profession* indicates the aspiration of all educators and provides standards by which to judge conduct.

The remedies specified by the NEA and/or its affiliates for the violation of any provision of this *Code* shall be exclusive and no such provision shall be enforceable in any form other than one specifically designated by the NEA or its affiliates.

## Principle I

**Commitment to the Student**   The educator strives to help each student realize his or her potential as a worthy and effective member of society. The educator therefore works to stimulate the spirit of inquiry, the acquisition of knowledge and understanding, and the thoughtful formulation of worthy goals.

In fulfillment of the obligation to the student, the educator—

1   Shall not unreasonably restrain the student from the independent action in the pursuit of learning.
2   Shall not unreasonably deny the student access to varying points of view.
3   Shall not deliberately suppress or distort subject matter relevant to the student's progress.
4   Shall make reasonable effort to protect the student from conditions harmful to learning or to health and safety.
5   Shall not intentionally expose the student to embarrassment or disparagement.
6   Shall not on the basis of race, color, creed, sex, national origin, marital status, political or religious beliefs, family, social or cultural background, or sexual orientation, unfairly—
    a   Exclude any student from participation in any program
    b   Deny benefits to any student
    c   Grant any advantage to any student.
7   Shall not use professional relationships with students for private advantage.
8   Shall not disclose information about students obtained in the course of professional service, unless disclosure serves a compelling professional purpose or is required by law.

## Principle II

**Commitment to the Profession**   The education profession is vested by the public with a trust and responsibility requiring the highest ideals of professional service.

In the belief that the quality of the services of the education profession directly influences the nation and its citizens, the educator shall exert every effort to raise professional standards, to promote a climate that encourages the exercise of professional judgment, to achieve conditions which attract persons worthy of the trust to careers in education, and to assist in preventing the practice of the profession by unqualified persons.

In fulfillment of the obligation to the profession, the educator—

1   Shall not in an application for a professional position deliberately make a false statement or fail to disclose a material fact related to competency and qualifications.
2   Shall not misrepresent his/her professional qualifications.
3   Shall not assist any entry into the profession of a person known to be unqualified in respect to character, education, or other relevant attribute.
4   Shall not knowingly make a false statement concerning the qualifications of a candidate for a professional position.
5   Shall not assist a noneducator in the unauthorized practice of teaching.
6   Shall not disclose information about colleagues obtained in the course of professional service unless disclosure serves a compelling professional purpose or is required by law.
7   Shall not knowingly make false or malicious statements about a colleague.
8   Shall not accept any gratuity, gift, or favor that might impair or appear to influence professional decisions or action.

Reprinted by permission of National Education Association, Washington, D.C.

# Appendix C

## Sample Lesson Plans

### Elementary Mathematics    Grade 3

A. Performance (Behavioral) Objective
   Given two numbers (two-digit numerals), the student will compute the sum when regrouping is required.

B. Major Concepts
   Addition
   Regrouping (renaming, "carrying")

C. Materials
   Flannel board and felt cutouts
   Counting men*
   Place value chart
   Instructional chart
   (Beansticks*/abacus)

D. Activities and Procedures
   1  Use the word problem: "I have twenty-three small red stars and eighteen small blue stars. How many small stars do I have altogether?"
   2  Represent the number sentence $23 + 18 = \square$ with felt cutouts on a flannel board.

*Counting men are sets of materials used for developing place value concepts and computational skills. Beansticks are sets of materials made of beans glued to sticks; they are also used for developing place value concepts and computational skills.

3  Ask the students to group the stars into sets of tens and ones. Ask the students to trade each group of ten small stars for one large star. (The sum will be represented by four large stars and one small star.)

4  Provide counting men as student aids and verbally guide the students through the process of representing the problem on their counting men.

5  Use place value chart to illustrate the solution:

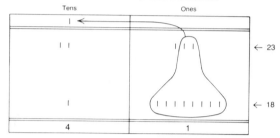

6  Use expanded notation, leading to the shortened form (on instructional charts)

```
                                                                                  1
   23          2 tens +   3 ones          23 = 20 +   3               23
  +18          1 ten  +   8 ones         +18 = 10 +   8              +18
               3 tens + 11 ones                30 + 11               41
               4 tens +   1 one               = 41
   41
```

7  *Alternative Activity*: Use beansticks to represent the idea of regrouping of 26 + 19.

E. Evaluation
   1  Ask students to do the following with this word problem:
      Bill has fifteen stamps and Betty has thirty-seven stamps. How many stamps do Bill and Betty have altogether?
      a.  Write the number sentence.
      b.  Use squares of paper to group into sets of tens and ones, trading each group of ten small squares for one large square of paper.
      c.  Find sum, using counting men.
      d.  Illustrate solution on a place value chart.
      e.  Use expanded notation and shortened form.

F. Assignment
   1  Word problems and exercises on page 78 of textbook.

# Secondary English (Written Composition)*
## Grade 11 or 12

I. Objectives
   General Aim: To make students aware of the fine distinctions in communication of language; to help them learn how to write more clearly and effectively.

*Reprinted with permission of Marsha Daugherty.

Specific Aim: To teach students to recognize the ambiguous elements in our language and how to avoid using them in their writing.

II. Content
Old Knowledge: Students have already learned about stress, pitch, and juncture in their language study.
New Knowledge: Types of structurally ambiguous sentences, distinguishing between the two meanings that can be attributed to one ambiguous sentence, and how to avoid writing ambiguous sentences.

III. Materials: Mimeographed sheets, list of ambiguous sentences

IV. Activities and Procedures
When students come into class, this sentence will be written on the board:

Girl hunter says father sets example

I will ask the class what this newspaper headline means to them. (I hope they will give me two different meanings; if they provide only one, I will tell them how it can have a completely different meaning from that one.)

To further introduce my subject for the lesson, I will tell them an amusing story about the misunderstanding by a coal deliveryman of the sentence "Empty sack in kitchen" and the funny consequences of this misunderstanding.

After I feel they sufficiently understand that sentences or even sequences of words they write may convey one meaning to themselves and quite another to someone else, I will enumerate and discuss with them six major sources of ambiguity and confusion in sentence structure.

I will ask students to add to the examples I give of each type of ambiguity. My examples will be on mimeographed sheets. The types of ambiguity are:

(1) One-stress pattern words—stress patterns of words are same, but certain words can function (grammatically) two ways in some sentences. Example:

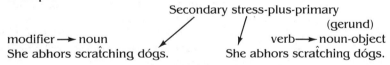

Secondary stress-plus-primary

(gerund)

modifier → noun                                        verb → noun-object
She abhors scratching dógs.                    She abhors scratching dógs.

(2) Overlap of stress patterns—some words have separate stress patterns for certain grammatical connotations.
Examples:
Secondary-plus-primary                                   Primary-plus-third

modifier → noun                                          compound nouns
dârk róom                                                     dárkroòm
bluê bóok                                                      blúeboòk

(3) Form and position duality of certain words—same word can identify with two parts of speech and mean two entirely different things.

Example:

The girl in the back seat looked *forward* (adverbial—ahead?)

$$\text{or}$$

$$\text{(adjectival—brash and unladylike?)}$$

(Verb *looked* also has two meanings in this connection)

Example:

He likes to spear muskrats and fish.

(Fish—noun object or infinitive?)

(. . . to spear muskrats and fish?)

$$\text{or}$$

(. . . to spear muskrats and to fish?)

(4)  Duality of sentence pattern

Example:

He found her an amateur. (indirect obj. plus direct obj.?)

$$\text{or}$$

$$\text{(direct object plus obj. complement?)}$$

(5)  Absence of stress, pitch, and juncture signals carried by speaking voice to indicate which of two meanings implied.

Example:

Do you know how happy people ought to be?

Do you know how happy⌐———➤⌐people ought to be?

Wanted: Baby-sitting in my apartment

Wanted: Baby⌐———➤⌐sitting in my apartment.

Did you ever stop to think how little men know about women?

Did you ever stop to think how little⌐———➤⌐men know about women?

(6)  Modification by position—word order and position

(This is an easier one for students to correct in their writing.)

Example:

He washed the chair on the patio.  (On the patio he washed the chair?)

$$\text{or}$$

$$\text{(The chair on the patio he washed?)}$$

After this discussion, I will explain several ways by which errors in ambiguity of this type (6) can be corrected. They are:

gender                        number      coordination
person—thing signals    position    punctuation
  (pers—rel pronouns)

To clarify this, I will give the students practice in trying to correct some ambiguous phrases. I will pass out sheets with these six phrases on them:

1.  The man in the chair with the tattered look.

(the/*its*)—gender

2.  The pet of the girl that was lying in the sand.

(who/*which*)—person—thing signals

3.  The boats at the dock which seemed far from our house.

(was/*were*)—number

4.  A discussion on gambling in the dormitory.

(in the dormitory on gambling)—position

5.  The novel that stood beside his dictionary which he loved to pore over.                  (*and that* he)—coordination

6.  A small room heater

(small-room heater or small room-heater)—punctuation

V. Evaluation: I will give the students a list of sentences (much like the above-mentioned phrases) that are structurally ambiguous and ask them to improve them according to the six criteria above.

   To make sure they understand this study of ambiguity thoroughly and completely, I will employ a reversal technique in which the students must deliberately think up about ten ambiguous sentences (including at least one to illustrate each of the six types of ambiguity I have introduced in class discussion) and be able to tell what is wrong with each of them.

VI. Assignments: The next day I will have the students read and discuss some of their made-up sentences in class. After that, we will discuss the best ways to correct the sentences on the sheet I gave them to work on the night before.

   To make them more aware of structural ambiguity and its frequent occurrence in writing (magazines, books, their own themes), I will announce a standing assignment to be due every Friday throughout the term. For a few minutes on these days, students will tell the class about examples of ambiguity they have noticed in a book or magazine. Also, since themes are returned every Friday, I will bring to the students' attention the ambiguous statements I have discovered in their writing and have them tell me why the statements are ambiguous and then correct them.

# Appendix D

## Sample Unit Plans

### Elementary Science*

#### Introductory Overview

This resource unit has been developed to introduce a third grade class to the study of fish. Through discussion, observation, and participation in activities, the students will gain an understanding of the basic characteristics of fish, their life processes, and their relative importance to man.

#### General Objectives

1   To help children develop an understanding of some generalizations of scientific principles they will be able to utilize in solving problems in their everyday lives.
2   To develop in children the ability to think and solve problems effectively and creatively.
3   To develop in children a scientific attitude.
4   To create in children an interest in and appreciation for the world in which we live.

*Reprinted with permission from Wilber S. Slawson, *A Guide for Teaching the Science of Our Environment* (Knoxville, Tenn.: University of Tennessee, 1981), pp. 136–51.

### Specific Objectives

Key concepts: given an appropriate learning experience, the students should be able to:

*1 Classify fish as vertebrates and members of the animal phylum chordata. IA–1, 2, 3, 5. DA–1, 2, 3, 4, 8a, 8b, 9, 10, 11, 17, 18. CA–1, 2, 3.

2 Recognize that most fish are alike in that they live only in water, have bodies covered with scales, have a head, trunk, and tail, and are cold-blooded. IA–2, 4, 5, 6. DA–3, 4, 7, 8a, 14, 17, 18, 20. CA–1, 2, 3.

3 Recognize that variations in color and sharp teeth sometimes serve to protect fish from their enemies. IA–2, 4, 5, 6. DA–3, 4, 8a, 17, 18. CA–1, 2, 3.

4 Realize that fish swim by the use of fins, a tail, and an air bladder. IA–2, 4, 5, 6. DA–1, 2, 4, 8a, 8b, 14, 17, 18. CA–1, 2, 3.

5 Identify that fish breathe through structures called gills and by opening and closing their mouths. IA–2, 4, 5, 6. DA–1, 2, 4, 6, 8a, 17, 18. CA–1, 2, 3.

6 State that fish eat plants; animals such as insects, worms, crayfish, snails; and other fish. IA–2, 4, 5. DA–3, 6, 8a, 13, 17, 18, 19. CA–1, 2, 3.

7 Understand that although the young of some fish develop inside the female's body and are born alive, most fish reproduce by the process of laying eggs called *spawning*. IA–2, 4, 5. DA–3, 4, 5, 8a, 8b, 16, 17, 18, 21. CA–1, 2, 3, 4, 5. RA–2, 4.

8 Appreciate that fish are valuable to man as sources of food, for sport and recreation, and for certain industrial products. IA–3, 6. DA–3, 8a, 17, 18. CA–1, 2, 3, 6, 7. RA–1, 5.

9 Realize that relatives of the bony fish are the lampreys, shark, and ray. IA–4, 5. DA–8a, 17, 18. CA–1, 2, 3. RA–3, 6.

**Process Skills**   Given an appropriate learning experience, the student will be able to:

1 Identify the common physical characteristics of fish. IA–1, 2, 4, 5, 6. DA–1, 2, 3, 4, 7, 8a, 8b, 9, 10, 11, 13, 17, 18, 20. CA–1, 2, 3.

2 Observe and describe the way in which fish breathe. IA–2, 4, 5, 6. DA–1, 2, 4, 8a, 8b, 12, 14, 15, 17, 18, 22. CA–1, 2, 3.

3 Observe and describe the way in which fish swim. IA–2, 4, 5, 6. DA–1, 2, 4, 8a, 8b, 14, 17, 18. CA–1, 2, 3.

4 List the types of food fish eat. IA–2, 4, 5. DA–3, 6, 8a, 13, 17, 18, 19. CA–1, 2, 3.

5 Explain the different processes of reproduction in fish. IA–2, 4, 5. DA–3, 4, 5, 8a, 8b, 16, 17, 18, 21. CA–1, 2, 3, 5. RA–2, 4.

6 State the importance of fish to humans. IA–2, 5, 6. DA–3, 8a, 17, 18. CA–1, 2, 3, 6, 7. RA–1, 5, 6.

*Key on p. 259.

### Content Outline

A.  The body of fish
 1. They are vertebrates.
 2. There are three parts to a fish's body.
  a. Head
  b. Trunk
  c. Tail
 3. Their skeletons are inside their bodies.
 4. The body of a fish is streamlined and tapered at both ends.
B.  How fish are alike
 1. Fish live only in water.
  a. Oceans
  b. Lakes
  c. Rivers
  d. Ponds
 2. Their bodies are covered with overlapping scales.
 3. Fish give off a slime that oozes between the scales and covers the body.
 4. Fish are cold-blooded.
C.  How fish breathe
 1. Fish breathe through respiratory organs called *gills* located on each side of the head.
 2. Most fish breathe by opening and closing their mouths.
  a. When a fish opens its mouth, water rushes in.
  b. When a fish closes its mouth, the water is forced out through two openings on each side at the back of the head.
  c. There are four or five gills in each opening.
  d. As the water is forced out over the gills, dissolved oxygen in the water passes through the thin walls of blood vessels and is picked up by the blood.
  e. The blood gets rid of its carbon dioxide and picks up fresh oxygen.
D.  How fish swim
 1. A fish swims forward rapidly by moving its tail and tail fins from side to side.
 2. A fish's fins serve several functions.
  a. Maintain balance
  b. Help the fish steer to the right or left
  c. Help the fish swim backward
 3. Most fish have an air bladder inside their bodies.
  a. Gases from the body can enter or leave the air bladder, making it inflate or deflate.
  b. The air bladder helps the fish to rise, sink, or stay at a particular depth.
E.  What fish eat
 1. Some fish eat only algae and other water plants.
 2. Some fish eat other animals such as insects, worms, crayfish, snails, and other fish.
 3. Fish that eat other animals have many sharp teeth.

F.  How fish reproduce
    1.  Most fish develop from eggs the female lays outside her body.
        a.  The female lays a large number of eggs in a process called spawning.
        b.  The male swims over the eggs and gives off a liquid which fertilizes them.
        c.  The fertilized eggs eventually hatch into tiny fish.
    2.  The young of some fish develop inside the female's body and are born alive.
    3.  Some fish have very unusual spawning habits.
        a.  Eel
        b.  Salmon
G.  Value of fish
    1.  They are important sources of food.
    2.  Many people catch fish for sport and recreation as well as for food.
    3.  Fish are used in the manufacture of many industrial products.
        a.  Paints
        b.  Glue
        c.  Vitamins A and D
H.  Relatives of the bony fish
    1.  The lamprey is a simple, primitive kind of fish.
    2.  The shark is very much like the bony fish but has characteristics that put it in its own group.
    3.  The ray belongs to the same group of fish as the shark.

## Initiating Activities

1   Have the children draw their interpretation of a fish. KC–2, PS–1.
2   Set up an aquarium in the room. To prepare an aquarium, put about 2 inches of sand on the bottom of the tank or bowl. Add pond or well water, if available. The water level should be at least an inch below the top of the tank. Let the sand settle, then put in the water plants. If you must use tap water, let it stand in the tank for a week before adding the plants. Tap water may have chlorine in it, which will pass off in this time. After the plants are in place, let the aquarium stand in medium light for another week. Then you can put in the fish. A fish about an inch long requires about a gallon of water. Feed the fish a pinch of food every two days. KC–2,3,4,5,6,7, PS–1,2,3,4,5.
3   Make a mobile about the importance of fish to people. KC–2, PS–6.
4   Visit a zoo to observe the aquariums. KC–2,3,4,5,6,7,9, PS–1,2,3,4,5.
5   Show the film "Swimmy." (Connecticut Films, Inc., 6 Cobble Hill Road, Westport, Connecticut, 06880. 1969.) 6 min., color. KC–all, PS–all.
6   For an extracurricular activity, with the permission and assistance of parents and school administration, take the children fishing on a Saturday, afternoon, or holiday. KC–2,3,4,5,8, PS–1,2,3,6.

### Developmental Activities

1 Draw a fish on the board showing the head, trunk, tail, gills, and fins. KC–2,4,5, PS–1,2,3.
2 Make or obtain charts and display them for children to see how fish are alike. KC–2,4,5, PS–1,2,3.
3 Collect pictures of fish and see if the children can tell how they are different. KC–2,3,6,7,8, PS–1,4,5,6.
4 Obtain a dead fish and dissect it to observe the different external and internal parts. KC–1,2,3,4,5,7, PS–1,2,3,5.
5 Obtain some fish eggs and observe them. KC–7, PS–5.
6 Very quickly, place a small fish (goldfish) in a jar of sealed-in plants and water and reseal. Watch for days and weeks and observe that both thrive in the sealed jar. KC–5,6, PS–2,4.
7 Observe scales under a microscope. KC–2, PS–1.
8 Obtain a diagram of the internal structures of modern fish and relate it to
  a. Evolution of fish. KC–all, PS–all.
  b. Dissection activity. (DA–4), KC–1,4,5,7, PS–1,2,3,5.
9 Secure some vertebrae of fish. Have the class examine them for the opening through which the spinal cord passes. Students may notice smaller openings through which nerves or blood vessels enter the bones. KC–1, PS–1.
10 Bones of vertebrate animals contain, among other elements, calcium and phosphorus. The compounds of calcium can be dissolved by placing the bones in vinegar or weak hydrochloric acid, then washing them in water. Have the students feel them and compare them with the original bones. (The remaining material is soft and flexible, indicating the function of calcium in making the bones rigid.) KC–1, PS–1.
11 Some of the more advanced students might clean and mount skeletons of fish. The flesh is easily removed if the fish is cooked in boiling water. As the flesh is removed from each body part, students should make drawings of the positions of the bones, then place the bones in an envelope. When all bones have been cleaned, they can be mounted on cardboard with glue. KC–1, PS–1.
12 Ask the students to observe the fish in an aquarium carefully for one five-minute period. Ask them particularly to watch the gill movements. After their observations, ask them whether the water enters the fish's mouth and goes out the gills, or enters the gills and goes out through the mouth. You will probably find supporters of both beliefs. The answer can be determined with the aid of a soda straw, a few drops of food coloring, and a fish. With the soda straw, place a drop of food coloring near the head of the fish to permit observation of water currents. You may wish to put the fish in a small container for better observation and for ease in introducing the food coloring. KC–5, PS–2.
13 Try feeding some fish in the room a variety of foods and observe. Ask: How does the fish know the food is there? Where

are the fish's eyes? How does the fish get its food? Which food did the fish prefer? KC–6, PS–4.

14  Obtain a few dead, whole perch. Have the children observe the streamlined body, scales, and fins of the perch. Afterwards, lift the flap covering the gills and observe the gills of the perch. Demonstrate the continuous passage from the mouth to the gills by passing a probe or a pencil from one through the other. This would be a good time to let an observant child watch live fish and notice that the mouth and the gill covering close alternately rather than simultaneously, thereby facilitating the flow of water over the gills. KC–2,4,5, PS–1,2,3.

15  To determine whether or not water has air in it for fish to live on, fill a glass with cold water. Let it stand in a warm room for a few hours. Look along the sides of the glass. What do you see? Use a pencil or toothpick to rub the inside of the glass. Tell what happens. What makes the bubbles? KC–5, PS–2.

16  Have students observe the essential features of sexual reproduction. Although brine shrimp are not fish, you can see them hatch from eggs. Obtain some fertilized brine shrimp eggs. You will also need a baking pan, salt, and water. Put two quarts of water into the pan. If you use tap water, let it stand for at least a day in an uncovered container. Add five teaspoons of salt to the water and stir. Place one-half teaspoon of brine shrimp eggs in the salt water. Place the pan in a warm place, but not in sunlight. Observe the eggs every day. Use a magnifying lens. How long does it take the eggs to hatch? Do you see any changes inside the eggs? After the eggs hatch, remove a few drops of water containing shrimp and place them on a glass slide. Observe the shrimp with a hand lens or microscope. A tiny brine shrimp continues to grow after it hatches from an egg, and its body cells keep dividing until the shrimp is fully grown. KC–7, PS–5.

17  Invite a member of the Fish and Game Service to visit the class. KC–all, PS–all.

18  Have the children do group reports on different aspects of fish, letting them decide on their own topic. KC–all, PS–all.

19  Design a felt board with pictures of different fishes and the various foods they eat. Let the children assist you in matching the fish with the appropriate foods. KC–6, PS–4.

20  Observe a fish in a bowl or glass tank. Note especially the absence of eyelids. Have the children speculate on how the fish sleeps at night. KC–2, PS–1.

21  Fill two glass bowls with water. Put some water plants into each bowl. Place a lighted desk lamp over one bowl. The burning light bulb will increase the temperature of the water. Keep the other bowl at room temperature. Place a pair of guppies into each bowl. Observe the guppies over a period of three months. Keep a record of the number of baby guppies that are born. Ask: How did the temperature affect the breeding of the guppies? How did it affect the gestation period? KC–7, PS–5.

22  Do a simulation activity of breathing. Have a small group of students act out the breathing process in fish. Draw a large fish

out of paper or outline one in tape on the floor. Have a few students stand at the mouth of the fish and have the mouth closed. Then have them spread out and another group of students enter through the mouth as water. Right inside, have two students act as the valve that closes after the water flows through. Have four students act as the gills, two on each side of the fish's head. As the valve closes, the gills contract and force the water out over a series of folds. Have a few students act as these folds. Blood in the gills gives up carbon dioxide and takes oxygen from the water. The students can trade signs or cards that say "carbon dioxide" for signs that say "oxygen." KC–5, PS–2.

### Culminating Activities

1   Let the children devise a way of taking roll using concepts of fish they have learned. KC–all, PS–all.
2   Make a notebook and/or scrapbook illustrating one of the process skills chosen by the student. KC–all, PS–all.
3   Visit a hatchery and/or trout farm. KC–7, PS–5.
4   Make a bulletin board pertaining to fish defenses. KC–3.
5   Have the children write stories about fish after visiting an aquarium, a hatchery or a trout farm. KC–all, PS–all.
6   Divide the class into groups and have each group make up poems, songs, stories, pantomimes, or puppet shows about how fish are affected by environmental pollution, and have them present them to the class. KC–8, PS–6.
7   Have the students make a mural of a large lake with fish common to the area. KC–3,8, PS–6.

### Related Activities

1   Make a "fish map" of the United States showing fish associated with various regions. KC–8, PS–6.
2   Make a poster with drawings and pictures showing the salmon's journey to its spawning waters. KC–7, PS–5.
3   At the zoo (if feasible) and through pictures, films, and filmstrips, observe relatives of fish and other water inhabitants (shark, dolphin, ray, lamprey, etc.) KC–9.
4   Breed some tropical fish. KC–7, PS–5.
5   Make a list and chart of fish common to the area. KC–8, PS–6.
6   To study the effects of pollution on fish, observe a goldfish that has been in pure water for awhile and one that has been in polluted water for the same amount of time. Note differences in their conditions. KC–9, PS–6.
*KEY*
Key concepts = KC
Process skills = PS
Initiating activity = IA
Developmental activity = DA
Culminating activity = CA
Related activity = RA

**Evaluation**

1   Give each child a piece of paper and let him illustrate the concept on the task card he has been given. When the children have finished, tape the pictures together to form a filmstrip and show it to the class.

2   To motivate a class discussion for oral examination and review, set up a "fish pond" in which children fish for their questions. Each child will attempt to answer the question, and then the class will discuss the answer. Make the fish pond with yardsticks, paper clips, magnets, string, and construction paper.

3   Use a card game to evaluate the children in groups. Make cards out of index cards, construction paper, etc. On one card, write a concept that has been learned, such as "Most fish reproduce by —————." On the card that will match, write the term and/or picture that completes the concept, such as a drawing of some fish eggs. Play the game as you would play "Old Maid," with a picture of a fish as the "Old Maid." Let the children play in groups while you observe how quickly and how well they identify the books of cards. Groups can play at different times of the day—during study periods, breaks, and homeroom—to enable the teacher to observe all groups.

4   By taping down pieces of colored construction paper, outline the floor space into a large maze. Around the maze, have different sets of questions on construction paper of the same colors as the maze. The children will take individual turns, roll dice, and take as many steps as the dice indicate. When they land on a color, they will take a question of the same color. The question might be something like "If you can name the journey the salmon makes to reproduce, go forward 2 steps; if not, go back 1 step." The number of steps forward and backward will depend on the difficulty of the questions. The first child to reach the end of the maze in the fewest number of turns wins. The teacher will observe the children to evaluate how much they have learned in the unit and/or lesson on fish.

5   Unscramble these words: 1. sligl 2. shif 3. brertveate 4. ifns 5. threabe 6. miws 7. karsh 8. thoum 9. lascses

**Across**

1   The bodies of all fish are covered with —————.
4   All fish have a ——————, trunk, and tail.
5   A relative of the fish which is flat and looks rather strange is the ——————.
6   Although mammals are warm blooded, fish are —————— blooded.
8   All fish live in ——————.
10  Some fish vary in —————— which helps protect them.
11  Fish have pairs of —————— which help them swim.
12  Fish breathe with structures called ——————.
14  Some fish eat animals, but some eat —————— in the water.
16  The young of some fish develop —————— the female's body instead of by laying eggs.
17  Fish are important to people as a source of ——————.

## Down

2  Fish are members of the phylum _____.
3  A relative of the bony fish with large sharp teeth is the _____.
7  Fish move about by _____.
9  Animals with backbones are called _____.
13 The process of fish laying eggs is known as _____.
15 A structure inside the fish's body which helps it swim is the _____ _____.

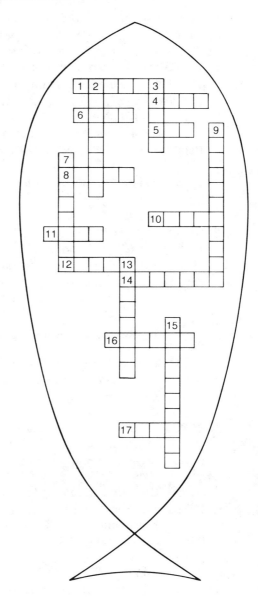

# Materials and Resources

## A. Books for the teacher

*Animal Life and Love: Fascinating and Improbable Facts About the Ways Of Mammals, Birds, Reptiles, and Amphibians, Fishes, Insects, and Other Invertebrates.* New York: Harper and Row, 1963.

Dean, Bashford. *Bibliography of Fishes,* 3 vols. ed. C.R. Eastman. New York: American Museum of Natural History, 1916–23.

*Ecology of Fishes.* New York: Academic Press, 1963.

Firth, Frank E., ed. *The Encyclopedia of Marine Resources.* New York: Van Nostrand Reinhold, 1969.

*The Fishes.* Morristown, N.J.: Silver Burdette, 1963.

*The Fishes,* Young Readers Ed. Morristown, N.J.: Silver Burdette, 1967.

*Fish and Wildlife: The Story of the Work of Fish and Wildlife Services.* New York: Putnam's, 1969.

*Golden Nature Guide: Fishes.* New York: Western, 1969.

Herald, Earl S. *Living Fishes of the World.* Garden City, N.Y.: Doubleday, 1961.

Inner, William T. *Exotic Aquarium Fishes.* 19th ed. New York: E.P. Dutton, 1964.

*The Life Story of the Fish,* 2nd rev. ed. New York: Dover, 1949.

*Nature Guide: Fishes.* New York: Western, 1969.

*Teach Yourself Indoor Aquarium.* New York: Dover, 1970.

Villard, Paul. *Exotic Fish as Pets.* Garden City, N.Y.: Doubleday, 1971.

Zim, Herbert S., and Hurst H. Shoemaker. *Fishes: A Guide to Fish and Saltwater Species.* Racine, Wis.: Golden Press, Western, 1956.

## B. Books for student and teacher

*Animal World in Color,* vol. 3. Chicago: Childrens Press, 1969. 12 vols.

Bendick, Jeanne. *The First Book of Fishes.* New York: Franklin Watts, 1965.

Berrill, Jacquelyn. *Wonders of Animal Migration.* New York: Dodd, Mead, 1964.

Buck, Margaret Waring. *In Ponds and Streams.* Nashville, Tenn.: Abingdon Press, 1955.

Buck, Margaret Waring. *Lots From the Pond.* Nashville, Tenn.: Abingdon Press, 1958.

Burger, Carl. *All About Fish.* New York: Random House, 1960.

Cooper, Elizabeth K. *Science on the Shores and Bunkers.* New York: Harcourt, Brace and World, 1960.

Earle, Olive L. *Strange Fishes of the Sea.* New York: William Morrow, 1968.

Fletcher, Alan Mark. *Fishes Dangerous to Man.* New York: Addison-Wesley, 1969.

Fletcher, Alan Mark. *Unusual Aquarium Fishes.* Philadelphia: J.B. Lippincott, 1968.

Hyde, Margaret O. *Animal Clocks and Compasses.* New York: McGraw-Hill, 1960.

LaGorce, John Oliver, ed. *The Book of Fishes,* rev. ed. Washington, D.C.: National Geographic Society, 1952.

Mason, George F. *Animal Homes.* New York: William Morrow, 1947.

Mason, George F. *Animal Teeth.* New York: William Morrow, 1965.

Morgan, Alfred. *Aquarium Book for Boys and Girls.* New York: Scribner's, 1959.

National Geographic Society. *Wondrous World of Fishes.* Washington, D.C.: National Geographic Society, 1965.

Ommanney, F.D. *The Fishes,* Young Readers Ed. New York: Time-Life Books, 1967.

Parker, Bertha Morris. *The New Golden Treasury of Natural History.* New York: Golden Press, 1968.

Paysaw, Klaus. *Aquarium Fish from Around the World.* Minneapolis, Minn.: Lerner, 1970.

Pettit, Ted S. *A Guide to Nature Projects.* New York: W.W. Norton, and Grosset and Dunlap, 1966.

Place, Marian T. *Let's Go To a Fish Hatchery.* New York: Putnam's, 1967.

Selsam, Millicent E. *The Language of Animals.* New York: Four Winds Press, 1969.

Selsam, Millicent E. *Underwater Zoo.* New York: William Morrow, 1961.

Shapp, Martha, and Charles Shapp. *Let's Find Out About Fishes.* New York: Franklin Watts, 1965.

Shaw, Evelyn. *Fish Out of School.* New York: Harper and Row, 1970.

Wildsmith, Brian. *Brian Wildsmith's Fishes.* New York: Franklin Watts, 1968.

Wong, Herbert, and Matthew F. Vessel. *My Goldfish.* Reading, Mass.: Addison-Wesley, 1969.

Woods, Loren P. *Fishes.* New York: Follett, 1969.

Zim, Herbert S., and Hurst H. Shoemaker. *Fishes.* New York: Golden Press, 1957.

## C. Films

"Aquarium Care." Garden City, N.Y.: Doubleday, 1964. 4 min., (Movie S 8 mm loop)

"Fish and Their Characteristics." Chicago: Coronet Films, 1970. (Movie 16 mm reel)

"Fish and Wildlife Conservation." Garden City, N.Y.: Doubleday, 1965. (Movie S 8 mm loop)

"Fish and Wildlife Conservation." Cenco Educational Aids, 1969. (Movie S 8 mm loop)

"Fish are Interesting." Los Angeles: Film Assoc. of California, 1954. (1 min., color)

"The Fish Embryo—From Fertilization to Hatching." Wilmette, Ill.: Encyclopaedia Britannica Films, 1963. (12 min., color)

"A Fish Family." Whittier, Calif.: Moody Institute of Science, Educational Film Division, 1957. (10 min., color)

"Food from the Sea." Bailey Film Assoc., 1969. (11 min., Movie S 8 mm reel)

"The Fish that Nearly Drowned." Garden City, N.Y.: Doubleday, 1969. (10 min., Movie 16 mm reel)

"The Fish That Turned Gold." Bloomington, Ind.: Indiana University Audio-visual Center. (16 min., Color & B&W)

"Goldfish Eggs Hatching." Garden City, N.Y.: Doubleday, 1964. (Movie S 8 mm loop)

"How do Fish Swim?" Sterling Educational Films, 1969. (24 min., Movie 16 mm reel)

"Introducing Fish." Chicago: Coronet Films, 1970. (Movie S 8 mm loop)

"Salmon Run." Garden City, N.Y.: Doubleday, 1966. (4 min., Movie S 8 mm loop)

"Wonder of Reproduction." Whittier, Calif.: Moody Institute of Science, Educational Film Division, 1969. (12 min., Movie 16 mm)

### D. Filmstrips

"Animal Life in the Sea." Filmstrip House, 1970.

"Animals with Backbones." Wilmette, Ill.: Encyclopaedia Brittanica Films.

"Classification—Different Kinds of Animals." Filmstrip House, 1970.

"Discovering Fishes." Wilmette, Ill.: Encyclopaedia Britannica, Educational Corp.

"Fish." Curriculum Materials, 1969.

"How Fish Get Their Food." Curriculum Materials, 1969.


## Secondary Social Studies*

I.  Topic
    The Spanish-American War is often glossed over or neglected entirely in surveys of American history, yet it is an excellent vehicle for examining American values at the turn of the century as well as America's perceived role in international affairs. The period itself (1898–1900) and its aftermath showcase a moral dilemma concerning American foreign policy, and eventually a resurgent "nationalism" that profoundly affects the events of ensuing decades. This is a five-day plan.

II. Students' background
    This unit is designed for a college-bound eleventh grade American history class with a small-town or suburban background.

III. Suggested resources for students
    A.  Anti-Imperialism
        *Twelve Against Empire*, Robert Beisner    } Copies in the library
        *U.S. Expansionism*, David Healy           } on reserve

*Reprinted with permission of Paul Aebischer, 122 Montana Ave., Oak Ridge, Tennessee 37830

Textbook
Encyclopedia
Xeroxed material on resource table            } May be used in class or
*Reader's Guide to Periodical Literature*      } checked out overnight

B.  Philippine Insurrection
    *Little Brown Brother*, Leon Wolff    } copies in library on reserve
    Textbook
    Encyclopedia
    *Reader's Guide to Periodical Literature*
    Xeroxed material on resource table

C.  1900 Presidential Election
    Encyclopedia
    Various political histories in library
    *History of American Presidential Elections*,   }        Library
        Arthur Schlesinger, editor                  }    reference area
    Textbook

D.  Foreign Policy
    *U.S. Expansionism*, David Healy } copies in the library on reserve
    Textbook
    Encyclopedia
    Reader's Guide

IV.  Teacher's Bibliography
     A.  Textbooks
         *America! America!*
         *America: A Portrait in History*

     B.  Secondary Sources
         Richard Hofstedter, ``Manifest Destiny . . .'' in Daniel Aaron's
             *America in Crisis.*
         Robert Beisner, *Twelve Against Empire*
         Frank Friedel, *The Splendid Little War*
         David Healy, *American Expansionism*
         Arthur Schlesinger, ed. *History of American Presidential Elections*,
             vol. III
         Joseph E. Wisah, *The Cuban Crisis as Reflected in the New York
             Press*
         Leon Wolff, *Little Brown Brother*
     C.  Periodicals
         Robert Beisner, ``30 Years After Manila: E.L. Godkin, Carl Schurz,
             and Anti-Imperialism in the Gilded Age,'' *The Historian*, vol. XXX,
             1968, pp. 561–76. (Portion of this article will be xeroxed for
             the resource table.)
         D.J. Tweton, ``Imperialism vs. Prosperity,'' *North Dakota Quar-
             terly*, vol. XXX, 1962, pp. 50–52.
     D.  Primary sources: Published documents listed under W.J. Bryan,
         E.L. Godkin, Carl Schurz, and T. Roosevelt. Also copies of W.R.
         Hearst's *New York Journal* and J. Pulitzer's *World*.

E.  Audiovisual: Films dealing with destruction of battleship "Maine."
    Note: For further information on this topic, refer to "anti-imperialism"
    or "Spanish-American War" headings in *Harvard Guide to American
    History.*

IV.  Objectives
     A.  To familiarize students with historical developments leading to the
         Spanish-American conflict.
     B.  To trace the course of the Spanish-Cuban conflict prior to U.S.
         intervention.
     C.  To recognize factors influencing the U.S. decision to enter the war.
     D.  To consider the role of the media and of public opinion as a potent
         force in politics.
     E.  To place the entire event in the context of the evolution of U.S.
         foreign policy.
     F.  To explore the consequences and implications of U.S. postwar
         policy, particularly in the Philippines.
     G.  To develop group discussion and problem-solving skills.
     H.  To develop research and writing skills.

V.  Procedures: Daily Activities
    Introduction
    A.  Monday
        1.  Introductory lecture. Topic is "Historical Background for the
            Spanish-American War." Lecture will cover the following:
            Spanish interests in the Caribbean—potential conflicts with
                the U.S.
            Unrest in Cuba—the revolution in 1895 to throw off Spanish
                power.
            U.S. economic interests and humanitarian interests—develop-
                ments in the Cuban-Spanish Conflict up to and including
                the explosion aboard *The Maine.* (20 minutes)
        2.  Show class the short film concerning activities surrounding the
            "Maine" incident. (20 minutes)
        3.  Introduce the class to the resource table where various docu-
            ments, primary materials, and articles concerning the Spanish-
            American War can be found.
            Explain to class that unit grade will be determined by:
                Participation in discussions
                Quiz
                Unit exam
                Individual project
            Distribute ditto sheets explaining the project requirements.

### Projects for Spanish-American War Unit (Culminating Activity)

Each student will complete one of the following:

A.  After reading letters and articles concerning the anti-Imperialists, sum-
    marize in a three–five page essay the sentiments of two of these people—
    Carl Schurz, E.L. Godkin, W.J. Bryan, Samuel Gompers.

    B.   Use outside resources to prepare a three–five page paper on the Philippine Insurrection.

    C.   Use outside resources to prepare a three–five page paper on how the Spanish-American War affected the presidential campaign of 1900.

    D.   Write a three–five page essay explaining how the Spanish-American War might have been a turning point in American foreign policy. Use specific examples.

    E.   Prepare a bulletin board or other audiovisual presentation dealing with some aspect of the Spanish-American War.

    F.   Get teacher's approval to develop your own project.

Distribute ditto sheets of the student's bibliography and research guide. (10 minutes)

Assignment:

> Read Chapter 30 in textbook (*America! America!*) in preparation for a short cognitive quiz on Tuesday.

*Body*

B.   Tuesday

    1.   20-point standardized cognitive quiz on Chapter 30 in textbook. (20 minutes)

    2.   Lecture. Topic is "U.S. Intervention: The Spanish-American War." Lecture will cover situations which convinced U.S. to enter the war, especially the "de Lome letter" and the "Maine" incident; President McKinley's role; suggestions that U.S. was eager to show off power, to seek "World Power" status; the course of the war before U.S. intervention; the course of the war after U.S. intervention; Admiral Dewey. (20 minutes)

    3.   Assignment/Activity. Distribute copies of an illustrative article from William Randolph Hearst's *New York Journal.* Allow remaining class time to read article. Distribute the following questions to be considered for discussion on Wednesday.

        a.   Is the article biased? What does it intend its readers to believe? Isolate specific examples of "sensationalism."

        b.   Do you think the media reflect public values or create them? Why?

        c.   How important is public opinion in an event such as the Spanish-American War? Do you think President McKinley was pressured by public opinion?

C.   Wednesday

    1.   Class is broken into groups of eight for discussion of above questions. Teacher appoints discussion leader, discussion monitor (to record who participates and how often), secretary, and reporter (can be the same person). Groups will be allowed three minutes to report their conclusions to the entire group. (20 minutes for discussion, 10 minutes for reports)

2.  Lecture. Topic is "Public Opinion: Emerging Nationalism." Lecture will cover concept and philosophy of nativism, manifest destiny, and the "White Man's Burden"; review America's history as an isolationist nation (Declaration of Independence, Washington's Farewell Address, Monroe Doctrine); describe "Yellow journalism," "jingoism," and the role of popular opinion; and introduce the anti-expansionist philosophy. (20 minutes)

D.  Thursday
    1.  Lecture. Topic is "Moral Dilemma-The Question of Empire." Lecture will cover crux of the Philippine issue. McKinley wrestles with four alternatives; humanitarian or economic? The anti-imperialists— ideology, philosophy, distinguished members, methods used, results; William Jennings Bryan— election of 1900 as a last gasp for an anti-imperialistic administration, the "Bryan" dilemma for Democrats; the Philippine insurrection—why did it occur? Acquisition of Philippines as a crossroads in American foreign policy. Point to future events: Caribbean policy; World War I. (20 minutes)
    2.  Explain nature of Friday's unit examination: Five out of eight identifications (50 points) and two out of three essays (50 points). (5 minutes)
    3.  Questioning techniques with entire group. Distribute handout from Philippine Islands.
        a.  How does this account differ from what you've read? How would you account for differences?
        b.  Main question: Should a nation be allowed the right of national self-determination? If they say Yes, "Suppose another powerful nation—such as Spain—would overrun the Philippines if the U.S. didn't acquire it?"
            If they say No, "How would U.S. have developed without this right? Could Philippines develop similarly?" (25 minutes)
            (If discussion stalls prematurely, time may be spent on projects.)

E.  Friday—Unit Exam (Entire Period)
    (Remind students that projects are due Monday)
    Part I.  Identification
    Identify and briefly explain the significance of five (5) of the following:
        Isolationism
        de Lome letter
        William Jennings Bryan
        Manifest Destiny
        "jingoism"
        the anti-Imperialists
        Admiral Dewey
    Part II.  Essay
    Respond to two (2) of the following questions. Responses should be in the form of a concise (three–four paragraphs), well organized, and cohesive essay.

1. Support or attack the following statement:
   "The Spanish-American War was a blemish on the United States' diplomatic record. A misinformed nation acted on misperceived threats with territorial gains primarily in mind."
2. "Theodore Roosevelt referred to the Spanish-American conflict as a 'Splendid Little War.' In reality, this war—fought on Cuba's behalf, against Spain, in the Philippines—was a major turning point in American foreign policy." Support or refute this statement.
3. Trace the role of public opinion—both during the war itself and in ensuing events—in the Spanish-American War Period. What importance would you ascribe to the power of public thinking? Be sure to consider political issues, economic aspirations, and "yellow journalism."
   Note: For those who finish before end of period—work on projects.

# Appendix E

## Sample Learning Center

### Learning Center on the Existing Relationships of Various Elements in the Environment

Rationale statement:

These materials are to be used as an introductory unit dealing with the elements of the environment. The three segments of the environment will be introduced. There is no intended grade level nor intended time allocation. The center is coded with symbols and organized as follows:

Introductory Activities— ▭ —rectangle
Key Concept I— △ —triangle
Key Concept II— ◯ —circle
Key Concept III— ▱ —parallelogram
Required Activities—R
Optional Activities—OP
Extension Activities—E
Example: This symbol △ᴿ 4 is to be interpreted to be a required activity and the fourth activity related to Key Concept I.

Key concepts

I. One segment of all environments is the *atmosphere.*
   A. The earth's atmosphere has many common characteristics regardless of a specific environment.
      1. Air has many physical properties.

Reprinted with permission from Wilber S. Slawson, *A Guide for Teaching the Science of Our Environment* (Knoxville, Tenn.: University of Tennessee, 1981), pp. 82–90.

2. Air exerts pressure which can be measured.

3. The atmosphere is layered, with each layer having definite characteristics.

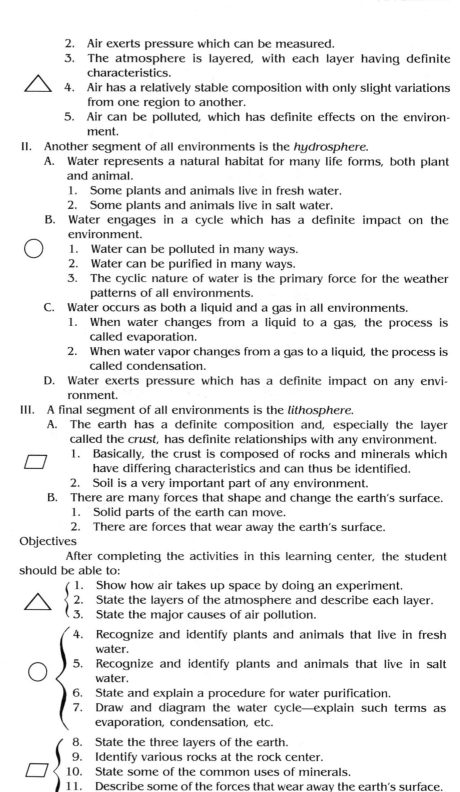

4. Air has a relatively stable composition with only slight variations from one region to another.

5. Air can be polluted, which has definite effects on the environment.

II. Another segment of all environments is the *hydrosphere.*

    A. Water represents a natural habitat for many life forms, both plant and animal.

        1. Some plants and animals live in fresh water.

        2. Some plants and animals live in salt water.

    B. Water engages in a cycle which has a definite impact on the environment.

        1. Water can be polluted in many ways.

        2. Water can be purified in many ways.

        3. The cyclic nature of water is the primary force for the weather patterns of all environments.

    C. Water occurs as both a liquid and a gas in all environments.

        1. When water changes from a liquid to a gas, the process is called evaporation.

        2. When water vapor changes from a gas to a liquid, the process is called condensation.

    D. Water exerts pressure which has a definite impact on any environment.

III. A final segment of all environments is the *lithosphere.*

    A. The earth has a definite composition and, especially the layer called the *crust,* has definite relationships with any environment.

        1. Basically, the crust is composed of rocks and minerals which have differing characteristics and can thus be identified.

        2. Soil is a very important part of any environment.

    B. There are many forces that shape and change the earth's surface.

        1. Solid parts of the earth can move.

        2. There are forces that wear away the earth's surface.

Objectives

After completing the activities in this learning center, the student should be able to:

1. Show how air takes up space by doing an experiment.

2. State the layers of the atmosphere and describe each layer.

3. State the major causes of air pollution.

4. Recognize and identify plants and animals that live in fresh water.

5. Recognize and identify plants and animals that live in salt water.

6. State and explain a procedure for water purification.

7. Draw and diagram the water cycle—explain such terms as evaporation, condensation, etc.

8. State the three layers of the earth.

9. Identify various rocks at the rock center.

10. State some of the common uses of minerals.

11. Describe some of the forces that wear away the earth's surface.

12. State the definitions of words on the vocabulary list.

Pre-Posttest for the Three Segments of the Environment.
☐ Pretest

△ {
  1. There are three parts of the environment—name them.
  2. Can you think of and describe an experiment that would show the concept, "Air exerts pressure which can be measured"?

○ {
  3. Name three plants and animals that live in fresh water.
  4. Name three plants and animals that live in salt water.
  5. Define evaporation.
  6. Define condensation.

▱ {
  7. Name the three layers of the earth.
  8. Name three types of rocks you find on the earth's crust.
  9. What is a mineral?
  10. What is an earthquake?

Posttest

△ {
  1. From the experiment using a bowl half filled with water and a glass tumbler, describe the concept illustrated.
  2. Draw a diagram of the earth's atmosphere and label each layer.
  3. What are the major causes of air pollution?
     What can you do to help prevent air pollution?

○ {
  4. Beside each plant and animal name, write either fresh water or salt water to indicate where it is found:

     algae          kelp
     starfish       bass
     guppy          sailfish
     seaweed        coral
     trout          snail darter
     shark          crab
  5. State a procedure for water purification.
  6. Draw the water cycle. Be sure to label it appropriately.
  7. Define condensation.

▱ {
  8. Identify three rocks shown at the front of the room.
  9. Label the diagram with the layers of the earth.
  10. Name some common uses of minerals in your home. Name at least three.
  11. Explain what happens when the earth cracks. (What causes an earthquake?)
  12. Name two forces that wear away the earth's surface.

Bonus: Define *Seismograph.*

Complete this experiment and record the results in your file.

△ R₁    Concept: Air takes up space.
        Materials:  bowl half full of water
                    glass tumbler
                    small piece of styrofoam

Method:  Turn tumbler upside down and push it straight into a bowl of water. Show that you have caught air in the tumbler. Float styrofoam in the water and try the same thing. Show that styrofoam is at a lower level because of the air in the tumbler.

Check this off on your checklist.

Air moves things. Make a pinwheel. What happens when we blow the pinwheel?

Complete this experiment and record your results in your file.

A.  Problem: Can air pressure hold water in a tumbler?
B.  Materials:
1.  Glass tumbler
2.  Water
3.  Piece of cardboard
4.  Basin or sink
C.  Procedure:
1.  Fill the glass tumbler completely full of water.
2.  Place a piece of cardboard on top of the glass and hold it in place with your hand.
3.  Over basin or sink, being careful not to let any bubble of air enter between the cardboard and the glass, invert the tumbler while holding the cardboard in place.
4.  Remove your hand carefully from the cardboard, being careful not to jar either the glass or the cardboard.

Write the results of your experiment; check this off on your checklist.

From your textbook and additional resources, make up a poem that mentions the layers of our atmosphere. Include something about each layer. During show and tell time, you may teach the class your poem. After you have completed this activity, check it off on your checklist.

Air pollution: The facts are clear—the air is not! What causes air pollution? Draw and/or cut out pictures of things that cause air pollution. What can *you* do to help stop air pollution?

After exploring the topic of air pollution, write a song with new words to fit an existing melody. (Sample tunes: "Old MacDonald," "She'll be Coming 'Round the Mountain.")

Make a list in your file of vocabulary words. All new words you come upon should be included.

On a rainy day, have the class (as a group) complete a homemade filmstrip about "The Hydrosphere." In this activity, students will get an introduction to Key Concepts II. After the class has finished the filmstrip, you may check this activity off on your checklist.

This activity combines science and writing. Select an animal that lives in either fresh water or salt water, and be that animal for a day. What kind of adventures would you have? What would you be able to do? How would you live? What part of the world would you live in and what would you eat? This activity requires some background information. You may use any references to write your paper. Draw a picture of the animal you have chosen when you finish the paper. After you have proofread your paper, check off this activity on your list.

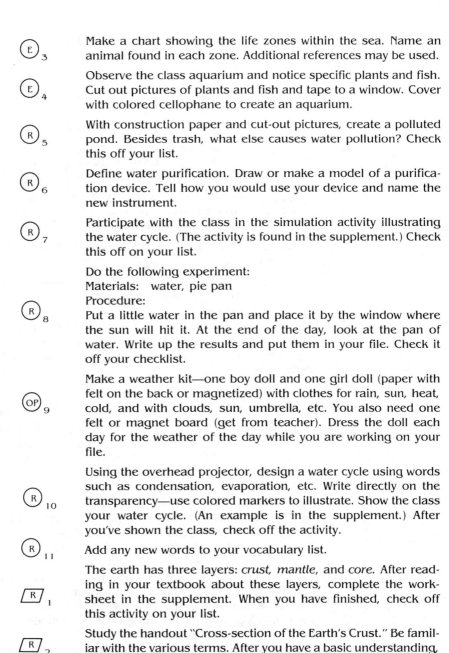

(E)₃  Make a chart showing the life zones within the sea. Name an animal found in each zone. Additional references may be used.

(E)₄  Observe the class aquarium and notice specific plants and fish. Cut out pictures of plants and fish and tape to a window. Cover with colored cellophane to create an aquarium.

(R)₅  With construction paper and cut-out pictures, create a polluted pond. Besides trash, what else causes water pollution? Check this off your list.

(R)₆  Define water purification. Draw or make a model of a purification device. Tell how you would use your device and name the new instrument.

(R)₇  Participate with the class in the simulation activity illustrating the water cycle. (The activity is found in the supplement.) Check this off on your list.

(R)₈  Do the following experiment:
Materials:  water, pie pan
Procedure:
Put a little water in the pan and place it by the window where the sun will hit it. At the end of the day, look at the pan of water. Write up the results and put them in your file. Check it off your checklist.

(OP)₉  Make a weather kit—one boy doll and one girl doll (paper with felt on the back or magnetized) with clothes for rain, sun, heat, cold, and with clouds, sun, umbrella, etc. You also need one felt or magnet board (get from teacher). Dress the doll each day for the weather of the day while you are working on your file.

(R)₁₀  Using the overhead projector, design a water cycle using words such as condensation, evaporation, etc. Write directly on the transparency—use colored markers to illustrate. Show the class your water cycle. (An example is in the supplement.) After you've shown the class, check off the activity.

(R)₁₁  Add any new words to your vocabulary list.

[R]₁  The earth has three layers: *crust, mantle,* and *core.* After reading in your textbook about these layers, complete the worksheet in the supplement. When you have finished, check off this activity on your list.

[R]₂  Study the handout "Cross-section of the Earth's Crust." Be familiar with the various terms. After you have a basic understanding, check this activity off on your list.

Bring in at least five different rocks you've found. Take the rocks to the "rock center" and identify the rocks.

[R]₃  In the rock center, you will find reference books, charts of rocks, pictures of rocks, and rock collections. Show your rocks to the class and explain the procedure you followed to identify the rocks. Add this procedure to your file. Check this activity in your file.

□R□ ₄ During sharing time, teach the concept: What are some of the common uses of minerals? Pick a common use and build a short lesson around it. Do not choose a common use that has been taught. Examples are coal, sand, or salt (table or epsom). Many minerals have practical applications at home and at work. To end your lesson, teach the class a song or poem to review the concept. Check off the activity in your file.

□R□ ₅ On the opaque projector, show the class forces that wear away the earth's surface. Pictures may be found in library books, your text, the encyclopedia, etc. Check off this activity.

□OP□ ₆ Define *seismograph*. How many smaller words can you make from the letters in seismograph? List them. Put the list in your file. (Examples: is, graph, sap)

□R□ ₇ Add any new words to your vocabulary list.

Homemade Filmstrip □R□ ₁

The class will participate together in making the filmstrip. This is a culminating activity for the class, to review the key concepts.

Put card # here

[ ]

Put name here
1. Respond to directions on card
2. Use your textbook or other resources
3. Be colorful, neat, use entire sheet
4. Leave materials on desk when finished and proceed with extending activity

Card 1—Title page, "The Environment"
Card 2—Copy this statement: "One segment of all environments is the atmosphere."
Card 3—Copy this statement: "Air has many physical properties."
Card 4—Name some physical properties of air.
Card 5—Copy this statement: "Air exerts pressure which can be measured."
Card 6—Give examples of air pressure.
Card 7—Copy this statement: "The atmosphere is layered."
Card 8—Name the layers of the atmosphere.
Card 9—Which layer of the atmosphere do we live in?
Card 10—Copy this statement: "Air can be polluted; this has definite effects on the environment."
Card 11—Draw or cut out pictures of things that pollute the air.
Card 12—Copy this statement: "Another segment of all environments is the hydrosphere."
Card 13—Copy this statement: "Some plants and animals live in salt water."
Card 14—Name four animals and four plants that live in salt water. Draw and color their pictures.
Card 15—Copy this statement: "Some plants and animals live in fresh water."
Card 16—Name four plants and four animals that live in fresh water. Draw and color their pictures.

Card 17—Copy this statement: "Water can be polluted in many ways." Name several ways water can be polluted.

Card 18—Define water purification.

Card 19—Define evaporation.

Card 20—Define condensation.

Card 21—Draw the water cycle.

Card 22—Copy this statement: "A final segment of all environments is the lithosphere."

Card 23—Name the rocks and minerals found in the crust.

Card 24—Copy this statement: "Soil is a very important part of the environment."

Card 25—Copy this statement: "Solid parts of the earth move."

Card 26—Describe a method in which a solid part of the earth can move. (Example: earthquake)

Card 27—Copy this statement: "There are forces that wear away the earth's surface."

Card 28—Draw some forces that wear away the earth's surface.

Card 29—Make an end page.

Extending Activities

Have the first three students who finish put the filmstrip together in numerical order.

Have a group of students compose a poem about the layers of the atmosphere.

Play a game: I pollute the air—what am I?

(Example: smoke from factory, car exhaust)

Sing a song about the rocks and minerals in the soil to the tune of "Mary Had A Little Lamb."

Do a demonstration with pictures of various plants and animals; do they live in fresh water or salt water?

Do an experiment to show evaporation.

Make a bulletin board on the effects of an earthquake.

**Game:**              $\boxed{R}_2$

Secret Message

| S | C | I | E | N | C | E | I | S | F | U | N |
|---|---|---|---|---|---|---|---|---|---|---|---|
| 1 | 2 | 3 | 4 | 5 | 6 | 7 | 8 | 9 | 10 | 11 | 12 |

Answer each question. Put the underlined letter in the corresponding secret message. What does it say?

1. The layer of earth we live on is the C R U S T.
                                          1

2. When water vapor changes from a gas to a liquid the process is called C O N D E N S A T I O N.
   2

3. Smoke from factories is called air P O L L U T I O N.
                                         3

4. A goldfish lives in F R E S H water.
                         4

5. A pin wheel can show how the W I N D blows.
                                   5

6. The centermost layer of the earth is the _C O R E_.
6

7. _E V A P O R A T I O N_ is when water changes from a liquid to
7
a gas.

8. The third largest ocean in terms of total area is the _I N D I A N_
Ocean.                                                                        8

9. The experiment using a glass tumbler, water, a piece of cardboard,
and a basin illustrates the concept of air _P R E S S U R E_.
9

10. The aquarium in the class contains _F R E S H_ water.
10

11. When it is raining outside you should carry an _U M B R E L L A_.
11

12. The middle layer of the earth is called the _M A N T L E_.
12

After the class completes its file, have the students participate in a game: Divide the class into tournament groups (probably four teams). Play password, using words from the vocabulary lists. Have each team play all of the other teams. After several rounds, a winning team will be selected. Other suitable games are variations of The Match Game, Hollywood Squares, and Chain Reaction.

# Appendix F

## Handwriting Refresher

### Individualized Performance-Based Handwriting (Manuscript and Cursive) Program

Materials enclosed:

1 Manuscript Alphabet Sheet
2 Cursive Alphabet Sheet
3 Handwriting Position Illustrations
4 Peer-teaching Evaluation Form

Experiences to be completed:

Session 1.  Practice of manuscript letters
Session 2.  Practice of cursive letters
Session 3.  Study of handwriting positions and analysis of handwriting samples (manuscript and cursive)
Session 4.  Prepare manuscript experience chart or transparency
Session 5.  Teach a handwriting skill to a peer (and be taught), completing an evaluation form.
Session 6.  Proficiency performance of manuscript and cursive letters and connected writing

Introduction:

This small set of materials has been prepared to help you achieve greater skill in your own handwriting, both manuscript and cursive. The objectives of this packet are to enable you to:

1   Practice writing on chalkboard and paper (manuscript letters, cursive letters, and numerals 1 to 10) until they are comparable to the Zaner-Bloser samples.

2   Evaluate a student's manuscript and cursive writing sample, with suggestions for improvement. Mark it in terms of the following items:

Letter form: Correct shape of letters

Proportion: Uniformity of letter size

Spacing: Uniform spacing between letters and between words

Alignment: Bottom of unlooped letters on line, not above or below

Slant: Manuscript letters written straight up and down; cursive letters slanted to the right

Line quality: Not too light (difficult to see); not too heavy (caused by retracing)

## MANUSCRIPT ALPHABET SHEET

## UPPER CASE LETTERS

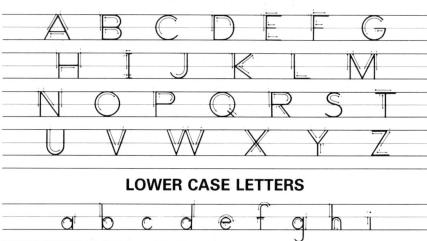

## LOWER CASE LETTERS

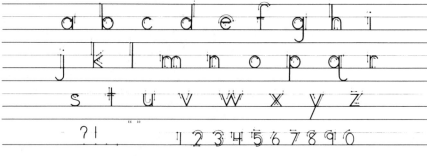

3  With a group of students, prepare an experience chart or overhead transparency in *manuscript*, such as:

| | |
|---|---|
| We went to the zoo. | Today we read *Animal Farm*. |
| We saw many animals. | We discussed different aspects of it. |
| They were having lunch. | We summarized its message. |
| It was fun to watch them. | We drew some conclusions of our own. |

4  Teach a basic group of letters (manuscript or cursive) to a peer,
applying the six basic steps as measured on a critique form
completed by a peer. Basic groups of manuscript letters include:

Straight line group (i, l, t)
Slant line group (v, y, w, x, z, k)
Circle (a, b, c, d, e, g, o, p, q)
Tall letters (b, d, f, h, k, l, t)
Hump letters (h, m, n, r, u)
Double curve (s)
Tail letters (j, g, p, q, y)
Similar capital letters (E, F, H, I, L, T)
Underturn letters (J, U)
Tall slant-line letters (K, N, W, Y, A, M, V, X, Z)
Big circle letters (C, D, G, O, Q)
Side-turn letters (B, P, D, R)

## CURSIVE ALPHABET

Basic groups of cursive letters include:

      Undercurve beginnings (i, u, w, e, r, s)
      Intermediate letters (t, d, p)
      Upper-loop letters, undercurve beginning (l, f, b, h, k)
      Hump-letters, overcurve beginning (m, n, v, x, y, z, h)
      Small-oval letters, downcurve beginning (a, d, g, q, o, c)
      Lower-loop letters (j, g, p, y, z, q, f)
      Check-stroke letters (v, w, b, o, r, s)
      Direct-oval capital letters (O, C, E, A, D)
      Upper-loop capital letters (S, G, L, I, J)
      Cane-stem letters (H, K, M, N, U, V, W, X, Y, Z, Q)
      Compound-curve letters (T, F, L, K, S)
      Lower-loop letters (J, Y, Z)
      Indirect-oval letters (P, B, R)
      Boat-ending letters (T, S, I, F, G, B)

Peer Teaching Evaluation Form

      Rate yourself and also have your peers rate your handwriting lesson as to whether or not you included each of these items.

Clearly defined objective of the lesson
Gave attention to interest of the student throughout the lesson
Legibly demonstrated the handwriting features presented in the lesson
Provided appropriate student practice
Encouraged the student to evaluate handwriting strengths/weaknesses
Used diagnosed weaknesses for corrective instruction

5  Take a timed test to determine proficiency in both manuscript and cursive writing and in writing numerals 1 to 10. You will be given two minutes for the manuscript portion, two minutes for the cursive portion, and one additional minute for the numerals. You may write numerals in either manuscript or cursive form, but they must be consistent. The test will be evaluated according to the Zaner-Bloser evaluation scale.

      You will then be given two minutes to write this connected prose in manuscript, and two minutes to write it in cursive:

      Thirty days hath September,
      April, June, and November
      All the rest have thirty-one;
      February twenty-eight alone,
      Except in leap year, at which time
      February's days are twenty-nine.

# CORRECT WRITING POSITION ILLUSTRATION

The writing tool should be held lightly between the thumb and the first two fingers, about one inch above the point.

The hand should be resting on the last two fingers with them acting as gliders.

The arm should be resting on the desk as shown in the figure to the right.

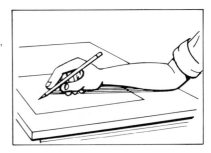

Left handed children should use the same position but with the writing tool in their left hand.

Right Hand Manuscript Paper Position

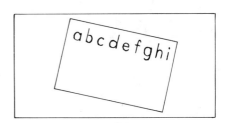

Left Hand Manuscript Paper Position

Right Hand Cursive Paper Position

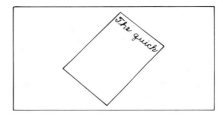

Left Hand Cursive Paper Position

# INDEX